Classic Readings of Humanities in English Book I

英语人文经典选读

（第一册）

徐浩　王海 / 主编
卞丽　茹静　王海萍 / 副主编

北京大学出版社
PEKING UNIVERSITY PRESS

图书在版编目(CIP)数据

英语人文经典选读.第一册/徐浩,王海主编.—北京:北京大学出版社,2017.11
ISBN 978-7-301-28933-4

Ⅰ.①英… Ⅱ.①徐… ②王… Ⅲ.①英语—阅读教学—高等学校—教学参考资料 Ⅳ.①H319.37

中国版本图书馆CIP数据核字(2017)第266944号

书　　　名	英语人文经典选读(第一册) YINGYU RENWEN JINGDIAN XUANDU(DI-YI CE)
著作责任者	徐　浩　王　海　主编
责 任 编 辑	朱梅全　刘秀芹
标 准 书 号	ISBN 978-7-301-28933-4
出 版 发 行	北京大学出版社
地　　　址	北京市海淀区成府路205号　100871
网　　　址	http://www.pup.cn　　新浪微博:@北京大学出版社
电 子 信 箱	zpup@pup.cn
电　　　话	邮购部 010-62752015　发行部 010-62750672　编辑部 021-62071998
印 　刷 　者	三河市北燕印装有限公司
经 销 者	新华书店
	730毫米×980毫米　16开本　15.75印张　241千字 2017年11月第1版　2023年8月第3次印刷
定　　　价	45.00元

未经许可,不得以任何方式复制或抄袭本书之部分或全部内容。
版权所有,侵权必究
举报电话: 010-62752024　电子信箱: fd@pup.cn
图书如有印装质量问题,请与出版部联系,电话: 010-62756370

编 者 说 明

为深化大学英语教学改革,适应大学通识教育改革的需要,充分发挥大学英语拓宽人文视野、传递人文精神、培育人文素养的职能,华东政法大学外语学院大学英语阅读教研室组织编写了"英语人文经典选读"系列教材。

本套教材是大学英语分级教学改革的一次经验总结。近十年来,随着中小学英语教育,甚至幼儿英语教育的普及和发展,非英语专业本科生的英语基础明显提高,这在分级教学高级班学生身上表现得尤为明显,现行的以词汇、句法、篇章为主要内容的大学英语教学与他们的知识需求出现了较大偏差。同时也应看到,这些学生虽然有良好的语言基础,但绝大多数还不具备阅读英语经典著作的能力,甚至从未接触过经典阅读、严肃阅读,他们的英语水平和人文视野仍有提高、拓展的空间。针对这种情况,来自教学第一线的编写组成员在先期教学实践中主动探索以经典原著为主要内容的授课模式,受到了学生的广泛欢迎,而编写一套英语人文经典教材便成了一线教师和学生的共同心愿。

本套教材以英语人文经典原著为主要内容,涵盖文化、文学、政治、经济、教育、心理、伦理等多个论题,突出人文性、经典性和拓展性,大幅提高阅读难度和阅读量,淡化传统教材所偏重的语法、词汇练习,旨在以经典名篇为导引,向学生开启人文经典阅读的大门,培养学生深度阅读的能力、习惯和兴趣,拓展学生的人文视野,使学生通过阅读经典,在提高英语语言能力的同时,获取人文知识,培育人文素养,塑造人文精神,使语言学习同时成为人文学习,使大学英语教学成为通识教育不可分割的一部分。

本套教材由华东政法大学外语学院大学英语阅读教研室负责编写,编写组成员全部拥有英语语言文学博士学位,并有着多年的大学英语一线教学经验,曾主编或参编多部大学英语教材。本套教材主要供非英语专业大学英语分级教学高级班和模块拓展班学生使用,也可作为英语专业学生、研究生、广大英语爱好者和科研人员的参考用书。

  本套教材的编写和出版离不开华东政法大学外语学院领导的关心和帮助,学院书记余素青教授审阅了书稿并提出修改意见,副院长张朱平副教授全程指导了教材的编写工作,为教材的出版付出了极大努力。复旦大学外国语言文学学院曾建彬教授为教材的编写和出版提出了宝贵的建议,北京大学出版社的刘秀芹编辑为教材的出版付出了辛勤的劳动,在此一并表示感谢。

  由于本教材编写时间仓促,编者才识有限,又兼选题范围广泛,疏漏错讹在所难免,请专家、教师同仁和读者诸君不吝赐教,以便及时修正完善。

徐 浩

2017年8月于华政集英楼

目录 Contents

Unit 1　Chinese Culture ……………………………………………………… (1)

　　Text A　Eating and Drinking ……………………… Lin Yutang　(1)

　　Text B　The Spirit of the Chinese People ……… Gu Hongming　(12)

　　Text C　The Chinese Character ………………… Bertrand Russell　(20)

Unit 2　Foreign Impressions ……………………………………………… (36)

　　Text A　Here Is New York ………………… Elwyn Brooks White　(36)

　　Text B　Flowery Tuscany …………… David Herbert Lawrence　(44)

　　Text C　What I Saw in America …… Gilbert Keith Chesterton　(50)

Unit 3　Politics ………………………………………………………………… (63)

　　Text A　The Spirit of Laws ………… Charles de Montesquieu　(63)

　　Text B　Of the Beginning of Political Societies …… John Locke　(72)

　　Text C　The Declaration of Independence

　　　　　　………………………………… Thomas Jefferson, et al.　(83)

Unit 4　Education ……………………………………………………………… (92)

　　Text A　A Liberal Education ………… Thomas Henry Huxley　(92)

　　Text B　Importance of Education ……………………… Plato　(102)

　　Text C　Education and Discipline ……………… Bertrand Russell　(110)

Unit 5　Women　(120)

　　Text A　Professions for Women ……… Virginia Woolf　(120)

　　Text B　Beauty ……………………………… Susan Sontag　(131)

　　Text C　The Tragedy of Woman's Emancipation
　　　　　　………………………………………… Emma Goldman　(137)

Unit 6　Methodology　(149)

　　Text A　The Demarcation Between Science and Pseudo-Science
　　　　　　………………………………………… Karl R. Popper　(149)

　　Text B　Discourse on Method ……………… René Descartes　(160)

　　Text C　The Myths of Objectivism and Subjectivism
　　　　　　………………… George Lakoff and Mark Johnson　(172)

Unit 7　Speeches　(185)

　　Text A　I Have a Dream …………… Martin Luther King, Jr.　(185)

　　Text B　Richard M. Nixon's Resignation Address
　　　　　　………………………………………… Richard M. Nixon　(196)

　　Text C　We Shall Fight on the Beaches
　　　　　　………………………………………… Winston Churchill　(202)

Unit 8　Literature　(216)

　　Text A　A Rose for Emily ……………… William Faulkner　(216)

　　Text B　Solitude ……………………… Henry David Thoreau　(232)

　　Text C　The Waste Land ……………………… T. S. Eliot　(238)

Unit 1

Chinese Culture

Text A   Eating and Drinking
Text B   The Spirit of the Chinese People
Text C   The Chinese Character

Text A

Eating and Drinking①

Lin Yutang

<u>1</u> The question has often been asked as to what we eat. The answer is that we eat all the **edible** things on this earth. We eat crabs **by preference**, and often eat barks by necessity. Economic necessity is the mother of our inventions in food. We are too over-populated and famine is too common for us not to eat everything we can **lay our hands on.** And it **stands to reason** that in this positively **exhaustive** experiment on edibles, we should have **stumbled upon** important discoveries, as most scientific or medical discoveries have been stumbled upon. For one thing, we have discovered the magic **tonic** and building qualities of **ginseng**, for which I am willing to give personal **testimony** as to its being the most enduring and most energy-giving tonic known to mankind, distinguished by the slowness and gentleness of its action. But

---

① Excerpted from Lin Yutang's *My Country and My People*.

apart from such accidental discoveries of medical or **culinary** importance, we are undoubtedly the only truly **omnivorous** animals on earth, and so long as our teeth last, we should continue to occupy that position. Some day a dentist will yet discover that we have the best teeth as a nation. Gifted with these teeth and driven by famine, there is no reason why we should not at some particular time of our national life suddenly discover that roasted beetles and fried bees' **chrysalis** are great delicacies. The only thing we have not discovered and will not eat is cheese. The Mongols could not persuade us to eat cheese, and the Europeans do not have a greater chance of doing so.

2   It is useless to use logical reasoning in the matter of our food, which is determined by prejudices. We eat **mussels** with the Europeans and eat **clams** with the Americans, but we don't eat **oysters** raw as the Americans do. It is useless, for instance, for anybody to convince me that snake's meat tastes like chicken. I have lived in China forty years without eating a snake, or seeing any of my relatives do so. Tales of eating snakes travel faster than tales of eating chicken, but actually we eat more chickens and better chickens than the white people, and snake-eating is as much a curiosity to the Chinese as it is to the foreigners.

3   All one can say is that we are very **catholic** in our tastes, and that any rational man can take anything off a Chinese table without any **qualm** of conscience. What famine dictates is not for us human mortals to choose. There is nothing that a man will not eat when hard pressed by hunger. And no one **is entitled to** condemn until he knows what famine means. Some of us have been forced in times of famine to eat babies and even this must be humanly rare but, thank God, we do not eat them raw as the English eat their beef!

4   If there is anything we are serious about, it is neither religion nor learning, but food. We openly acclaim eating as one of the few joys of this human life. This question of attitude is very important, for unless we are

honest about it we will never be able to lift eating and cooking into an art. The difference of attitude regarding the problem of food is represented in Europe by the French and the English. The French eat enthusiastically, while the English eat **apologetically**. The Chinese national genius decidedly leans toward the French in the matter of feeding ourselves.

<u>5</u>   The danger of not taking food seriously and allowing it to degenerate into a **slipshod** business may be studied in the English national life. If they had known any taste for food their language would reveal it. The English language does not provide a word for **cuisine**; they call it just "cooking." They have no proper word for "chef"; they just call him a "cook". They do not speak about their "menu", but know only what are called "dishes." And they have no word for "**gourmet**"; they just call him "Greedy Gut" in their **nursery rhymes**. The truth is, the English do not admit that they have a stomach. No stomach is fit for conversation unless it happens to be "sick" or "aching." The result is that while the Frenchman will talk about the cuisine of his chef with what seems to the English mind immodest gestures, the Englishman can hardly venture to talk about the "food" of his "cook" without **impairing** the beauty of his language. When hard pressed by his French host he might be willing to **mutter** between his teeth that "that pudding is awfully good" and there let the matter rest. Now if a pudding is good it is good for some definite reasons, and about these problems the Englishman does not bother himself. All the English are interested in is how to strengthen themselves against influenza, as with Bovril①, and save the doctor's bills.

<u>6</u>   We are unashamed of our eating. We have "Su Tungp'o pork" and "Kiang bean-curd". In England, a Wordsworth steak or Galsworthy **cutlet** would be unimaginable. Wordsworth sang about "simple living and high thinking," but he failed to note that good food, especially fresh-cut bamboo

---

① Bovril is the trademarked name of a thick, salty meat extract, developed in the 1870s by John Lawson Johnston.

shoots and mushrooms, counts among the real joys of a simple rural life. The Chinese poets, with a more **utilitarian** philosophy, have frankly sung about the "**minced perch and shun vegetable soup**" of their native home. This thought is regarded as so poetic that officials in their **petition** for resignation will say that they are "thinking of vegetable" as a most elegant expression. Actually our love of fatherland is largely a matter of recollection of the keen sensual pleasures of our childhood. The loyalty to Uncle Sam is the loyalty to American doughnuts but the Americans will not admit it. Many Americans, while abroad, sigh for their ham and sweet potatoes at home, but they will not admit that this makes them think of home, nor will they put it in their poetry.

7 The Chinese accept food as they accept sex, women and life in general. No great English poet or writer would **condescend** to write a *Cook Book*, which they regard as belonging outside the realms of literature and worthy of the efforts of Aunt Susan only. But the great poet-dramatist Li Liweng did not consider it beneath his dignity to write about the cooking of mushrooms and all kinds of vegetarian and non-vegetarian foods. Another great poet and scholar, Yuan Mei, wrote a whole book on cooking, besides writing a most wonderful essay on his cook. He described his cook as Henry James described the English **butler**, as a man carrying himself with dignity and understanding in his profession. But H. G. Wells, who of all English minds is the one most likely to write about English food, evidently cannot write it, and no hope is to be expected from the less **encyclopaedic** minds.

8 Two principles distinguish Chinese from European cooking. One is that we eat food for its **texture**, the **elastic** or crisp effect it has on our teeth, as well for fragrance, flavor and color. Li Liweng said that he was a slave to crabs, because they had the combination of fragrance, flavor and color. The idea of texture is seldom understood, but a great part of the popularity of bamboo-shoots is due to the fine resistance the young shoots give to our

teeth. The appreciation of bamboo-shoots is probably the most typical example of our taste. Being not oily, it has a certain fairy-like "**fugitive**" quality about it. But the most important principle is that it lends flavor to meat (especially pork) cooked with it, and, on the other hand, it receives the flavor of the pork itself. This is the second principle, that of mixing of flavors. The whole culinary art of China depends on the art of mixture. While the Chinese recognize that many things, like fresh fish, must be cooked in their own juice, in general they mix flavors a great deal more than Western cooks do. No one, for instance, knows how cabbage tastes until he has tasted it when properly cooked with chicken, and the chicken flavor has gone into the cabbage and the cabbage flavor has gone into the chicken. From this principle of mixture, any number of fine and delicate combinations can be developed. **Celery**, for instance, may be eaten raw and alone, but when Chinese see, in a foreign dinner, vegetables like **spinach** or **carrots** cooked separately and then served on the same plate with pork or roast goose, they smile at the **barbarians**.

9   The Chinese, whose sense of **proportion** is so wonderfully **acute** in painting and architecture, seem to have completely lost it in the matter of food, to which they give themselves wholeheartedly when they seat themselves around a dinner table. Any big **course**, like the fat duck, coming after twelve or thirteen other courses, should be a sufficient meal in itself for any human being. This is due to a false standard of **courtesy**, and to the fact that as course after course is served during dinners, the people are supposed to be occupied in different wine-games or contests of poetry during the intervals, which naturally lengthens the time required and gives more time for the stomach to **assimilate** the food. Most probably the relatively lower efficiency of Chinese government officials is due directly to the fact that all of them are subjected to an inhuman routine of three or four dinners a night. One-fourth of their food goes to **nourish** them and three-fourths to kill them.

That **accounts for** the **prevalence** of rich men's **ailments**, like diseases of the liver and the kidneys, which are periodically announced in the newspapers when these officials see fit to retire from the political **arena** for reasons of convenience.

10　　As to drinks, we are naturally moderate except as regarding tea. Owing to the comparative absence of **distilled** liquor one very seldom sees drunkards in the streets. But tea-drinking is an art in itself. It amounts with some persons almost to a **cult**. There are special books about tea-drinking as there are special books about **incense** and wine and rocks for house decoration. More than any other human invention of this nature, the drinking of tea has colored our daily life as a nation, and gives rise to the institution of tea-houses which are **approximate** equivalents of Western cafes for the common people. People drink tea in their homes and in the tea-houses, alone and in company, at committee meetings and at the settling of disputes. They drink tea before breakfast and at midnight with a teapot. A Chinese is happy wherever he is. It is a universal habit, and it has no **deleterious** effect whatsoever, except in very rare cases, as in my native district where according to tradition some people have drunk themselves bankrupt. This is only possible with extremely costly tea, but the average tea is cheap, and the average tea in China is good enough for a prince. The best tea is mild and gives a "back-flavor" which comes after a minute or two, when its chemical action has **set in** on the **salivary glands**. Such good tea puts everybody in good humor. I have no doubt that it **prolongs** Chinese lives by aiding their digestion and maintaining their **equanimity** of temper.

Vocabulary

edible ['edəbl] a.	to be safe to eat and not poisonous 可食用的
by preference	按照喜好
bark [bɑːk] n.	the tough material that covers the outside of a tree 树皮
lay hands on	得到，找到

stand to reason	合乎道理
exhaustive [ig'zɔstiv] a.	thorough and complete 详尽的,彻底的
stumble upon	偶然发现
tonic ['tɔnik] n.	a medicine that makes you feel stronger, healthier, and less tired 补药
ginseng ['dʒinseŋ] n.	高丽参,人参
testimony ['testiməni] n.	a formal statement that they make about what they saw someone do or what they know of a situation, after having promised to tell the truth 证词,证言,证据
apart from	除……之外,且不说,并且
culinary ['kʌlinəri] a.	of or relating to or used in cooking 厨房的,烹调用的
omnivorous [ɔm'nivərəs] a.	eating all kinds of food, including both meat and plants 杂食的,无所不吃的
chrysalis ['krisəlis] n.	蝶蛹,虫茧
mussel ['mʌsəl] n.	蚌,贻贝
clam [klæm] n.	蛤
oyster ['ɔistə] n.	牡蛎
catholic ['kæθəlik] a.	to be very varied 宽容的,宽宏大量的,气量大的
qualm [kwa:m] n.	uneasiness about the fitness of an action 疑虑,不安
be entitled to	有权,有……的资格
apologetically [əpɔlə'dʒetikli] ad.	带有歉意地
slipshod ['slipʃɔd] a.	marked by great carelessness 潦草的,马虎的
cuisine [kwi'zi:n] n.	the practice or manner of preparing food or the food so prepared 烹饪,厨艺,菜系,美食
gourmet ['guəmei] n.	a person devoted to refined sensuous enjoyment 美食家
nursery rhymes	童谣,儿歌
impair [im'pɛə] vt.	make worse or less effective 损害,削弱,减少
mutter ['mʌtə] v.	talk indistinctly; usually in a low voice 咕哝,喃喃自语
cutlet ['kʌtlit] n.	肉片,炸肉排,炸肉片
utilitarian [ju:tili'tɛəriən] a.	having utility often to the exclusion of values 功利的,功利主义的
minced perch and shun vegetable soup	鲈脍莼羹
petition [pi'tiʃən] n.	a formal message requesting something that is submitted to an authority 请愿,请愿书,祈求;[法]诉状
condescend [kɔndi'send] vi.	do something that one considers to be below one's dignity 屈尊,俯就
butler ['bʌtlə] n.	a manservant 男管家,仆役长

encyclopaedic [en,saikləu'pi:dik] a.	broad in scope or content 百科全书的，广博的，如百科辞典的
texture ['tekstʃə] n.	the feel of a surface or a fabric 肌理，纹理，质地
elastic [i'læstik] a.	capable of resuming original shape after stretching or compression; springy 有弹性的
fugitive ['fju:dʒitiv] a.	逃亡的，无常的，易变的
celery ['seləri] n.	芹菜
spinach ['spinidʒ] n.	菠菜
carrot ['kærət] n.	胡萝卜
barbarian [ba:'bɛəriən] n.	without civilizing influences 原始人，野蛮人，未开化的人
proportion [prə'pɔ:ʃən] n.	the quotient obtained when the magnitude of a part is divided by the magnitude of the whole 比例
acute [ə'kju:t] a.	having or experiencing a rapid onset and short but severe course 尖锐的，急性的，严重的
course [kɔ:s] n.	part of a meal served at one time 一道菜
courtesy ['kə:tisi] n.	politeness, respect, and consideration for others 礼貌，好意，恩惠
assimilate [ə'simileit] v.	take (gas, light or heat) into a solution 吸收，使同化
nourish ['nʌriʃ] vt.	to provide with the food that is necessary for life, growth, and good health 滋养
account for	对……负有责任，对……作出解释
prevalence ['prevələns] n.	the quality of prevailing generally; being widespread 流行，普遍，广泛
ailment ['eilmənt] n.	an often persistent bodily disorder or disease; a cause for complaining 小病
arena [ə'ri:nə] n.	a place where sports, entertainments, and other public events take place, it has seats around it where people sit and watch 舞台，竞技场
distilled [dis'tild] a.	extracted by the process of distillation 由蒸馏得来的
cult [kʌlt] n.	a situation in which people regard that thing as very important or special 狂热崇拜，迷信
incense ['insens] n.	香
approximate [ə'prɔksimət] a.	be close or similar 近似的，大概的
deleterious [deli'tiəriəs] a.	harmful to living things 有毒的，有害的
set in	开始
salivary glands	唾液腺
prolong [prə'lɔŋ] vt.	lengthen or extend in duration or space 延长，拖延
equanimity [ekwə'nimiti] n.	steadiness of mind under stress 平静，镇定

I. Vocabulary Building

a/an-: without

e. g. , amoral, atheism, apolitical, amorphous, anarchism, anharmonic, anechoic, anonymous

il-, ir-: the opposite

e. g. , illegal, illiterate, illogical, illimitable, irregular, irrational, irrelative, irresolute, irreproachable, irrefutable, irresistible, irrevocable

im-, in-: the opposite

e. g. , immoral, impartial, impassive, impeccable, immortal, immutable, inhuman, injustice, incorrigible, inconstant, indifferent, innocuous, inimitable, insubordinate

un-: the opposite

e. g. , unequal, unabashed, unassuming, uncommitted, unscrupulous, unconditional, unambitious, unconscionable, unfailing, unworldly, uncivilized, unalloyed, uncharted

II. Discussion

Discuss the following questions with your own words.

1. According to the writer, what makes Chinese people the only truly omnivorous animals on the earth?

2. What is the meaning of the following lines: "The result is that while the Frenchman will talk about the cuisine of his chef with that seems to the English mind modest gestures, the Englishman can hardly venture to talk about the 'food' of his 'cook' without impairing the beauty of his language"?

3. Why did the writer use the derogatory word "condescend" in Para. 7? What are the cultural differences between Britons and Chinese so far as

writing a cook book is concerned according to the writer?

4. What do you think of the two principles which distinguish Chinese from European cooking?

5. Why is drinking tea so important to average Chinese?

III. Translation A

Translate the following sentences selected from the text into Chinese.

1. The question has often been asked as to what we eat. The answer is that we eat all the edible things on this earth. We eat crabs by preference, and often eat barks by necessity. Economic necessity is the mother of our inventions in food. We are too over-populated and famine is too common for us not to eat everything we can lay our hands on. And it stands to reason that in this positively exhaustive experiment on edibles, we should have stumbled upon important discoveries, as most scientific or medical discoveries have been stumbled upon. (Para. 1)

2. All one can say is that we are very catholic in our tastes, and that any rational man can take anything off a Chinese table without any qualm of conscience. What famine dictates is not for us human mortals to choose. There is nothing that a man will not eat when hard pressed by hunger. And no one is entitled to condemn until he knows what famine means. Some of us have been forced in times of famine to eat babies and even this must be humanly rare but, thank God, we do not eat them raw as the English eat their beef! (Para. 3)

3. The danger of not taking food seriously and allowing it to degenerate into a slipshod business may be studied in the English national life. If they had known any taste for food their language would reveal it. (Para. 5)

4. The Chinese poets, with a more utilitarian philosophy, have frankly sung about the "minced perch and shun vegetable soup" of their native home. This thought is regarded as so poetic that officials in their petition for

resignation will say that they are "thinking of vegetable" as a most elegant expression. (Para. 6)

5. This is due to a false standard of courtesy, and to the fact that as course after course is served during dinners, the people are supposed to be occupied in different wine-games or contests of poetry during the intervals, which naturally lengthens the time required and gives more time for the stomach to assimilate the food. (Para. 9)

IV. Translation B
Translate the following passage into Chinese.

We in the West make a fetish of "progress," which is the ethical camouflage of the desire to be the cause of changes. If we are asked, for instance, whether machinery has really improved the world, the question strikes us as foolish: it has brought great changes and therefore great "progress." What we believe to be a love of progress is really, in nine cases out of ten, a love of power, an enjoyment of the feeling that by our fiat we can make things different. For the sake of this pleasure, a young American will work so hard that, by the time he has acquired his millions, he has become a victim of dyspepsia, compelled to live on toast and water, and to be a mere spectator of the feasts that he offers to his guests. But he consoles himself with the thought that he can control politics, and provoke or prevent wars as may suit his investments. It is this temperament that makes Western nations "progressive." (Excerpted from Text C)

V. Writing Exercise

Please make your comments on the following lines: "The traditional family table is round. No corners. No sides. No head. No tail. Everything is smooth. The food is in the center, and each family member reaches over the same distance. Someone you love is next to you on each side, and no one is last or at the end. The person farthest away from you is also the person facing you."

Text B

The Spirit of the Chinese People①

Gu Hongming

A Paper that was to have been read before the Oriental Society of Peking

1 I say that the total impression which the Chinese type of humanity makes upon you is that he is gentle, that he is inexpressibly gentle. When you analyse this quality of inexpressible gentleness in the real Chinaman②, you will find that it is the product of a combination of two things, namely, sympathy and intelligence. I have compared the Chinese type of humanity to a **domesticated** animal. Now what is that which makes a domesticated animal so different from a wild animal? It is something in the domesticated animal which we recognise as distinctively human. But what is distinctively human as distinguished from what is animal? It is intelligence. But the intelligence of a domesticated animal is not a thinking intelligence. It is not an intelligence which comes to him from reasoning. Neither does it come to him from instinct, such as the intelligence of the fox, the **vulpine** intelligence which knows where eatable chickens are to be found. This intelligence which comes from instinct, of the fox, all, even wild, animals have. But this, what

---

① Excerpted from Gu Hongming's *The Spirit of the Chinese People*.
② "Chinaman"一词在早期的词典(如1913年版的韦氏字典)中没有负面含义,与"Englishman, Frenchman, Irishman"等并列使用。但在现代英语中,该词具有歧视意味,泛指华人和亚洲人,已不再使用。

may be called human intelligence of a domesticated animal is something quite different from the vulpine or animal intelligence. This intelligence of a domesticated animal is an intelligence which comes not from reasoning, nor from instinct, but from sympathy, from a feeling of love and attachment. A **thorough-bred** Arab horse understands his English master not because he has studied English grammar nor because he has an instinct for the English language, but because he loves and **is attached to** his master. This is what I call human intelligence, as distinguished from mere vulpine or animal intelligence. It is the possession of this human quality which distinguishes domesticated from wild animals. In the same way, I say, it is the possession of this sympathetic and true human intelligence, which gives to the Chinese type of humanity, to the real Chinaman, his inexpressible gentleness.

2 I once read somewhere a statement made by a foreigner who had lived in both countries, that the longer a foreigner lives in Japan the more he dislikes the Japanese, whereas the longer a foreigner lives in China the more he likes the Chinese. I do not know if what is said of the Japanese here, is true. But, I think, all of you who have lived in China will agree with me that what is here said of the Chinese is true. It is well-known fact that the liking—you may call it the taste for the Chinese—grows upon the foreigner the longer he lives in this country. There is an indescribable something in the Chinese people which, in spite of their want of habits of cleanliness and **refinement**, in spite of their many defects of mind and character, makes foreigners like them as foreigners like no other people. This indescribable something which I have defined as gentleness, softens and **mitigates**, if it does not **redeem**, the physical and moral defects of the Chinese in the hearts of foreigners. This gentleness again is, as I have tried to show you, the product of what I call sympathetic or true human intelligence—an intelligence which comes not from reasoning nor from instinct, but from sympathy—from the power of sympathy. Now what is the secret of the power of sympathy of the Chinese

people?

<u>3</u>　　I will here venture to give you an explanation—a **hypothesis**, if you like to call it so—of the secret of this power of sympathy in the Chinese people and my explanation is this. The Chinese people have this power, this strong power of sympathy, because they live wholly, or almost wholly, a life of the heart. The whole life of Chinaman is a life of feeling—not feeling in the sense of sensation which comes from the bodily organs, nor feeling in the sense of passions which flow, as you would say, from the nervous system, but feeling in the sense of emotion or human affection which comes from the deepest part of our nature—the heart or soul. Indeed I may say here that the real Chinaman lives so much a life of emotion or human affection, a life of the soul, that he may be said sometimes to neglect more than he ought to do, even the necessary requirements of the life of the senses of a man living in this world composed of body and soul. That is the true explanation of the insensibility of the Chinese to the physical discomforts of unclean surroundings and want of refinement. But that is neither here nor there.

<u>4</u>　　The Chinese people, I say, have the power of sympathy because they live wholly a life of the heart—a life of emotion or human affection. Let me here, first of all, give you two **illustrations** of what I mean by living a life of the heart. My first illustration is this. Some of you may have personally known an old friend and colleague of mine in Wuchang—known him when he was Minister of the Foreign Office here in Peking—Mr. Liang Tun-yen, Mr. Liang told me, when he first received the appointment of the Customs Taotai of Hankow, that what made him wish and strive to become a great **mandarin**, to wear the red button, and what gave him pleasure then in receiving this appointment, was not because he cared for the red button, not because he would henceforth be rich and independent, and we were all of us very poor then in Wuchang, but because he wanted to rejoice, because this promotion and advancement of his would gladden the heart of his old mother

in **Canton**. That is what I mean when I say that the Chinese people live a life of the heart—a life of emotion or human affection.

5 My other illustration is this. A Scotch friend of mine in the Customs told me he once had a Chinese servant who was a perfect **scamp**, who lied, who "squeezed," and who was always gambling, but when my friend fell ill with **typhoid fever** in an **out-of-the-way** port where he had no foreign friend to attend to him, this awful scamp of a Chinese servant nursed him with a care and devotion which he could not have expected from an intimate friend or near relation. Indeed I think what was once said of a woman in the Bible may also be said, not only of the Chinese servant, but of the Chinese people generally: "Much is forgiven them, because they love much." The eyes and understanding of the foreigner in China see many defects and **blemishes** in the habits and in the character of the Chinese, but his heart is attracted to them, because the Chinese have a heart, or, as I said, live a life of the heart—a life of emotion or human affection.

6 Now we have got, I think, a clue to the secret of sympathy in the Chinese people—the power of sympathy which gives to the real Chinaman that sympathetic or true human intelligence, making him so inexpressibly gentle. Let us next put this clue or hypothesis to the test. Let us see whether with this clue that the Chinese people live a life of the heart we can explain not only **detached** facts such as the two illustrations I have given above, but also general characteristics which we see in the actual life of the Chinese people.

7 First of all let us take the Chinese language. As the Chinese live a life of the heart, the Chinese language, I say, is also a language of the heart. Now it is a well-known fact that children and uneducated persons among foreigners in China learn Chinese very easily, much more so than grown-up and educated persons. What is the reason of this? The reason, I say, is because children and uneducated persons think and speak with the language of the

heart, whereas educated men, especially men with the modern intellectual education of Europe, think and speak with the language of the head or intellect. In fact, the reason why educated foreigners find it so difficult to learn Chinese, is because they are too educated, too intellectually and scientifically educated. As it is said of the Kingdom of Heaven, so it may also be said of the Chinese language: "Unless you become as little children, you cannot learn it."

<u>8</u>　　Next let us take another well-known fact in the life of the Chinese people. The Chinese, it is well-known, have wonderful memories. What is the secret of this? The secret is: the Chinese remember things with the heart and not with the head. The heart with its power of sympathy, acting as **glue**, can retain things much better than the head or intellect which is hard and dry. It is, for instance, also for this reason that we, all of us, can remember things which we learnt when we were children much better than we can remember things which we learnt in mature life. As children, like the Chinese, we remember things with the heart and not with the head.

<u>9</u>　　Let us next take another generally admitted fact in the life of the Chinese people—their politeness. The Chinese are, it has often been remarked, a peculiarly polite people. Now what is the essence of true politeness? It is consideration for the feelings of others. The Chinese are polite because, living a life of the heart, they know their own feelings and that makes it easy for them to show consideration for the feelings of others. The politeness of the Chinese, although not **elaborate** like the politeness of the Japanese, is pleasing because it is, as the French beautifully express it, *la politesse du coeur*, the politeness of the heart. The politeness of the Japanese, on the other hand, although elaborate, is not so pleasing, and I have heard some foreigners express their dislike of it, because it is what may be called a rehearsal politeness—a politeness learnt by heart as in a theatrical piece. It is not a **spontaneous** politeness which comes direct from the heart. In fact the

politeness of the Japanese is like a flower without fragrance, whereas the politeness of a really polite Chinese has a perfume like the **aroma** of a precious ointment—instar unguenti fragrantis①—which comes from the heart.

10 Last of all, let us take another characteristic of the Chinese people, by calling attention to which the Rev. Arthur Smith has made his reputation, **viz.**: want of exactness. Now what is the reason for this want of exactness in the ways of the Chinese people? The reason, I say again, is because the Chinese live a life of the heart. The heart is a very delicate and sensitive balance. It is not like the head or intellect, a hard, stiff, rigid instrument. You cannot with the heart think with the same steadiness, with the same **rigid** exactness as you can with the head or intellect. At least, it is extremely difficult to do so. In fact, the Chinese pen or pencil which is a soft brush, may be taken as a symbol of the Chinese mind. It is very difficult to write or draw with it, but when you have once mastered the use of it, you will, with it, write and draw with a beauty and grace which you cannot do with a hard steel pen.

11 Now the above are a few simple facts connected with the life of the Chinese people which anyone, even without any knowledge of Chinese, can observe and understand, and by examining these facts, I think, I have made good my hypothesis that the Chinese people live a life of the heart.

12 Now it is because the Chinese live a life of the heart, the life of a child, that they are so primitive in many of their ways. Indeed, it is a remarkable fact that for a people who have lived so long in the world as a great nation, the Chinese people should to this day be so primitive in many of their ways. It is this fact which has made superficial foreign students of China think that the Chinese have made no progress in their civilization and that the Chinese civilization is a **stagnant** one. Nevertheless, it must be admitted that, as far

---

① It refers to "a sweet ointment".

as pure intellectual life goes, the Chinese are, to a certain extent, a people of arrested development. The Chinese, as you all know, have made little or no progress not only in the physical, but also in the pure abstract sciences such as mathematics, logic and **metaphysics**. Indeed the very words "science" and "logic" in the European languages have no exact equivalent in the Chinese language. The Chinese, like children who live a life of the heart, have no taste for the abstract sciences, because in these the heart and feelings are not engaged. In fact, for everything which does not engage the heart and feelings, such as tables of statistics, the Chinese have a dislike amounting to **aversion**. But if tables of statistics and the pure abstract sciences fill the Chinese with aversion, the physical sciences as they are now pursued in Europe, which require you to cut up and mutilate the body of a living animal in order to **verify** a scientific theory, would inspire the Chinese with **repugnance** and horror.

<u>13</u> The Chinese, I say, as far as pure intellectual life goes, are to a certain extent, a people of arrested development. The Chinese to this day live the life of a child, a life of the heart. In this respect, the Chinese people, old as they are as a nation, are to the present day, a nation of children. But then it is important you should remember that this nation of children, who live a life of the heart, who are so primitive in many of their ways, have yet a power of mind and rationality which you do not find in a primitive people, a power of mind and rationality which has enabled them to deal with the complex and difficult problems of social life, government and civilization with a success which, I will venture to say here, the ancient and modern nations of Europe have not been able to attain—a success so **signal** that they have been able practically and actually to keep in peace and order a greater portion of the population of the Continent of Asia under a great Empire.

<u>14</u> In fact, what I want to say here, is that the wonderful peculiarity of the Chinese people is not that they live a life of the heart. All primitive people

also live a life of the heart. The Christian people of **medieval** Europe, as we know, also lived a life of the heart. Matthew Arnold① says: "The poetry of medieval Christianity lived by the heart and imagination." But the wonderful peculiarity of the Chinese people, I want to say here, is that, while living a life of the heart, the life of a child, they yet have a power of mind and rationality which you do not find in the Christian people of medieval Europe or in any other primitive people. In other words, the wonderful peculiarity of the Chinese is that for a people, who have lived so long as a grown-up nation, as a nation of adult reason, they are yet able to this day to live the life of a child—a life of the heart.

Vocabulary

domesticated [də'mestikeitid] a.	converted or adapted to domestic use 家养的,驯服的
vulpine ['vʌlpain] a.	resembling or characteristic of a fox 狐狸的,诡计多端的
thorough-bred ['θʌrəbred] a.	having a list of ancestors as proof of being a purebred animal 良种的,受过严格训练的
be attached to	喜爱,附属于
refinement [ri'fainmənt] n.	a highly developed state of perfection; having a flawless or impeccable quality 精致,文雅
mitigate ['mitigeit] v.	make less severe or harsh 缓和,减轻
redeem [ri'di:m] vt.	save from sins 赎回,挽回
hypothesis [hai'pɔθisis] n.	a proposal intended to explain certain facts or observations 假设
illustration [ilə'streiʃən] n.	a visual representation (a picture or diagram) that is used make some subject more pleasing or easier to understand 例证,图解
mandarin ['mændərin] n.	a high public official of imperial China 清代官吏,官话
Canton ['kæntən] n.	广州(旧称)
scamp [skæmp] n.	one who is playfully mischievous 流氓
typhoid fever	伤寒热
out-of-the-way ['autəvðə'wei] a.	偏僻的
blemish ['blemiʃ] n.	a mark or flaw that spoils the appearance of something 瑕疵,污点,缺点

---

① Matthew Arnold (1822—1888) was an English poet and cultural critic.

detached [di'tætʃt] a.	no longer connected or joined 分离的，分开的
glue [gluː] n.	cement consisting of a sticky substance that is used as an adhesive 胶，各种胶合物
elaborate [i'læbərət] a.	marked by complexity and richness of detail （煞费）苦心的，费力的
spontaneous [spɔn'teiniəs] a.	happening or arising without apparent external cause 自发的，自然的
aroma [ə'rəumə] n.	a distinctive odor that is pleasant 芳香
viz. abbr.	也就是，即是
rigid ['ridʒid] a.	incapable of compromise or flexibility 严格的，精确的
stagnant ['stægnənt] a.	not growing or changing; without force or vitality 停滞的，迟钝的
metaphysics [metə'fiziks] n.	the philosophical study of being and knowing 玄学，形而上学
aversion [ə'vəːʃən] n.	a feeling of intense dislike 厌恶
verify ['verifai] vt.	confirm the truth of 核实，查证
repugnance [ri'pʌgnəns] n.	intense aversion 反感，厌恶
signal ['signəl] a.	notably out of the ordinary 显著的
medieval [medi'iːvl] a.	relating to or belonging to the Middle Ages 中世纪的

Text C

The Chinese Character①

Bertrand Russell

1   There is a theory among **Occidentals** that the Chinaman is **inscrutable**, full of secret thoughts, and impossible for us to understand. It may be that a greater experience of China would have brought me to share this opinion; but I could see nothing to support it during the time when I was working in that country. I talked to the Chinese as I should have talked to English people,

---

① Excerpted from Bertrand Russell's *The Problem of China*.

and they answered me much as English people would have answered a Chinese whom they considered educated and not wholly unintelligent. I do not believe in the **myth** of the "Subtle **Oriental**"; I am convinced that in a game of mutual deception an Englishman or American can beat a Chinese nine times out of ten. But as many comparatively poor Chinese have dealings with rich white men, the game is often played only on one side. Then, no doubt, the white man is deceived and **swindled**; but not more than a Chinese mandarin would be in London.

<u>2</u>   One of the most remarkable things about the Chinese is their power of securing the affection of foreigners. Almost all Europeans like China, both those who come only as tourists and those who live there for many years. In spite of the Anglo-Japanese Alliance, I can recall hardly a single Englishman in the Far East who liked the Japanese as well as the Chinese. Those who have lived long among them tend to acquire their outlook and their standards. New arrivals are struck by obvious evils: the beggars, the terrible poverty, the **prevalence** of disease, the **anarchy** and corruption in politics. Every energetic Westerner feels at first a strong desire to reform these evils, and of course they ought to be reformed.

<u>3</u>   But the Chinese, even those who are the victims of preventable misfortunes, show a vast passive indifference to the excitement of the foreigners; they wait for it to **go off**, like the **effervescence** of soda-water. And gradually strange hesitations creep into the mind of the bewildered traveller; after a period of indignation, he begins to doubt all the maxims he has **hitherto** accepted without question. Is it really wise to be always guarding against future misfortune? Is it **prudent** to lose all enjoyment of the present through thinking of the disasters that may come at some future date? Should our lives be passed in building a **mansion** that we shall never have leisure to inhabit?

<u>4</u>   The Chinese answer these questions in the negative, and therefore have

to **put up with** poverty, disease, and anarchy. But, to **compensate** for these evils, they have **retained**, as industrial nations have not, the capacity for civilized enjoyment, for leisure and laughter, for pleasure in sunshine and philosophical discourse. The Chinese, of all classes, are more laughter-loving than any other race with which I am acquainted; they find amusement in everything, and a dispute can always be softened by a joke.

5   I remember one hot day when a party of us were crossing the hills in chairs—the way was rough and very steep, the work for the **coolies** very severe. At the highest point of our journey, we stopped for ten minutes to let the men rest. Instantly they all sat in a row, brought out their pipes, and began to laugh among themselves as if they had not a care in the world. In any country that had learned the virtue of **forethought**, they would have devoted the moments to complaining of the heat, in order to increase their tip. We, being Europeans, spent the time worrying whether the automobile would be waiting for us at the right place. Well-to-do Chinese would have started a discussion as to whether the universe moves in cycles or progresses by a **rectilinear** motion; or they might have set to work to consider whether the truly virtuous man shows *complete* self-**abnegation**, or may, on occasion, consider his own interest.

6   One comes across white men occasionally who suffer under the delusion that China is not a civilized country. Such men have quite forgotten what constitutes civilization. It is true that there are no **trams** in Peking, and that the electric light is poor. It is true that there are places full of beauty, which Europeans **itch to** make **hideous** by digging up coal. It is true that the educated Chinaman is better at writing poetry than at remembering the sort of facts which can be looked up in *Whitaker's Almanac*. A European, in recommending a place of residence, will tell you that it has a good train service; the best quality he can conceive in any place is that it should be easy to get away from. But a Chinaman will tell you nothing about the trains; if

you ask, he will tell you wrong. What he tells you is that there is a palace built by an ancient emperor, and a retreat in a lake for scholars **weary** of the world, founded by a famous poet of the Tang dynasty. It is this outlook that strikes the Westerner as barbaric.

<u>7</u>   The Chinese, from the highest to the lowest, have an **imperturbable** quiet dignity, which is usually not destroyed even by a European education. They are not **self-assertive**, either individually or nationally; their pride is too profound for self-assertion. They admit China's military weakness in comparison with foreign Powers, but they do not consider efficiency in **homicide** the most important quality in a man or a nation. I think that, at bottom, they almost all believe that China is the greatest nation in the world, and has the finest civilization. A Westerner cannot be expected to accept this view, because it is based on traditions utterly different from his own. But gradually one comes to feel that it is, **at any rate**, not an absurd view; that it is, in fact, the logical outcome of a self-consistent standard of values. The typical Westerner wishes to be the cause of as many changes as possible in his environment; the typical Chinaman wishes to enjoy as much and as delicately as possible. This difference is at the bottom of most of the contrast between China and the English-speaking world.

<u>8</u>   We in the West make a **fetish** of "progress," which is the ethical **camouflage** of the desire to be the cause of changes. If we are asked, for instance, whether machinery has really improved the world, the question strikes us as foolish: it has brought great changes and therefore great "progress." What we believe to be a love of progress is really, in nine cases out of ten, a love of power, an enjoyment of the feeling that by our **fiat** we can make things different. For the sake of this pleasure, a young American will work so hard that, by the time he has acquired his millions, he has become a victim of **dyspepsia, compelled** to live on toast and water, and to be a mere spectator of the feasts that he offers to his guests. But he **consoles**

himself with the thought that he can control politics, and provoke or prevent wars as may suit his investments. It is this **temperament** that makes Western nations "progressive."

9   There are, of course, ambitious men in China, but they are less common than among ourselves. And their ambition takes a different form—not a better form, but one produced by the preference of enjoyment to power. It is a natural result of this preference that **avarice** is a widespread failing of the Chinese. Money brings the means of enjoyment, therefore money is passionately desired. With us, money is desired chiefly as a means to power; politicians, who can acquire power without much money, are often content to remain poor. In China, the *tuchuns* (military governors), who have the real power, almost always use it for the sole purpose of **amassing** a fortune. Their object is to escape to Japan at a suitable moment; with sufficient **plunder** to enable them to enjoy life quietly for the rest of their days. The fact that in escaping they lose power does not trouble them in the least. It is, of course, obvious that such politicians, who spread **devastation** only in the provinces committed to their care, are far less harmful to the world than our own, who ruin whole continents in order to win an election campaign.

10 The corruption and anarchy in Chinese politics do much less harm than one would be inclined to expect. But for the **predatory** desires of the Great Powers—especially Japan—the harm would be much less than is done by our own "efficient" Governments. Nine-tenths of the activities of a modern Government are harmful; therefore the worse they are performed, the better. In China, where the Government is lazy, corrupt, and stupid, there is a degree of individual liberty which has been wholly lost in the rest of the world.

11 The laws are just as bad as elsewhere; occasionally, under foreign pressure, a man is imprisoned for **Bolshevist** propaganda, just as he might be in England or America. But this is quite exceptional; as a rule, in practice,

there is very little interference with free speech and a free press. The individual does not feel obliged to **follow the herd**, as he has in Europe since 1914, and in America since 1917. Men still think for themselves, and are not afraid to announce the conclusions at which they arrive. Individualism has perished in the West, but in China it survives, for good as well as for evil. Self-respect and personal dignity are possible for every coolie in China, to a degree which is, among ourselves, possible only for a few leading financiers.

<u>12</u> The business of "saving face," which often strikes foreigners in China as **ludicrous**, is only the **carrying-out** of respect for personal dignity in the sphere of social manners. Everybody has "face," even the humblest beggar; there are humiliations that you must not inflict upon him, if you are not to outrage the Chinese **ethical** code. If you speak to a Chinaman in a way that transgresses the code, he will laugh, because your words must be taken as spoken **in jest** if they are not to constitute an offense.

<u>13</u> Once I thought that the students to whom I was lecturing were not as industrious as they might be, and I told them so in just the same words that I should have used to English students in the same circumstances. But I soon found I was making a mistake. They all laughed uneasily, which surprised me until I saw the reason. Chinese life, even among the most modernized, is far more polite than anything to which we are accustomed. This, of course, interferes with efficiency, and also (what is more serious) with sincerity and truth in personal relations. If I were Chinese, I should wish to see it mitigated. But to those who suffer from the brutalities of the West, Chinese **urbanity** is very restful. Whether on the balance it is better or worse than our frankness, I shall not venture to decide.

<u>14</u> The Chinese remind one of the English in their love of compromise and in their habit of bowing to public opinion. Seldom is a conflict pushed to its ultimate brutal issue. The treatment of the Manchu Emperor may be taken as a case in point. When a Western country becomes a Republic, it is customary

to cut off the head of the **deposed monarch**, or at least to cause him to fly the country. But the Chinese have left the Emperor his title, his beautiful palace, his troops of **eunuchs**, and an income of several million dollars a year. He is a boy of sixteen, living peaceably in the Forbidden City. Once, in the course of a civil war, he was nominally restored to power for a few days; but he was deposed again, without being in any way punished for the use to which he had been put.

15   Public opinion is a very real force in China, when it can be roused. It was, **by all accounts**, mainly responsible for the downfall of the An Fu party in the summer of 1920. This party was pro-Japanese and was accepting loans from Japan. Hatred of Japan is the strongest and most widespread of political passions in China, and it was stirred up by the students in fiery **orations**. The An Fu party had, at first, a great **preponderance** of military strength; but their soldiers melted away when they came to understand the cause for which they were expected to fight. In the end, the opponents of the An Fu party were able to enter Peking and change the Government almost without firing a shot.

16   The same influence of public opinion was decisive in the teachers' strike, which was on the point of being settled when I left Peking. The Government, which is always **impecunious**, owing to corruption, had left its teachers unpaid for many months. At last they struck to enforce payment, and went on a peaceful **deputation** to the Government, accompanied by many students. There was a clash with the soldiers and police, and many teachers and students were more or less severely wounded. This led to a terrific outcry, because the love of education in China is profound and widespread. The newspapers **clamoured** for revolution. The Government had just spent nine million dollars in corrupt payments to three Tuchuns who had descended upon the capital to **extort** blackmail. It could not find any colourable pretext for refusing the few hundred thousands required by the teachers, and it

capitulated in panic. I do not think there is any Anglo-Saxon country where the interests of teachers would have roused the same degree of public feeling.

17   Nothing astonishes a European more in the Chinese than their patience. The educated Chinese are well aware of the foreign **menace**. They realize acutely what the Japanese have done in Manchuria and Shantung. They are aware that the English in Hong-Kong are doing their utmost to bring to **naught** the Canton attempt to introduce good government in the South. They know that all the Great Powers, without exception, look with greedy eyes upon the undeveloped resources of their country, especially its coal and iron. They have before them the example of Japan, which, by developing a brutal militarism, a **cast-iron** discipline, and a new reactionary religion, has succeeded in holding at bay the fierce lusts of "civilized" industrialists. Yet they neither copy Japan nor submit tamely to foreign domination. They think not in decades, but in centuries. They have been conquered before, first by the Tartars and then by the Manchus; but in both cases they absorbed their conquerors. Chinese civilization persisted, unchanged; and after a few generations the invaders became more Chinese than their subjects.

18   Manchuria is a rather empty country, with abundant room for colonization. The Japanese assert that they need colonies for their surplus population, yet the Chinese immigrants into Manchuria exceed the Japanese a hundredfold. Whatever may be the temporary political status of Manchuria, it will remain a part of Chinese civilization, and can be recovered whenever Japan happens to be in difficulties. The Chinese derive such strength from their four hundred millions, the toughness of their national customs, their power of passive resistance, and their unrivalled national **cohesiveness**—in spite of the civil wars, which merely ruffle the surface—that they can afford to despise military methods, and to wait till the feverish energy of their oppressors shall have exhausted itself in **internecine** combats.

19   China is much less a political entity than a civilization—the only one that

has survived from ancient times. Since the days of Confucius, the Egyptian, Babylonian, Persian, Macedonian, and Roman Empires have perished; but China has persisted through a continuous evolution. There have been foreign influences—first Buddhism, and now Western science. But Buddhism did not turn the Chinese into Indians, and Western science will not turn them into Europeans. I have met men in China who knew as much of Western learning as any professor among ourselves; yet they had not been thrown off their balance, or **lost touch with** their own people. What is bad in the West—its brutality, its restlessness, its readiness to oppress the weak, its preoccupation with purely material aims—they see to be bad, and do not wish to adopt. What is good, especially its science, they do wish to adopt.

20   The old **indigenous** culture of China has become rather dead; its art and literature are not what they were, and Confucius does not satisfy the spiritual needs of a modern man, even if he is Chinese. The Chinese who have had a European or American education realize that a new element, is needed to vitalize native traditions, and they look to our civilization to supply it. But they do not wish to construct a civilization just like ours; and it is precisely in this that the best hope lies. If they are not **goaded** into militarism, they may produce a genuinely new civilization, better than any that we in the West have been able to create.

21   So far, I have spoken chiefly of the good sides of the Chinese character; but of course China, like every other nation, has its bad sides also. It is disagreeable to me to speak of these, as I experienced so much courtesy and real kindness from the Chinese, that I should prefer to say only nice things about them. But for the sake of China, as well as for the sake of truth, it would be a mistake to conceal what is less admirable. I will only ask the reader to remember that, on the balance, I think the Chinese one of the best nations I have come across, and am prepared to draw up a graver **indictment** against every one of the Great Powers. Shortly before I left China, an

eminent Chinese writer pressed me to say what I considered the chief defects of the Chinese. With some reluctance, I mentioned three: avarice, cowardice and **callousness**. Strange to say, my **interlocutor**, instead of getting angry, admitted the justice of my criticism, and proceeded to discuss possible remedies. This is a sample of the intellectual integrity which is one of China's greatest virtues.

22 The callousness of the Chinese is bound to strike every Anglo-Saxon. They have none of that humanitarian impulse which leads us to devote one per cent of our energy to mitigating the evils **wrought** by the other ninety-nine per cent. For instance, we have been forbidding the Austrians to join with Germany, to emigrate, or to obtain the raw materials of industry. Therefore the Viennese have starved, except those whom it has pleased us to keep alive from **philanthropy**. The Chinese would not have had the energy to starve the Viennese, or the philanthropy to keep some of them alive. While I was in China, millions were dying of famine; men sold their children into slavery for a few dollars, and killed them if this sum was unobtainable. Much was done by white men to relieve the famine, but very little by the Chinese, and that little **vitiated** by corruption. It must be said, however, that the efforts of the white men were more effective in soothing their own consciences than in helping the Chinese. So long as the present birth-rate and the present methods of agriculture persist, famines are bound to occur periodically; and those whom philanthropy keeps alive through one famine are only too likely to perish in the next.

23 Famines in China can be permanently cured only by better methods of agriculture combined with emigration or birth-control on a large scale. Educated Chinese realize this, and it makes them indifferent to efforts to keep the present victims alive. A great deal of Chinese callousness has a similar explanation, and is due to perception of the vastness of the problems involved. But there remains a **residue** which cannot be so explained. If a dog

is run over by an automobile and seriously hurt, nine out of ten passers-by will stop to laugh at the poor **brute's** howls. The spectacle of suffering does not of itself rouse any sympathetic pain in the average Chinaman; in fact, he seems to find it mildly agreeable. Their history, and their **penal code** before the revolution of 1911, show that they are by no means **destitute** of the impulse of active cruelty; but of this I did not myself come across any instances. And it must be said that active cruelty is practised by all the great nations, to an extent concealed from us only by our **hypocrisy.**

24　　Cowardice is **prima facie** a fault of the Chinese; but I am not sure that they are really lacking in courage. It is true that, in battles between rival tuchuns, both sides run away, and victory rests with the side that first discovers the flight of the other. But this proves only that the Chinese soldier is a rational man. No cause of any importance is involved, and the armies consist of mere **mercenaries.** When there is a serious issue, as, for instance, in the Tai-Ping rebellion, the Chinese are said to fight well, particularly if they have good officers. Nevertheless, I do not think that, in comparison with the Anglo-Saxons, the French, or the Germans, the Chinese can be considered a courageous people, except in the matter of passive endurance. They will endure torture, and even death, for motives which men of more **pugnacious** races would find insufficient—for example, to conceal the hiding-place of stolen plunder. In spite of their comparative lack of *active* courage, they have less fear of death than we have, as is shown by their readiness to commit suicide.

25　　Avarice is, I should say, the gravest defect of the Chinese. Life is hard, and money is not easily obtained. For the sake of money, all except a very few foreign-educated Chinese will be guilty of corruption. For the sake of a few pence, almost any coolie will run an **imminent** risk of death. The difficulty of combating Japan has arisen mainly from the fact that hardly any Chinese politician can resist Japanese bribes. I think this defect is probably due to the fact that, for many ages, an honest living has been hard to get; in which case it will be lessened as economic conditions improve. I doubt if it is any worse now in China than it was in Europe in the eighteenth century. I have not heard of any Chinese general more corrupt than Marlborough①, or of any politician more corrupt than Cardinal Dubois②. It is, therefore, quite likely that changed industrial conditions will make the Chinese as honest as we are—which is not saying much.

26 I have been speaking of the Chinese as they are in ordinary life, when they appear as men of active and **sceptical** intelligence, but of somewhat **sluggish** passions. There is, however, another side to them: they are capable of wild excitement, often of a collective kind. I saw little of this myself, but there can be no doubt of the fact. **The Boxer** rising was a case in point, and one which particularly affected Europeans. But their history is full of more or less **analogous** disturbances. It is this element in their character that makes them incalculable, and makes it impossible even to guess at their future. One can imagine a section of them becoming fanatically Bolshevist, or anti-Japanese, or Christian, or devoted to some leader who would ultimately declare himself Emperor. I suppose it is this element in their character that makes them, in spite of their habitual caution, the most reckless gamblers in the world. And many emperors have lost their thrones through the force of romantic love, although romantic love is far more despised than it is in the West.

27 To sum up the Chinese character is not easy. Much of what strikes the foreigner is due merely to the fact that they have preserved an ancient civilization which is not industrial. All this is likely to pass away, under the pressure of the Japanese, and of European and American financiers. Their

---

① John Churchill, 1st Duke of Marlborough (1650—1722), was an English general and statesman.
② Guillaume Dubois (1656—1723) was a French cardinal and statesman.

art is already perishing, and being replaced by crude imitations of second-rate European pictures. Most of the Chinese who have had a European education are quite incapable of seeing any beauty in native painting, and merely observe **contemptuously** that it does not obey **the laws of perspective.**

28 The obvious charm which the tourist finds in China cannot be preserved; it must perish at the touch of industrialism. But perhaps something may be preserved, something of the ethical qualities in which China is supreme, and which the modern world most desperately needs. Among these qualities I place first the **pacific** temper, which seeks to settle disputes on grounds of justice rather than by force. It remains to be seen whether the West will allow this temper to persist, or will force it to give place, in self-defence, to a frantic militarism like that to which Japan has been driven.

Vocabulary

Occidental [ɔksi'dentəl] n.	denoting or characteristic of countries of Europe and the Western hemisphere 西方人,欧美人
inscrutable [in'skrutəbl] a.	of an obscure nature 神秘的,不可理解的,不能预测的,不可思议的
myth [miθ] n.	a traditional story accepted as history; serves to explain the world view of a people 神话,虚构的人,虚构的事
Oriental [ori'entəl] n.	a member of an Oriental race; the term is regarded as offensive by Asians (especially by Asian Americans) 东方人
swindle ['swindl] v.	deprive of by deceit 被骗
prevalence ['prevələns] n.	the quality of prevailing generally; being widespread 流行,普遍,广泛
anarchy ['ænəki] n.	a state of lawlessness and disorder (usually resulting from a failure of government) 无政府状态,混乱,无秩序
go off	离开,进行
effervescence [efə'ves(ə)ns] n.	the process and the property of bubbling as gas escapes 冒泡,(化工)泡腾
hitherto [hiðə'tu] ad.	used in negative statement to describe a situation that has existed up to this point or up to the present time 迄今,至今

prudent ['prudnt] a.	careful and sensible; marked by sound judgment 谨慎的，精明的，节俭的
mansion ['mænʃən] n.	a large and imposing house 大厦，宅邸
put up with	容忍
compensate ['kɔmpenset] v.	make amends for; pay compensation for 补偿，赔偿
retain [ri'ten] v.	hold within 保持
coolie ['kuli] n.	an offensive name for an unskilled Asian laborer 苦力，小工
forethought ['fɔr'θɔt] n.	planning or plotting in advance of acting 深谋远虑
rectilinear [rekti'liniə] a.	characterized by a straight line or lines 直线运动的
abnegation [æbni'geʃən] n.	the denial and rejection of a doctrine or belief 克制
trams [træms] n.	a conveyance that transports passengers or freight in carriers suspended from cables and supported by a series of towers 有轨电车
itch to	恨不得
hideous ['hidiəs] a.	grossly offensive to decency or morality; causing horror 可怕的，丑恶的
weary ['wiri] a.	疲倦的，厌烦的
imperturbable [impə'tə:bəbəl] a.	get tired of something or somebody 冷静的，泰然自若的
self-assertive a.	confidently aggressive 维护自身的
homicide ['hɔmisaid] n.	the killing of a human being by another human being 杀人，杀人罪，过失杀人
at any rate	无论如何
fetish ['fetiʃ] n.	excessive or irrational devotion to some activity 恋物，迷信
camouflage ['kæmə'flɑʒ] n.	the act of concealing the identity of something by modifying its appearance 伪装，掩饰
fiat ['fi:æt] n.	a legally binding command or decision entered on the court record (as if issued by a court or judge) 命令，许可
dyspepsia [dis'pepʃə] n.	a disorder of digestive function characterized by discomfort or heartburn or nausea（内科）消化不良
compel [kəm'pel] vt.	force or compel somebody to do something 强迫，迫使
console ['kɔnsəul] vt.	give moral or emotional strength to 慰藉，安慰
temperament ['temprəmənt] n.	your basic nature, especially as it is shown in the way that you react to situations or to other people 气质，性格
avarice ['ævəris] n.	reprehensible acquisitiveness; insatiable desire for wealth (personified as one of the deadly sins) 贪婪
amass [ə'mæs] vt.	collect or gather 积累
plunder ['plʌndə] n.	goods or money obtained illegally 掠夺品，战利品
devastation [devə'steiʃn] n.	the state of being decayed or destroyed 毁坏，荒废

predatory [ˈpredətəri] a.	living by or given to victimizing others for personal gain 掠夺的,掠夺成性的,食肉的
Bolshevist [ˈbɔlʃivist] a.	布尔什维克主义的
follow the herd	人云亦云,随大流
ludicrous [ˈludikrəs] a.	broadly or extravagantly humorous; resembling farce 滑稽的,荒唐的
carrying-out	实施,贯彻
ethical [ˈeθikl] a.	conforming to accepted standards of social or professional behavior 伦理的,道德的
in jest	开玩笑地,诙谐地
urbanity [əˈbænəti] n.	polished courtesy; elegance of manner 雅致,有礼貌
depose [diˈpəuz] v.	force to leave (an office) 废黜
monarch [ˈmɔnək] n.	a nation's ruler or head of state usually by hereditary right 君主
eunuch [ˈjuːnək] n.	a man who has been castrated and is incapable of reproduction 太监
by all accounts	人人都说
oration [ɔˈreiʃ(ə)n] n.	a formal speech made in public 演说
preponderance [priˈpɔndərəns] n.	superiority in power or influence 优势,占多数
impecunious [impiˈkjuniəs] a.	not having enough money to pay for necessities 没有钱的
deputation [depjuˈteiʃən] n.	a group of representatives or delegates 代表团,代表
clamour [ˈklæmə] v.	loud and persistent outcry from many people 大声地要求
extort [ikˈstɔrt] vt.	get from you using force, threats, or other unfair or illegal means 敲诈,侵占,强求
capitulate [kəˈpitʃulet] vi.	surrender under agreed conditions 认输,屈服
menace [ˈmenəs] n.	a threat or the act of threatening 威胁
naught [nɔt] n.	a quantity of no importance 无价值
cast-iron [ˈkaːstˈaiən] a.	extremely robust 坚固的,顽强的,铸铁的
cohesiveness [kəuˈhisivnis] n.	the state of cohering or sticking together 凝聚力
internecine [intəˈniːsain] a.	characterized by bloodshed and carnage for both sides 两败俱伤的
lost touch with	失去与……的联系
indigenous [inˈdidʒinəs] a.	originating where it is found 本土的,国产的,固有的
goad [gəud] v.	deliberately make someone feel angry or irritated, often causing them to react by doing something 被刺激,煽动,驱赶
indictment [inˈdaitmənt] n.	a formal document written for a prosecuting attorney charging a person with some offense 起诉书,控告

callousness ['kæləsnɪs] n.	devoid of passion or feeling; hardheartedness 麻木不仁
interlocutor [ɪntə'lɔkjutə] n.	a person who takes part in a conversation 对话者
wrought [rɔːt] v. wreak 的过去分词	cause to happen or to occur as a consequence 造成
philanthropy [fɪ'lænθrəpɪ] n.	voluntary promotion of human welfare 慈善事业
vitiate ['vɪʃɪeɪt] vt.	corrupt morally or by intemperance or sensuality 损坏，弄坏
residue ['rezɪdjuː] n.	something left after other parts have been taken away 残渣，剩余
brute [bruːt] n.	a cruelly rapacious person 畜生
penal code	刑法典
destitute ['destɪtjuːt] a.	completely wanting or lacking 缺乏的
hypocrisy [hɪ'pɔkrɪsɪ] n.	insincerity by virtue of pretending to have qualities or beliefs that you do not really have 伪善
prima facie (Latin) ['praɪmə'feɪʃɪ] a.	乍一看的
mercenary ['mɜːsɪn(ə)rɪ] n.	a person hired to fight for another country than their own 雇佣兵
pugnacious [pʌg'neɪʃəs] a.	tough and callous by virtue of experience 好战的
imminent ['ɪmɪnənt] a.	close in time; about to occur 即将来临的
sceptical ['skeptɪk(ə)l] a.	marked by or given to doubt 怀疑的，怀疑论的
sluggish ['slʌgɪʃ] a.	with little movement; very slow 迟钝的，行动迟缓的，懒惰的
the Boxer	义和团
analogous [ə'næləgəs] a.	similar or equivalent in some respects though otherwise dissimilar 类似的，可比的
contemptuously [kən'temptjuəslɪ] ad.	without respect; in a disdainful manner 轻蔑地
the laws of perspective	透视法
pacific [pə'sɪfɪk] a.	disposed to peace or of a peaceful nature 和平的，温和的，平静的

Unit 2

Foreign Impressions

Text A   Here Is New York
Text B   Flowery Tuscany
Text C   What I Saw in America

Text A

Here Is New York[①]

Elwyn Brooks White

<u>1</u>   On any person who desires such queer prizes, New York will **bestow** the gift of loneliness and the gift of privacy. It is this **largess** that accounts for the presence within the city's walls of a considerable section of the population; for the residents of Manhattan are to a large extent strangers who have pulled up stakes somewhere and come to town, seeking **sanctuary** or fulfillment or some greater or lesser grail. The **capacity** to make such dubious gifts is a mysterious quality of New York. It can destroy an individual, or it can fulfill him, depending a good deal on luck. No one should come to New York to live unless he is willing to be lucky.

<u>2</u>   New York is the concentrate of art and commerce and sport and religion and entertainment and finance, bringing to a single compact arena the

---

①   Excerpted from Elwyn Brooks White's *Here Is New York*.

gladiator, the evangelist, the promoter, the actor, the trader, and the merchant. It carries on its lapel the **unexpungeable** odor of the long past, so that no matter where you sit in New York you feel the vibrations of great times and tall deeds, of queer people and events and undertakings. I am sitting at the moment in a **stifling** hotel room in 90-degree heat, halfway down an air shaft, in midtown. No air moves in or out of the room, yet I am curiously affected by **emanations** from the immediate surroundings. I am twenty-two blocks from where Rudolph Valentino lay in state, eight blocks from where Nathan Hale was executed, five blocks from the publisher's office where Ernest Hemingway hit Max Eastman on the nose, four miles from where Walt Whitman sat sweating out editorials for the Brooklyn Eagle, thirty-four blocks from the street Willa Cather lived in when she came to New York to write books about Nebraska, one block from where Marceline used to clown on the boards of the Hippodrome, thirty-six blocks from the spot where the historian Joe Gould kicked a radio to pieces in full view of the public, thirteen blocks from where Harry Thaw shot Stanford White, five blocks from where I used to usher at the Metropolitan Opera and only 112 blocks from the spot where Clarence Day the elder was washed of his sins in the Church of the **Epiphany** (I could continue this list indefinitely); and for that matter I am probably occupying the very room that any number of exalted and some wise memorable characters sat in, some of them on hot, breathless afternoons, lonely and private and full of their own sense of emanations from without.

3　　When I went down to lunch a few minutes ago I noticed that the man sitting next to me (about eighteen inches away along the wall) was Fred Stone. The eighteen inches are both the connection and the separation that New York provides for its inhabitants. My only connection with Fred Stone was that I saw him in the The Wizard of Oz around the beginning of the century. But our waiter felt the same stimulus from being close to a man from Oz, and after Mr. Stone left the room the waiter told me that when he (the waiter) was a young man just arrived in this country and before he could understand a word of English, he had taken his girl for their first theater date to The Wizard of Oz. It was a wonderful show, the waiter recalled—a man of straw, a man of tin. Wonderful! (And still only eighteen inches away.) "Mr. Stone is a very hearty eater," said the waiter thoughtfully, content with this **fragile** participation in destiny, this link with Oz.

4   New York blends the gift of privacy with the excitement of participation; and better than most dense communities it succeeds in insulating the individual (if he wants it, and almost every body wants or needs it) against all **enormous** and violent and wonderful events that are taking place every minute. Since I have been sitting in this **miasmic** air shaft, a good many rather splashy events have occurred in town. A man shot and killed his wife in a fit of jealousy. It caused no stir outside his block and got only small mention in the papers. I did not attend. Since my arrival, the greatest air show ever staged in all the world took place in town. I didn't attend and neither did most of the eight million other inhabitants, although they say there was quite a crowd. I didn't even hear any planes except a couple of **westbound** commercial airliners that habitually use this air shaft to fly over. The biggest oceangoing ships on the North Atlantic arrived and departed. I didn't notice them and neither did most other New Yorkers. I am told this is the greatest seaport in the world, with 650 miles of waterfront, and ships calling here from many exotic lands, but the only boat I've happened to notice since my arrival was a small **sloop** tacking out of the East River night before last on the ebb tide when I was walking across the Brooklyn Bridge. I heard the Queen Mary blow one midnight, though, and the sound carried the whole history of departure and longing and loss. The Lions have been in convention. I've seen not one Lion. A friend of mine saw one and told me about him. (He was lame, and was wearing a bolero.) At

the ball grounds and horse parks the greatest sporting spectacles have been enacted. I saw no ballplayer, no racehorse. The governor came to town. I heard the siren scream, but that was all there was to that—an eighteen-inch margin again. A man was killed by a falling **cornice**. I was not a party to the tragedy, and again the inches counted heavily.

<u>5</u>   I mention these events merely to show that New York is peculiarly constructed to absorb almost anything that comes along (whether a thousand-foot liner out of the East or twenty-thousand-man convention out of the West) without inflicting the event on its inhabitants; so that every event is, in a sense, optional, and the inhabitant is in the happy position of being able to choose his spectacle and so conserve his soul. In most **metropolises**, small and large, the choice is often not with the individual at all. He is thrown to the Lions. The Lions are overwhelming; the event is unavoidable. A cornice falls, that it hits every citizen on the head, every last man in town. I sometimes think that the only event that hits every New Yorker on the head is the annual St. Patrick's Day parade, which is fairly **penetrating**—the Irish are a hard race to tune out, there are 500 000 of them in residence, and they have the police force right in the family.

<u>6</u>   The quality in New York that **insulates** its inhabitants from life may simply weaken them as individuals. Perhaps it is healthier to live in a community where, when a cornice falls, you feel the blow; where, when the governor passes, you see at any rate his hat.

<u>7</u>   I am not defending New York in this regard. Many of its settlers are probably here merely to escape, not face, reality. But whatever it means, it is a rather rare gift, and I believe it has a positive effect on the creative capacities of New Yorkers—for creation is in part merely the business of forgoing the great and small distractions.

<u>8</u>   Although New York often imparts a feeling of great **forlornness** or **forsakenness**, it seldom seems dead or **unresourceful**; and you always feel that

either by shifting your location ten blocks or by reducing your fortune by five dollars you can experience **rejuvenation**. Many people who have no real independence of spirit depend on the city's tremendous variety and sources of excitement for spiritual **sustenance** and maintenance of morale. In the country there are a few chances of sudden rejuvenation—a shift in weather, perhaps, or something arriving in the mail. But in New York the chances are endless. I think that although many persons are here from some excess of spirit(which caused them to break away from their small town), some, too, are here from a deficiency of spirit, who find in New York a protection, or an easy **substitution.**

Vocabulary

bestow [bi'stəu] v.	give as a gift 赠给
largess [la:'dʒes] n.	liberality in bestowing gifts; extremely liberal and generous of spirit 慷慨赠予
sanctuary ['sæŋktʃuəri] n.	a shelter from danger or hardship 庇护所,圣所
capacity [kə'pæsəti] n.	ability to perform or produce 容量,才能
unexpungeable [ˌʌnik'spʌndʒəbl] a.	incapable of being subdued or overthrown 不可磨灭的
stifling ['staifliŋ] a.	characterized by oppressive heat and humidity 令人窒息的
emanation [ˌemə'neiʃn] n.	the act of emitting; causing to flow forth 散发
epiphany [i'pifəni] n.	a divine manifestation 顿悟,显灵
fragile ['frædʒail] a.	vulnerably delicate 脆弱的
enormous [i'nɔ:məs] a.	extraordinarily large in size or extent or amount or power or degree 庞大的
miasmic [mi'æzmik] a.	an unwholesome atmosphere 瘴气的
westbound ['westbaund] a.	moving toward the west 西行的
sloop [slu:p] n.	a sailing vessel with a single mast 单桅纵帆船
cornice ['kɔ:nis] n.	a molding at the corner between the ceiling and the top of a wall 屋檐
metropolises [mi'trɔpəlisiz] n.	the largest, busiest, and most important city in a country or region 大都会
penetrating ['penitreitiŋ] a.	having the power of entering or piercing 渗透性的
insulate ['insjuleit] v.	set apart 使孤立

forlornness [fə'lɔːnnis] n.	sadness resulting from being forsaken or abandoned 孤立,愁绪
forsakenness [fə'seikənnəs] n.	the state of being completely deserted or abandoned 被抛弃的状态
unresourceful [ˌʌnri'sɔːsfl] a.	not adroit or imaginative 一筹莫展
rejuvenation [riˌdʒuːvə'neiʃn] n.	the act of restoring to a more youthful condition 恢复活力
sustenance ['sʌstənəns] n.	a source of materials to nourish the body 养料
morale [mə'rɑːl] n.	a state of individual psychological well-being based upon a sense of confidence and usefulness 士气,精神面貌
substitution [ˌsʌbsti'tjuːʃn] n.	the act of putting one thing or person in the place of another 替代

I. Vocabulary Building

-ward/-wards: towards a certain direction

e. g. , toward, forward, upwards, downwards, homeward, inward, outward, seaward, westward, eastward

-wise: along..., in terms of...

e. g. , clockwise, counterclockwise, coastwise, crosswise, likewise

-dom: status, a field dominated by a certain status

e. g. , kingdom, officialdom, serfdom, martyrdom, bachelordom, stardom, filmdom, cockneydom

-cide/-icide: killing

e. g. , suicide, genocide, insecticide, herbicide, bactericide, ecocide, fratricide, homicide, matricide, patricide

II. Discussion

Discuss the following questions with your own words.

1. As is mentioned in the excerpt, "On any person who desires such queer prizes, New York will bestow the gift of loneliness and the gift of privacy," what is your interpretation of "such queer prizes"?

2. E. B. White's roam around Manhattan remains as a lyric and nostalgic "love letter" to the city. What is the haunting theme of his "love letter"?

3. In literary circles, E. B. White is also noted for his crystalline clarity of style. Besides short and witty comments, what are the quintessential elements of his style?

4. The author states at one point: "It is a miracle that New York works at all" referring to the fact that there is so much compressed in such a small area. Could you illustrate the miraculous quality of New York by citing some vivid instances from the excerpt?

5. In his short book *Here is New York* (1949), E. B. White concludes with a dark note touching upon the forces that may destroy the city that the writer loves. What may you reasonably infer about the destructive force?

III. Translation A

Translate the following sentences selected from the text into Chinese.

1. On any person who desires such queer prizes, New York will bestow the gift of loneliness and the gift of privacy. (Para. 1)

2. It carries on its lapel the unexpungeable odor of the long past, so that no matter where you sit in New York you feel the vibrations of great times and tall deeds, of queer people and events and undertakings. I am sitting at the moment in a stifling hotel room in 90-degree heat, halfway down an air shaft, in midtown. (Para. 2)

3. It was a wonderful show, the waiter recalled—a man of straw, a man of tin. Wonderful! (And still only eighteen inches away.) "Mr. Stone is a very hearty eater," said the waiter thoughtfully, content with this fragile participation in destiny, this link with Oz. (Para. 3)

4. Although New York often imparts a feeling of great forlornness or forsakenness, it seldom seems dead or unresourceful. (Para. 8)

5. Many people who have no real independence of spirit depend on the city's tremendous variety and sources of excitement for spiritual sustenance and maintenance of morale. (Para. 8)

IV. Translation B
Translate the following passage into Chinese.

But in the sunny countries, change is the reality and permanence is artificial and a condition of imprisonment. Hence, to the northerner, the phenomenal world is essentially tragical, because it is temporal and must cease to exist. Its very existence implies ceasing to exist, and this is the root of the feeling of tragedy. But to the southerner, the sun is so dominant that shadow, or dark, is only merely relative: merely the result of something getting between one and the sun. In the human race, the one thing that is always there is the shining sun, and dark shadow is an accident of intervention. (Excerpted from Text B)

V. Writing Exercise

As is observed by E. B. White, "There are roughly three New Yorks. There is, first, the New York of the man or woman who was born here, who takes the city for granted and accepts its size and its turbulences as natural and inevitable. Second, there is the New York of the commuter—the city that is devoured by locusts each day and spat out each night. Third, there is the New York of the person who was born somewhere else and came to New York in quest of something." On the basis of the above-mentioned observations, please write a relevant critical comment on the diverse features of the city life.

Text B

Flowery Tuscany[①]

David Herbert Lawrence

1   North of the Alps, the everlasting winter is interrupted by summers that struggle and soon **yield**; south of the Alps, the everlasting summer is interrupted by **spasmodic** and **spiteful** winters that never get a real hold, but that are mean and dogged. The in-between, in either case, is just as it may be. But the lands of the sun are south of the Alps, forever.

2   In the morning, the sun shines strong on the horizontal green cloud-puffs of the pines, the sky is clear and full of life, the water runs hastily, still browned by the last juice of crushed olives. And there the earth's bowl of crocuses is amazing. You cannot believe that the flowers are really still. They are open with such delight, and their pistil thrust（雌蕊花柱）is so red-orange, and they are so many, all reaching out wide and marvelous, that it suggests a perfect **ecstasy** of radiant, **thronging** movement, lit-up violet and orange, and surging in some invisible rhythm of concerted, delightful movement. You cannot believe they do not move, and make some sort of **crystalline** sound of delight. If you sit still and watch, you begin to move with them, like moving with the stars, and you feel the sound of their radiance. All the little cells of the flowers must be leaping with flowery life and **utterance.**

3   And now that it is March, there is a rush of flowers. Down by the other stream, which turns sideways to the sun, and **tangles** the brier（野蔷薇）and bramble（荆棘）, down where the hellebore（菟葵）has stood so wan and

---

①   Excerpted from David Herbert Lawrence's *The Year in Flowery Tuscany*.

dignified all winter, there are now white tufts of primroses (报春花), suddenly come. Among the tangle and near the water-lip, tufts and bunches of primroses, in **abundance**. Yet they look more **wan**, more **pallid**, more flimsy than English primroses. They lack some of the full wonder of the northern flowers. One tends to overlook them, to turn to the great, **solemn**-faced purple violets that rear up from the bank, and above all, to the wonderful little towers of the grape hyacinth (风信子). This is the time, in March, when the sloe (黑刺李) is white and misty in the hedgetangle (灌木乱丛) by the stream, and on the slope of land the peach tree stands pink and alone. The almond blossom, silvery pink, is passing, but the peach, deep-toned, bluey, not at all **ethereal**, this reveals itself like flesh, and the trees are like isolated individuals, the peach and the apricot (杏子). It is so **conspicuous** and so individual, that pink among the coming green of spring, because the first flowers that emerge from winter seem always white or yellow or purple. Now the celandines (白屈菜) are out, and along the edges of the podere (博得里尔), the big, sturdy, black-purple anemones (银莲花), with black hearts.

<u>4</u>   The daisies are out too, in sheets, and they too red-mouthed. The first ones are big and handsome. But as March goes on, the **dwindle** to bright little things, like tiny buttons, clouds of them together. That means summer is nearly here.

<u>5</u>   In some places there are odd yellow tulips, slender, spiky and Chinese looking. They are very lovely, pricking out their dulled yellow in slim spikes. But they too soon lean, expand beyond themselves, and are gone like an **illusion**.

<u>6</u>   And when the tulips are gone, there is a moment's pause, before summer. Summer is the next move.

<u>7</u>   In the pause towards the end of April, when the flowers seem to hesitate, the leaves make up their minds to come out. For sometime, at the

very ends of the bare boughs of fig trees, **spurts** of pure green have been burning like little **cloven** tongues of green fire vivid on the tips of the **candelabrum.** Now these spurts of green spread out, and begin to take the shape of hands, feeling for the air of summer. And tiny green figs are below them, like glands（腺体）on the throat of a goat.

8   Now the aspens（山杨树）on the hill are all remarkable with the **translucent membranes** of blood-veined leaves. They are gold-brown, but not like autumn, rather like thin wings bats when like birds—call them birds—they wheel in clouds against the setting sun, and the sun glows through the stretched membrane of their wings, as through thin, brown-red **stained** glass. This is the red **sap** of summer, not the red dust of autumn.

9   The cherry tree is something the same, but more **sturdy.** Now, in the last week of April, the cherry blossom is still white, but **waning** and passing away: it is late this year, and the leaves are **clustering** thick and softly copper（铜）in their dark blood-filled glow. It is queer about fruit trees in this district. The pear and the peach were out together. But now the pear tree is a lovely thick softness of new and glossy green, vivid with a tender fullness of apple-green leaves, **gleaming** among all the other green of the landscape, the half-high wheat, **emerald,** and the grey olive, half-invisible, the browning green of the dark cypress（翠柏）, the black of the evergreen oak, the rolling of the heavy green **puffs** of the stone-pines, the **flimsy** green of small peach and almond trees, the sturdy young green of horse-chestnut（七叶树）. So many greens, all in flakes and shelves and **tilted** tables and round shoulders and plumes（羽毛饰）and shaggles（矮树丛）and uprisen bushes, of greens and greens, sometimes blindingly brilliant at evening, when the landscape looks as if it were on fire from inside, with greenness and with gold.

10   In the wood, the scrub-oak is only just coming **uncrumpled,** and the pines keep their hold on winter. They are wintry things, stone-pines. At

Christmas, their heavy green clouds are richly beautiful. When the cypresses rise their tall and naked bodies of dark green, and the **osiers** are vivid red-orange, on the still blue air, and the land is lavender; then, in mid-winter, the landscape is the most beautiful in colour, surging with colour.

<u>11</u>   Not that this week is flowerless. But the flowers are a little lonely things, here and there: the early purple orchid（兰花）, ruddy and very much alive, you come across occasionally, then the little groups of bee-orchids, with their ragged **concerted** indifference to their appearance. Also there are the huge bud-spikes of the **stout**, thick flowering pink orchid, huge buds like fat ears of wheat, hard-purple and splendid. But already odd grains of the wheat-ear are open, and out of the purple hangs the delicate pink rag of floweret（小花）. Also there are very lovely and choice cream-clouted orchids with brown spots on the long and delicate lip. These grow in the more moist places, and have exotic tender spikes, very rare-seeming. Another orchid is a little, pretty yellow one.

<u>12</u>   By May, the nightingale will sing an unbroken song, and the discreet, barely audible Tuscan cuckoo will be a little more audible. Then the lovely pale-lilac irises will come out in all their showering abundance of tender, proud, spiky bloom, till the air will gleam with mauve（淡紫色）, and a new crystalline lightness will be everywhere.

<u>13</u>   There will be tufts of irises（鸢尾花）everywhere, arising up proud and tender. When the rose-coloured wild gladiolus（剑兰，唐菖蒲）is **mingled** in the corn, and the love-in-the-mist（黑种草）opens blue: in May and June, before the corn is cut.

<u>14</u>   But as yet is neither May nor June, but the end of April, the pause between spring and summer, the nightingale singing uninterrupted, the bean-flowers dying in the bean-fields, the bean-perfume passing with spring, the little birds hatching in the nests, the olives **pruned**, and the vines, the last bit of late ploughing finished, and not much work to hand, now, not

until the peas are ready to pick, in another two weeks or so.

15 So the change, the endless and rapid change. In the sunny countries, the change seems more vivid, and more complete than in the grey countries. In the grey countries, there is a grey or dark **permanency**, over whose surface passes change **ephemeral**, leaving no real mark.

16 But in the sunny countries, change is the reality and permanence is artificial and a condition of **imprisonment**. Hence, to the northerner, the phenomenal world is essentially tragical, because it is **temporal** and must cease to exist. Its very existence implies ceasing to exist, and this is the root of the feeling of tragedy.

17 But to the southerner, the sun is so dominant that shadow, or dark, is only merely **relative**: merely the result of something getting between one and the sun.

18 In the human race, the one thing that is always there is the shining sun, and dark shadow is an accident of **intervention.**

19 For my part, if the sun always shines, and always will shine, in spite of millions of clouds of words. In the sunshine, even death is sunny. And there is no end to the sunshine.

20 That is why the rapid change of the Tuscan spring is **utterly** free, for me, of any senses of tragedy. The sun always shines. It is our fault if we don't think so.

Vocabulary

yield [jiːld] v.　　　　　　　　end resistance, especially under pressure or force 屈服
spasmodic [spæzˈmɔdik] a.　　occurring in spells and often abruptly 一阵阵的
spiteful [ˈspaitfl] a.　　　　　showing malicious ill will and a desire to hurt 恶意的
ecstasy [ˈekstəsi] n.　　　　　a state of elated bliss 狂喜
throng [θrɔŋ] n.　　　　　　　press tightly together or cram 蜂拥而至
crystalline [ˈkristəlain] a.　　transmitting light; able to be seen through with clarity 似水晶的

Unit 2
Foreign Impressions

utterance [ˈʌtərəns] n.	the use of uttered sounds for auditory communication 表达
tangle [ˈtæŋgl] v.	twist together or entwine into a confusing mass （使）缠结
abundance [əˈbʌndəns] n.	the property of a more than adequate quantity or supply 丰富
wan [wɔn] a.	pale and sickly 苍白的
pallid [ˈpælid] a.	abnormally deficient in color as suggesting physical or emotional distress 苍白的，病态的
solemn [ˈsɔləm] a.	dignified and somber in manner or character 庄重的
ethereal [iˈθiəriəl] a.	characterized by lightness; as impalpable or intangible as air 缥缈
conspicuous [kənˈspikjuəs] a.	obvious to the eye or mind 显而易见的
dwindle [ˈdwindl] v.	become smaller or lose substance 缩小
illusion [iˈluːʒn] n.	an erroneous mental representation 错觉,幻想
spurt [spəːt] v.	gush forth in a sudden stream or jet 突然喷出
cloven [ˈkləuvən] a.	used of hooves 劈开的
candelabrum [ˌkændəˈlaːbrəm] n.	branched candlestick 烛台
translucent [trænsˈluːsnt] a.	almost transparent; allowing light to pass through diffusely 半透明的
membranes [ˈmemˌbreinz] n.	a thin piece of skin which connects or covers parts of a person's or animal's body 薄膜
stained [steind] a.	marked or dyed or discolored with foreign matter 染色的
sap [sæp] n.	a watery solution of sugars, salts, and minerals that circulates through the vascular system of a plant 树液,活力
sturdy [ˈstəːdi] a.	having rugged physical strength 强壮的
waning [ˈweiniŋ] a.	a gradual decrease in magnitude or extent 衰落
cluster [ˈklʌstə(r)] n.	gather or cause to gather into a cluster 使聚集
gleaming [ˈgliːmiŋ] a.	bright with a steady but subdued shining 闪闪发光的
emerald [ˈemərəld] n.	the green color of an emerald 翡翠,翠绿色
puff [pʌf] n.	a short light gust of air 一阵(气味、烟雾等)
flimsy [ˈflimzi] a.	very thin and insubstantial 薄的
tilted [ˈtiltid] a.	departing from the true vertical or horizontal 倾斜的
uncrumpled [ʌnˈkrʌmpld] a.	having no wrinkles 衣冠整洁的
osier [ˈəuziə(r)] n.	any of various willows having pliable twigs used in basketry and furniture 柳树
concerted [kənˈsəːtid] a.	involving the joint activity of two or more 协调的
stout [staut] a.	having rugged physical strength 结实的

mingle ['miŋgl] v.	be all mixed up or jumbled together 混合
prune [pruːn] v.	cultivate, tend, and cut back the growth of 修剪
permanency ['pəːmənənsi] n.	the property of being able to exist for an indefinite duration 永存
ephemeral [i'femərəl] a.	enduring a very short time 朝生暮死的
imprisonment [im'priznmənt] n.	the act of confining someone in a prison (or as if in a prison) 关押，监禁
temporal ['tempərəl] a.	not eternal 暂存的
relative ['relətiv] a.	not absolute or complete 相对的
intervention [ˌintə'venʃn] n.	the act of intervening (as to mediate a dispute) 介入，干涉
utterly ['ʌtəli] ad.	completely; used informally as intensifiers 完全地，彻底地

Text C

What I Saw in America①

Gilbert Keith Chesterton

1   I have never managed to lose my old conviction that travel narrows the mind. At least a man must make a double effort of moral humility and imaginative energy to prevent it from narrowing his mind. Indeed there is something touching and even tragic about the thought of the thoughtless tourist, who might have stayed at home loving Laplanders, embracing Chinamen②, and clasping Patagonians to his heart in Hampstead or Surbiton, but for his blind and suicidal impulse to go and see what they looked like. This is not meant for nonsense; still less is it meant for the silliest sort of nonsense, which is **cynicism**. The human bond that he feels at

---

① Excerpted from Gilbert Keith Chesterton's *What I Saw in America*.

② "Chinaman"一词在早期的词典（如1913年版的韦氏字典）中没有负面含义，与"Englishman, Frenchman, Irishman"等并列使用。但在现代英语中，该词具有歧视意味，泛指华人和亚洲人，已不再使用。

home is not an **illusion**. On the contrary, it is rather an inner reality. Man is inside all men. In a real sense any man may be inside any men. But to travel is to leave the inside and draw dangerously near the outside. So long as he thought of men in the abstract, like naked **toiling** figures in some classic **frieze**, merely as those who labor and love their children and die, he was thinking the fundamental truth about them. By going to look at their unfamiliar manners and customs he is inviting them to disguise themselves in fantastic masks and costumes. Many modern internationalists talk as if men of different nationalities had only to meet and mix and understand each other. In reality that is the moment of supreme danger—the moment when they meet. We might **shiver**, as at the old **euphemism** by which a meeting meant a duel.

<u>2</u>   Travel ought to combine amusement with instruction; but most travelers are so much amused that they refuse to be instructed. I do not blame them for being amused; it is perfectly natural to be amused at a Dutchman for being Dutch or a Chinaman for being Chinese. Where they are wrong is that they take their own amusement seriously. They base on it their serious ideas of international instruction. It was said that the Englishman takes his pleasures sadly; and the pleasure of despising foreigners is one which he takes most sadly of all. He comes to **scoff** and does not remain to pray, but rather to **excommunicate.** Hence in international relations there is far too little laughing, and far too much **sneering.** But I believe that there is a better way which largely consists of laughter; a form of friendship between nations which is actually founded on differences.

<u>3</u>   Let me begin my American impressions with two impressions I had before I went to America. One was an incident and the other an idea; and when taken together they **illustrate** the attitude I mean. The first principle is that nobody should be ashamed of thinking a thing funny because it is foreign; the second is that he should be ashamed of thinking it wrong because

it is funny. The reaction of his senses and superficial habits of mind against something new, and to him **abnormal**, is a perfectly healthy reaction. But the mind which imagines that mere unfamiliarity can possibly prove anything about **inferiority** is a very **inadequate** mind. It is inadequate even in criticizing things that may really be inferior to the things involved here. It is far better to laugh at a Negro for having a black face than to sneer at him for having a sloping skull. It is **proportionally** even more preferable to laugh rather than judge in dealing with highly civilized peoples. Therefore I put at the beginning two working examples of what I felt about America before I saw it; the sort of thing that a man has a right to enjoy as a joke, and the sort of thing he has a duty to understand and respect, because it is the explanation of the joke.

4 When I went to the American consulate to regularize my passports, I was **capable** of expecting the American consulate to be American. Embassies and consulates are by tradition like islands of the soil for which they stand; and I have often found the tradition corresponding to a truth. I have seen the unmistakable French official living on omelettes and a little wine and serving his sacred **abstractions** under the last palm-trees frying in a desert. In the heat and noise of quarreling Turks and Egyptians, I have come suddenly, as with the cool shock of his own shower-bath, on the **listless amiability** of the English gentleman. The officials I interviewed were very American, especially in being very polite; for whatever may have been the mood or meaning of Martin Chuzzlewit, I have always found Americans by far the politest people in the world. They put in my hands a form to be filled up, to all appearances like other forms I had filled up in other passport offices. But in reality it was very different from any form I had ever filled up in my life. At least it was a little like a freer form of the game called "Confessions" which my friends and I invented in our youth; an examination paper containing questions like, "If you saw a rhinoceros in the front garden, what

would you do?" One of my friends, I remember, wrote, "Take the pledge." But that is another story, and might bring Mr. Pussyfoot Johnson on the scene before his time.

    One of the questions on the paper was, "Are you an **anarchist**?" To which a **detached** philosopher would naturally feel **inclined** to answer, "What the devil has that to do with you? Are you an atheist" along with some playful efforts to cross-examine the official about what constitutes atheist. Then there was the question, "Are you in favor of **subverting** the government of the United States by force?" Against this I should write, "I prefer to answer that question at the end of my tour and not the beginning." The inquisitor, in his more than **morbid** curiosity, had then written down, "Are you a **polygamist**?" The answer to this is, "No such luck" or "Not such a fool," according to our experience of the other sex. But perhaps a better answer would be that given to W. T. Stead when he circulated the **rhetorical** question, "Shall I slay my brother Boer"—the answer that ran, "Never interfere in family matters." But among many things that amused me almost to the point of treating the form thus disrespectfully, the most amusing was the thought of the **ruthless** outlaw who should feel compelled to treat it respectfully. I like to think of the foreign **desperado**, seeking to slip into America with official papers under official protection, and sitting down to write with a beautiful **gravity**, "I am an anarchist. I hate you all and wish to destroy you." Or, "I intend to subvert by force the government of the United States as soon as possible, sticking the long sheath-knife in my left trouser-pocket into your President at the earliest opportunity." Or again, "Yes, I am a polygamist all right, and my forty-seven wives are accompanying me on the voyage disguised as secretaries." There seems to be a certain **simplicity** of mind about these answers; and it is reassuring to know that anarchists and polygamists are so pure and good that the police have only to ask them questions and they are certain to tell no lies.

6   Now that is the model of the sort of foreign practice, founded on foreign problems, at which a man's first impulse is naturally to laugh. Nor have I any intention of apologizing for my laughter. A man is perfectly **entitled** to laugh at a thing because he happens to find it **incomprehensible.** What he has no right to do is to laugh at it as incomprehensible, and then criticise it as if he comprehended it. The very fact of its unfamiliarity and mystery ought to set him thinking about the deeper causes that make people so different from himself, and that without merely assuming that they must be inferior to himself.

7   Superficially this is rather a queer business. It would be easy enough to suggest that in this America has introduced a quite abnormal spirit of **inquisition**; an interference with liberty unknown among all the ancient **despotisms** and aristocracies. About that there will be something to be said later; but superficially it is true that this degree of officialism is comparatively unique. In a journey which I took only the year before I had occasion to have my papers passed by governments which many worthy people in the West would vaguely identify with **corsairs** and **assassins**; I have stood on the other side of Jordan, in the land ruled by a rude Arab chief, where the police looked so like **brigands** that one wondered what the brigands looked like. But they did not ask me whether I had come to subvert the power of the Shereef; and they did not exhibit the faintest curiosity about my personal views on the ethical basis of civil authority. These ministers of ancient Moslem despotism did not care about whether I was an anarchist; and naturally would not have minded if I had been a polygamist. The Arab chief was probably a polygamist himself. These slaves of Asiatic autocracy were content, in the old liberal fashion, to judge me by my actions; they did not inquire into my thoughts. They held their power as limited to the limitation of practice; they did not forbid me to hold a theory. It would be easy to argue here that Western democracy persecutes where even Eastern despotism

tolerates or **emancipates**. It would be easy to develop the fancy that, as compared with the sultans of Turkey or Egypt, the American Constitution is a thing like the Spanish Inquisition.

8   Only the traveler who stops at that point is totally wrong; and the traveler only too often does stop at that point. He has found something to make him laugh, and he will not suffer it to make him think. And the **remedy** is not to unsay what he has said, not even, so to speak, to unlaugh what he has laughed, not to deny that there is something unique and curious about this American inquisition into our abstract opinions, but rather to continue the train of thought, and follow the admirable advice of Mr. H. G. Wells, who said, "It is not much good thinking of a thing unless you think it out." It is not to deny that American officialism is rather peculiar on this point, but to inquire what it really is which makes America peculiar, or which is peculiar to America. In short, it is to get some ultimate idea of what America is; and the answer to that question will **reveal** something much deeper and grander and more worthy of our intelligent interest.

9   It may have seemed something less than a compliment to compare the American Constitution to the Spanish Inquisition. But oddly enough, it does involve a truth, and still more oddly perhaps, it does involve a compliment. The American Constitution does resemble the Spanish Inquisition in this: that it is founded on a **creed.** America is the only nation in the world that is founded on creed. That creed is set forth with **dogmatic** and even **theological** lucidity in the Declaration of Independence; perhaps the only piece of practical politics that is also theoretical politics and also great literature. It **enunciates** that all men are equal in their claim to justice, that governments exist to give them that justice, and that their authority is for that reason just. It certainly does **condemn** anarchism, and it does also by inference condemn atheism, since it clearly names the Creator as the ultimate authority from whom these equal rights are derived. Nobody expects a modern political

system to proceed logically in the application of such dogmas, and in the matter of God and Government it is naturally God whose claim is taken more lightly. The point is that there is a creed, if not about **divine**, at least about human things.

10 Now a creed is at once the broadest and the narrowest thing in the world. In its nature it is as broad as its scheme for a brotherhood of all men. In its nature it is limited by its definition of the nature of all men. This was true of the Christian Church, which was truly said to exclude neither Jew nor Greek, but which did definitely substitute something else for Jewish religion or Greek philosophy. It was truly said to be a net drawing in of all kinds; but a net of a certain pattern, the pattern of Peter the Fisherman. And this is true even of the most disastrous **distortions** or **degradations** of that creed; and true among others of the Spanish Inquisition. It may have been narrow about theology, it could not confess to being narrow about nationality or **ethnology**. The Spanish Inquisition might be admittedly Inquisitorial; but the Spanish Inquisition could not be merely Spanish. Such a Spaniard, even when he was narrower than his own creed, had to be broader than his own empire. He might burn a philosopher because he was **heterodox**; but he must accept a **barbarian** because he was **orthodox**. And we see, even in modern times, that the same Church which is blamed for making **sages** heretics is also blamed for making savages priests. Now in a much vaguer and more evolutionary fashion, there is something of the same idea at the back of the great American experiment; the experiment of a democracy of diverse races which has been compared to a melting-pot. But even that metaphor implies that the pot itself is of a certain shape and a certain substance; a pretty solid substance. The melting-pot must not melt. The original shape was **traced** on the lines of Jeffersonian democracy; and it will remain in that shape until it becomes shapeless. America invites all men to become citizens; but it implies the dogma that there is such a thing as citizenship. Only, so far as its

primary ideal is concerned, its exclusiveness is religious because it is not racial. The **missionary** can condemn a **cannibal**, precisely because he cannot condemn a Sandwich Islander. And in something of the same spirit the American may exclude a polygamist, precisely because he cannot exclude a Turk.

11 Now in America this is no idle theory. It may have been theoretical, though it was thoroughly sincere, when that great Virginian gentleman declared it in surroundings that still had something of the character of an English countryside. It is not merely theoretical now. There is nothing to prevent America being **literally** invaded by Turks, as she is invaded by Jews or **Bulgars**. In the most **exquisitely** inconsequent of the Bab Ballads, we are told concerning Pasha Bailey Ben:

12 One morning knocked at half-past eight A tall Red Indian at his gate. In Turkey, as you'r' p'raps (意为:you are perhaps) aware, Red Indians are extremely rare.

13 But the converse need by no means be true. There is nothing in the nature of things to prevent an **emigration** of Turks increasing and multiplying on the plains where the Red Indians wandered; there is nothing to necessitate the Turks being extremely rare. The Red Indians, alas, are likely to be rarer. And as I much prefer Red Indians to Turks, I speak without prejudice; but the point here is that America, partly by original theory and partly by historical accident, does lie open to racial **admixtures** which most countries would think **incongruous** or comic. That is why it is only fair to read any American definitions or rules in a certain light, and relatively to a rather unique position. It is not fair to compare the position of those who may meet Turks in the back street with that of those who have never met Turks except in the Bab Ballads. It is not fair simply to compare America with England in its regulations about the Turk. In short, it is not fair to do what almost every Englishman probably does; to look at the American international

examination paper, and laugh and be satisfied with saying, "We don't have any of that nonsense in England."

14 We do not have any of that nonsense in England because we have never attempted to have any of that philosophy in England. And, above all, because we have the **enormous** advantage of feeling it natural to be national, because there is nothing else to be. England in these days is not well governed; England is not well educated; England suffers from wealth and poverty that are not well distributed. But England is English—esto perpetua. England is English as France is French or Ireland is Irish; the great mass of men taking certain national traditions for granted. Now this gives us a totally different and a very much easier task. We have not got an inquisition, because we have not got a creed; but it is arguable that we do not need a creed, because we have got a character. In any of the old nations the national unity is preserved by the national type. Because we have a type we do not need to have a test.

15 Take that innocent question, "Are you an anarchist?" which is **intrinsically** quite as **impudent** as "Are you an **optimist**?" or "Are you a **philanthropist**?" I am not discussing here whether these things are right, but whether most of us are in a position to know them rightly. Now it is quite true that most Englishmen do not find it necessary to go about all day asking each other whether they are anarchists. It is quite true that the phrase occurs on no British forms that I have seen. But this is not only because most of the Englishmen are not anarchists. It is even more because even the anarchists are Englishmen. For instance, it would be easy to make fun of the American formula by noting that the cap would fit all sorts of bald academic heads. It might well be maintained that Herbert Spencer was an anarchist. It is practically certain that Auberon Herbert was an anarchist. But Herbert Spencer was an extraordinary typical Englishman of the Nonconformist middle class. And Auberon Herbert was an extraordinarily typical English

aristocrat of the old and genuine aristocracy.

16   Everyone knew in his head that the squire would not throw a bomb at the Queen, and the Nonconformist would not throw a bomb at anybody. Every one knew that there was something subconscious in a man like Auberon Herbert, which would have come out only in throwing bombs at the enemies of England; as it did come out in his son and namesake, the generous and unforgotten. who fell flinging bombs from the sky far beyond the German line. Every one knows that normally, in the last resort, the English gentleman is patriotic. Every one knows that the English Nonconformist is national even when he denies that he is patriotic. Nothing is more notable indeed than the fact that nobody is more stamped with the mark of his own nation than the man who says that there ought to be no nations. Somebody called Cobden the International Man; but no man could be more English than Cobden. Everybody recognises Tolstoy as the iconoclast of all patriotism; but nobody could be more Russian than Tolstoy. In the old countries where there are these national types, the types may be allowed to hold any theories. Even if they hold certain theories they are unlikely to do certain things. So the conscientious objector, in the English sense, may be and is one of the peculiar by-products of England. But the **conscientious** objector will probably have a conscientious objection to throwing bombs.

17   Now I am very far from intending to imply that these American tests are good tests or that there is no danger of tyranny becoming the temptation of America. I shall have something to say later on about that temptation or tendency. Nor do I say that they apply consistently this conception of a nation with the soul of a church, protected by religious and not racial selection. If they did apply that principle consistently, they would have to exclude **pessimists** and rich **cynics** who deny the democratic ideal; an excellent thing but a rather **improbable** one. What I say is that when we realise that

this principle exists at all, we see the whole position in a totally different perspective. We say that the Americans are doing something heroic or doing something **insane**, or doing it in an unworkable or unworthy fashion, instead of simply wondering what the devil they are doing.

Vocabulary

cynicism ['sinisizəm] n.	a cynical feeling of distrust 愤世嫉俗
illusion [i'lu:3n] n.	deception by creating illusory ideas 错觉,幻想
toiling ['tɔiliŋ] a.	doing arduous or unpleasant work 长时间或辛苦地工作
frieze [fri:z] n.	an architectural ornament consisting of a horizontal sculptured band between the architrave and the cornice 雕带
shiver ['ʃivə(r)] v.	tremble convulsively, as from fear or excitement 颤抖
euphemism ['ju:fəmizəm] n.	an inoffensive expression 委婉语
scoff [skɔf] v.	laugh at with contempt and derision 嘲弄
excommunicate [,ekskə'mju:nikeit] v.	oust or exclude from a group or membership by decree 把……逐出教会
sneering ['sniriŋ] v.	expressive of contempt 讥笑
illustrate ['iləstreit] a.	clarify by giving an example of 表明
abnormal [æb'nɔ:ml] a.	not normal; not typical or regular or conforming to a norm 异常的
inferiority [in,fiəri'ɔrəti] n.	the quality of being a competitive disadvantage 劣势,自卑情绪
inadequate [in'ædikwət] a.	not sufficient to meet a need 信心不足的
proportionally [prə'pɔ:ʃənəli] ad.	to a proportionate degree 按比例地
capable ['keipəbl] a.	possibly accepting or permitting 有能力的
abstraction [æb'strækʃn] n.	a concept or idea not associated with any specific instance 抽象概念
listless ['listləs] a.	marked by low spirits; showing no enthusiasm 无精打采的
amiability [,eimiə'biləti] n.	a cheerful and agreeable mood 和蔼可亲
anarchist ['ænəkist] n.	an advocate of anarchism 无政府主义者
detached [di'tætʃt] a.	showing lack of emotional involvement 超然的
subvert [səb'və:t] v.	cause the downfall of 颠覆
morbid ['mɔ:bid] a.	suggesting an unhealthy mental state 病态的
polygamist [pə'ligəmist] n.	someone who is married to two or more people at the same time 一妻多夫,一夫多妻

rhetorical [ri'tɔrikl] a.	concerned with effect or style of writing and speaking 修辞学的, 虚夸的
ruthless ['ru:θləs] a.	without mercy or pity 无情的, 冷酷的
desperado [ˌdespə'rɑ:dəu] n.	a bold outlaw 亡命徒, 暴徒
gravity ['grævəti] n.	a manner that is serious and solemn 庄重
simplicity [sim'plisəti] n.	a lack of penetration or subtlety 简单, 天真
incomprehensible [inˌkɔmpri'hensəbl] a.	difficult to understand 高深莫测的
inquisition [ˌinkwi'ziʃn] n.	a severe interrogation (often violating the rights or privacy of individuals) 调查, 审讯
despotism ['despətizəm] n.	dominance through threat of punishment and violence 专制
corsair [kɔ:'seə(r)] n.	a pirate along the Barbary coast 海盗
assassin [ə'sæsin] n.	a murderer (especially one who kills a prominent political figure) who kills by a treacherous surprise attack and often is hired to do the deed 刺客
brigand ['brigənd] n.	an armed thief who is (usually) a member of a band 土匪, 强盗
tolerate ['tɔləreit] v.	put up with something or somebody unpleasant 容忍
emancipate [i'mænsipeit] v.	free from slavery or servitude 解放
remedy ['remədi] n.	act of correcting an error or a fault or an evil 补救办法
reveal [ri'vi:l] v.	make clear and visible 揭示
creed [kri:d] n.	any system of principles or beliefs 信条
dogmatic [dɔg'mætik] a.	characterized by arrogant assertion of unproved principles 固执己见的
theological [ˌθi:ə'lɔdʒikl] a.	concerning theology 神学上的
enunciate [i'nʌnsieit] v.	express or state clearly 确切地说明
condemn [kən'dem] v.	express strong disapproval of 谴责
divine [di'vain] a.	emanating from God 神圣的
distortion [di'stɔ:ʃn] n.	the mistake of misrepresenting the facts 扭曲
degradation [ˌdegrə'deiʃn] n.	changing to a lower state (a less respected state) 堕落
ethnology [eθ'nɔlədʒi] n.	the branch of anthropology that deals with the division of humankind into races and with their origins and distribution and distinctive characteristics 人种学, 民族学
heterodox ['hetərədɔks] a.	characterized by departure from accepted beliefs or standards 异端的

barbarian [bɑːˈbeəriən] n.	a crude uncouth ill-bred person lacking culture or refinement 野蛮人
orthodox [ˈɔːθədɔks] a.	adhering to what is commonly accepted 公认的，正统的
sage [seidʒ] n.	a mentor in spiritual and philosophical topics who is renowned for profound wisdom 圣人，智者
heretic [ˈherətik] n.	a person who holds unorthodox opinions in any field 异教徒，异端分子
trace [treis] n.	follow, discover, or ascertain the course of development of something 追溯
missionary [ˈmiʃənri] n.	someone sent on a mission, especially a religious or charitable mission to a foreign country 传教士
cannibal [ˈkænibl] n.	a person who eats human flesh 食人者
literally [ˈlitərəli] ad.	without exaggeration 确实地
Bulgar [ˈbʌlgɑː] n.	保加利亚人
exquisitely [ekˈskwizitli] ad.	in a delicate manner 精致地，异常地
admixture [ədˈmikstʃə(r)] n.	the act of mixing together 混合
incongruous [inˈkɔŋgruəs] a.	lacking in harmony or compatibility or appropriateness 不和谐的
intrinsically [inˈtrinzikli] ad.	with respect to its inherent nature 从本质上
impudent [ˈimpjədənt] a.	improperly forward or bold 粗鲁的，无礼的
optimist [ˈɔptimist] n.	a person disposed to take a favorable view of things 乐天派
philanthropist [fiˈlænθrəpist] n.	someone who makes charitable donations intended to increase human well-being 慈善家
conscientious [ˌkɔnʃiˈenʃəs] a.	guided by or in accordance with conscience or sense of right and wrong 认真负责的
pessimist [ˈpesimist] n.	a person who expects the worst 厌世者
improbable [imˈprɔbəbl] a.	not likely to be true or to occur or to have occurred 不大可能的
insane [inˈsein] a.	characteristic of mental derangement 疯狂的

Unit 3
Politics

Text A   The Spirit of Laws
Text B   Of the Beginning of Political Societies
Text C   The Declaration of Independence

Text A

The Spirit of Laws[1]

Charles de Montesquieu

BOOK I. OF LAWS IN GENERAL

CHAP. I. Of the Relation of Laws to Different Beings

1 LAWS, in their most general signification, are the necessary relations arising from the nature of things. In this sense, all beings have their laws; the Deity His laws, the material world its laws, the intelligence superior to man their laws, the beasts their laws, man his laws.

2 They who assert, that a blind **fatality** produced the various effects we behold in this world, talk very absurdly; for can anything be more unreasonable than to pretend that a blind fatality could be productive of intelligent beings?

---

[1] Excerpted from Charles de Montesquieu's *The Spirit of Laws*.

3　　There is, then, a primitive reason; and laws are the relations **subsisting** between it and different beings, and the relations of these to one another.

4　　God is related to the universe as Creator and Preserver; the laws by which He created all things are those by which He preserves them. He acts according to these rules, because He knows them; He knows them, because He made them; and He made them, because they are relative to His wisdom and power.

5　　Since we observe that the world, though formed by the motion of matter, and void of understanding, subsists through so long a succession of ages, its motions must certainly be directed by invariable laws; and, could we imagine another world, it must also have constant rules, or it would inevitably **perish.**

6　　Thus the creation, which seems an arbitrary act, supposes laws as invariable as those of the fatality of the **Atheists**. It would be absurd to say, that the Creator might govern the world without those rules, since without them it could not subsist.

7　　These rules are a fixed and invariable relation. In bodies moved, the motion is received, increased, diminished, lost, according to the relations of the quantity of matter and **velocity**; each diversity is **uniformity**; each change is **constancy.**

8　　Particular intelligent beings may have laws of their own making; but they have some likewise which they never made. Before there were intelligent beings, they were possible; they had therefore possible relations, and consequently possible laws. Before laws were made, there were relations of possible justice. To say that there is nothing just or unjust, but what is commanded or forbidden by **positive laws,** is the same as saying that, before the describing of a circle, all the radii were not equal.

9　　We must therefore acknowledge relations of justice **antecedent** to the positive law by which they are established: as for instance, that, if human societies existed, it would be right to conform to their laws; if there were intelligent beings that had received a benefit of another being, they ought to show their gratitude; if one intelligent being had created another intelligent being, the latter ought to continue in its original state of dependence; if one intelligent being injures another, it deserves a **retaliation**; and so on.

<u>10</u>   But the intelligent world is far from being so well governed as the physical; for, though the former has also its laws, which of their own nature are invariable, it does not conform to them so exactly as the physical world. This is because, on the one hand, particular intelligent beings are of a finite nature, and consequently liable to error; and, on the other, their nature requires them to be free agents. Hence they do not steadily conform to their primitive laws; and even those of their own instituting they frequently **infringe**.

<u>11</u>   Whether brutes be governed by the general laws of motion, or by a particular movement, we cannot determine. Be that as it may, they have not a more intimate relation to God than the rest of the material world; and sensation is of no other use to them, than in the relation they have either to other particular beings, or to themselves.

<u>12</u>   By the **allurement** of pleasure they preserve the individual, and by the same allurement they preserve their species. They have natural laws, because they are united by sensation; positive laws they have none, because they are not connected by knowledge. And yet they do not invariably conform to their natural laws; these are better observed by vegetables, that have neither understanding nor sense.

<u>13</u>   **Brutes** are deprived of the high advantages which we have; but they have some which we have not. They have not our hopes, but they are without our fears; they are subject, like us, to death, but without knowing it; even most of them are more attentive than we to self-preservation, and do not make so bad a use of their passions.

14　　Man, as a physical being, is, like other bodies, governed by invariable laws. As an intelligent being, he incessantly transgresses the laws established by God, and changes those of his own instituting. He is left to his private direction, though a limited being, and subject, like all finite intelligences, to ignorance and error: even his imperfect knowledge he loses; and, as a sensible creature, he is hurried away by a thousand **impetuous** passions. Such a being might every instant forget his Creator; God has therefore reminded him of his duty by the laws of religion. Such a being is liable every moment to forget himself; philosophy has provided against this by the laws of morality. Formed to live in society, he might forget his fellow-creatures; legislators have, therefore, by political and civil laws, confined him to his duty.

CHAP. III. Of Positive Laws

15　　AS soon as mankind enter into a state of society, they lose the sense of their weakness; equality ceases, and then commences the state of war.

16　　Each particular society begins to feel its strength; whence arises a state of war **betwixt** different nations. The individuals likewise of each society become sensible of their force; hence the principal advantages of this society they endeavour to convert to their own emolument, which constitutes a state of war betwixt individuals.

17　　These two different kinds of states give rise to human laws. Considered as inhabitants of so great a planet, which necessarily contains a variety of nations, they have laws relative to their mutual **intercourse**, which is what we call the law of nations. As members of a society that must be properly supported, they have laws relative to the governors and the governed; and this we distinguish by the name of politic law. They have also another sort of laws, as they stand in relation to each other; by which is understood the civil law.

18　　The law of nations is naturally founded on this principle, that different nations ought in time of peace to do one another all the good they can, and in time of war as little injury as possible, without prejudicing their real interests.

19 The object of war is victory; that of victory is conquest; and that of conquest, preservation. From this and the preceding principle all those rules are derived which constitute the law of nations.

20 All countries have a law of nations, not excepting the Iroquois themselves, though they **devour** their prisoners; for they send and receive ambassadors, and understand the rights of war and peace. The **mischief** is, that their law of nations is not founded on true principles.

21 Besides the law of nations relating to all societies, there is a polity, or civil constitution, for each, particularly considered. No society can subsist without a form of government. "The united strength of individuals," as Gravina well observes, "constitutes what we call the body politic."

22 The general strength may be in the hands of a single person, or of many. Some think that, nature having established paternal authority, the most natural government was that of a single person. But the example of paternal authority proves nothing: for, if the power of a father be relative to a single government, that of brothers after the death of a father, and that of cousin-germans after the decease of brothers, refer to a government of many. The political power necessarily comprehends the union of several families.

23 Better is it to say, that the government most conformable to nature is that which best agrees with the humour and **disposition** of the people in whose favour it is established.

24 The strength of individuals cannot be united without a **conjunction** of all their wills. "The conjunction of those wills," as Gravina again very justly observes, "is what we call the civil state."

25 Law in general is human reason, inasmuch as it governs all the inhabitants of the earth; the political and civil laws of each nation ought to be

only the particular cases in which human reason is applied.

26   They should be adapted in such a manner to the people for whom they are framed, that it is a great chance if those of one nation suit another.

27   They should be relative to the nature and principle of each government; whether they form it, as may be said of political laws; or whether they support it, as in the case of civil institutions.

28   They should be relative to the climate of each country, to the quality of its soil, to its situation and extent, to the principal occupation of the natives, whether husbandmen, huntsmen, or shepherds: they should have a relation to the degree of liberty which the constitution will bear, to the religion of the inhabitants, to their inclinations, riches, numbers, commerce, manners, and customs. In fine, they have relations to each other, as also to their origin, to the intent of the **legislator**, and to the order of things on which they are established; in all which different lights they ought to be considered.

29   This is what I have undertaken to perform in the following work. These relations I shall examine, since all these together constitute what I call the Spirit of Laws.

30   I have not separated the political from the civil institutions; for, as I do not pretend to treat of laws, but of their spirit, and as this spirit consists in the various relations which the laws may have to different objects, it is not so much my business to follow the natural order of laws, as that of these relations and objects.

31   I shall first examine the relations which laws have to the nature and principle of each government; and, as this principle has a strong influence on laws, I shall make it my study to understand it **thoroughly**; and, if I can but once establish it, the laws will soon appear to flow thence as from their source. I shall proceed afterwards to other more particular relations.

Vocabulary

fatality [fə'tæləti] n.	a death that is caused in an accident or a war, or by violence or disease(事故、战争、疾病等中的)死亡
subsist [səb'sist] v.	(formal) to exist; to be valid 存在,有效
perish ['periʃ] v.	(literary) (of people or animals 人或动物) to die, especially in a sudden violent way 死亡,暴死
atheist ['eiθiist] n.	a person who believes that God does not exist 无神论者
velocity [və'lɔsəti] n.	(technical 术语) the speed of something in a particular direction(沿某一方向的)速度
uniformity [ˌjuːni'fɔːməti] n.	a condition in which everything is regular and unvarying 均匀性,单调,无变化
constancy ['kɔnstənsi] n.	the quality of staying the same and not changing 稳定性,持久不变,始终如一
positive laws	制定法
antecedent [ˌænti'siːdnt] n.	(formal) a thing or an event that exists or comes before another, and may have influenced it 前事,先例
retaliation [riˌtæli'eiʃn] n.	action that a person takes against somebody who has harmed them in some way 报复
infringe [in'frindʒ] n.	(of an action, a plan, etc. 行动、计划等) to break a law or rule 违背,触犯(法规)
allurement [ə'ljuəmənt] n.	attractiveness 诱惑
brute [bruːt] n.	a large strong animal 大野兽,牲畜
impetuous [im'petʃuəs] a.	acting or done quickly and without thinking carefully about the results 鲁莽的,冲动的,轻率的
betwixt [bi'twikst] v.	(literary, or old use) between 在……之间(或中间)
intercourse ['intəkɔːs] n.	(old-fashioned) communication between people, countries, etc. (人、国家等之间的)往来,交往,交际
devour [di'vauə(r)] v.	to eat all of something quickly, especially because you are very hungry(尤指因饥饿而)狼吞虎咽地吃光
mischief ['mistʃif] n.	(formal) harm or injury that is done to somebody or to their reputation 伤害,毁损
disposition [ˌdispə'ziʃn] n.	the natural qualities of a person's character 性格,性情
conjunction [kən'dʒʌŋkʃn] n.	a combination of events, etc., that causes a particular result (引起某种结果的事物等的)结合,同时发生
legislator ['ledʒisleitə(r)] n.	(formal) a member of a group of people that has the power to make laws 立法委员
thoroughly ['θʌrəli] ad.	very much, completely 非常,彻底,完全

I. Vocabulary Building

anti-: against

e. g., antibiotic, antiseptic, anti-war, anti-racist, antidepressant, antisocial, anti-Semitic, anti-consumerism, antifederalist, antioxidant

counter-: against

e. g., counteract, counterbalance, countercurrent, countermarch, counterpart, counterfactual, counterculture, counterrevolution, counteroffer, counterintuitive

pro-: to the front

e. g., progress, prologue, promote, propel, protrude, prominent, provoke, prospect, profuse, prosperous

pro-: for

e. g., pro-life, pro-choice, pro-American, pros and cons

II. Discussion

Discuss the following questions with your own words.

1. Why does the author argue that laws are the necessary relations arising from the nature of things?

2. Why are there similar laws that were not made by particular intelligent beings besides the laws of their own making?

3. Why must a human being be confined to his duty by political and civil laws?

4. What does the author think are the two different kinds of states that give rise to human laws?

5. Why does the author argue that the government most conformable to nature is that which best agrees with the humour and disposition of the people in whose favour it is established?

III. Translation A

Translate the following sentences selected from the text into Chinese.

1. There is then a primitive reason; and laws are the relations subsisting between it and different beings, and the relations of these to one another. (Para. 3)

2. These rules are a fixed and invariable relation. In bodies moved, the motion is received, increased, diminished, lost, according to the relations of the quantity of matter and velocity; each diversity is uniformity; each change is constancy. (Para. 7)

3. Such a being might every instant forget his Creator; God has therefore reminded him of his duty by the laws of religion. Such a being is liable every moment to forget himself; philosophy has provided against this by the laws of morality. Formed to live in society, he might forget his fellow-creatures; legislators have, therefore, by political and civil laws, confined him to his duty. (Para. 14)

4. All countries have a law of nations, not excepting the Iroquois themselves, though they devour their prisoners; for they send and receive ambassadors, and understand the rights of war and peace. The mischief is, that their law of nations is not founded on true principles. (Para. 20)

5. I have not separated the political from the civil institutions; for, as I do not pretend to treat of laws, but of their spirit, and as this spirit consists in the various relations which the laws may have to different objects, it is not so much my business to follow the natural order of laws, as that of these relations and objects. (Para. 30)

IV. Translation B

Translate the following passage into Chinese.

We hold these truths to be self-evident, that all men are created equal, that they are endowed by their Creator with certain unalienable Rights, that among these are Life, Liberty and the pursuit of Happiness. —That to secure these rights, Governments are instituted among Men, deriving their just powers from the consent of the governed, —That whenever any Form of Government becomes destructive of these ends, it is the Right of the People to alter or to abolish it, and to institute new Government, laying its foundation on such principles and organizing its powers in such form, as to them shall seem most likely to effect their Safety and Happiness. (Excerpted from Text C)

V. Writing Exercise

The Spirit of Laws is, without question, one of the central texts in the history of 18th-century thought of the West. Please summarize the historical impact of *The Spirit of Laws* on the evolution of the western political systems.

Text B

Of the Beginning of Political Societies①

John Locke

1 §95. MEN being, as has been said, by nature, all free, equal, and

---

① Excerpted from John Locke's *Two Treatises of Government*.

independent, no one can be put out of this estate, and subjected to the political power of another, without his own consent. The only way whereby any one **divests** himself of his natural liberty, and puts on the bonds of civil society, is by agreeing with other men to join and unite into a community, for their comfortable, safe, and peaceable living one amongst another, in a secure enjoyment of their properties, and a greater security against any, that are not of it. This any number of men may do, because it injures not the freedom of the rest; they are left as they were in the liberty of the state of nature. When any number of men have so consented to make one community or government, they are thereby presently **incorporated**, and make one body politic, wherein the majority have a right to act and conclude the rest.

§ 96. For when any number of men have, by the consent of every individual, made a community, they have thereby made that community one body, with a power to act as one body, which is only by the will and determination of the majority: for that which acts any community, being only the consent of the individuals of it, and it being necessary to that which is one body to move one way; it is necessary the body should move that way whither the greater force carries it, which is the consent of the majority; or else it is impossible it should act or continue one body, one community, which the consent of every individual that united into it, agreed that it should; and so every one is bound by that consent to be concluded by the majority. And therefore we see, that in assemblies, **impowered** to act by positive laws, where no number is set by that positive law which impowers them, the act of the majority passes for the act of the whole, and of course determines, as having, by the law of nature and reason, the power of the whole.

§ 97. And thus every man, by consenting with others to make one body politic under one government, puts himself under an obligation, to every one of that society, to **submit to** the determination of the majority, and to be concluded by it; or else this original compact, whereby he with others incorporates into one society, would signify nothing, and be no compact, if he be left free, and under no other ties than he was in before in the state of nature. For what appearance would there be of any compact? What new engagement if he were no farther tied by any **decrees** of the society, than he himself thought fit, and did actually consent to? This would be still as great a liberty, as he himself had before his compact, or any one else in the state of nature hath, who may submit himself, and consent to any acts of it if he thinks fit.

§ 98. For if the consent of the majority shall not, in reason, be received as the act of the whole, and conclude every individual; nothing but the consent of every individual can make any thing to be the act of the whole: but such a consent is next to impossible ever to be had, if we consider the **infirmities** of health, and **avocations** of business, which in a number, though much less than that of a commonwealth, will necessarily keep many away from the public assembly. To which if we add the variety of opinions, and **contrariety** of interests, which unavoidably happen in all collections of men, the coming into society upon such terms would be only like Cato's coming into the theatre, only to go out again. Such a constitution as this would make the mighty Leviathan of a shorter duration, than the **feeblest** creatures, and not let it outlast the day it was born in: which cannot be supposed, till we can think, that rational creatures should desire and constitute societies only to be dissolved: for where the majority cannot conclude the rest, there they cannot act as one body, and consequently will be immediately dissolved again.

§ 99. Whosoever therefore out of a state of nature unite into a community, must be understood to give up all the power, necessary to the ends for which they unite into society, to the majority of the community, unless they expressly agreed in any number greater than the majority. And this is done by barely agreeing to unite into one political society, which is all the compact that is, or needs be, between the individuals, that enter into, or make up a commonwealth. And thus that, which begins and actually constitutes any political society, is nothing but the consent of any number of freemen capable of a majority to unite and incorporate into such a society. And this is that, and that only, which did, or could give beginning to any lawful government in the world.

6 §100. To this I find two objections made.

7 First, That there are no instances to be found in story, of a company of men independent, and equal one amongst another, that met together, and in this way began and set up a government.

Secondly, It is impossible of right, that men should do so, because all men being born under government, they are to submit to that, and are not at liberty to begin a new one.

8 §101. To the first there is this to answer, That it is not at all to be wondered, that history gives us but a very little account of men, that lived together in the state of nature. The **inconveniences** of that condition, and the love and want of society, no sooner brought any number of them together, but they presently united and incorporated, if they designed to continue together. And if we may not suppose men ever to have been in the state of nature, because we hear not much of them in such a state, we may as well suppose the armies of Salmanasser or Xerxes were never children, because we hear little of them, till they were men, and **imbodied** in armies. Government is every where antecedent to records, and letters seldom come in amongst a people till a long continuation of civil society has, by other more necessary arts, provided for their safety, ease, and plenty: and then they

begin to look after the history of their founders, and search into their original, when they have outlived the memory of it: for it is with commonwealths as with particular persons, they are commonly ignorant of their own births and infancies: and if they know any thing of their original, they are beholden for it, to the accidental records that others have kept of it. And those that we have, of the beginning of any polities in the world, excepting that of the Jews, where God himself immediately **interposed**, and which favours not at all **paternal dominion**, are all either plain instances of such a beginning as I have mentioned, or at least have manifest footsteps of it.

§ 102. He must shew a strange inclination to deny evident matter of fact, when it agrees not with his hypothesis, who will not allow, that the beginning of Rome and Venice were by the uniting together of several men free and independent one of another, amongst whom there was no natural superiority or subjection. And if Josephus Acosta's word may be taken, he tells us, that in many parts of America there was no government at all. There are great and apparent **conjectures**, says he, that these men, speaking of those of Peru, for a long time had neither kings nor commonwealths, but lived in troops, as they do this day in Florida, the Cheriquanas, those of Brasil, and many other nations, which have no certain kings, but as occasion is offered, in peace or war, they choose their captains as they please, *l. i. c. 25*. If it be said, that every man there was born subject to his father, or the head of his family; that the subjection due from a child to a father took not away his freedom of uniting into what political society he thought fit, has been already proved. But be that as it will, these men, it is evident, were actually free; and whatever superiority some politicians now would place in any of them, they themselves claimed it not, but by consent were all equal, till by the same consent they set rulers over themselves. So that their politic societies all began from a **voluntary** union, and the mutual agreement of men freely acting in the choice of their governors, and forms of government.

<u>10</u> § 103. And I hope those who went away from Sparta with Palantus, mentioned by Justin *l. 3. c. 4* will be allowed to have been freemen independent one of another, and to have set up a government over themselves, by their own consent. Thus I have given several examples, out of history, of people free and in the state of nature, that being met together incorporated and began a commonwealth. And if the want of such instances be an argument to prove that government were not, nor could not be so begun, I suppose the **contenders** for paternal empire were better let it alone, than urge it against natural liberty: for if they can give so many instances, out of history, of governments begun upon paternal right, I think (though at best an argument from what has been, to what should of right be, has no great force) one might, without any great danger, yield them the cause. But if I might advise them in the case, they would do well not to search too much into the original of governments, as they have begun de facto, lest they should find, at the foundation of most of them, something very little **favourable** to the design they promote, and such a power as they contend for.

<u>11</u> § 104. But to conclude, reason being plain on our side, that men are naturally free, and the examples of history shewing, that the governments of the world, that were begun in peace, had their beginning laid on that foundation, and were made by the consent of the people; there can be little room for doubt, either where the right is, or what has been the opinion, or practice of mankind, about the first **erecting** of governments.

<u>12</u> § 105. I will not deny, that if we look back as far as history will direct us, towards the original of commonwealths, we shall generally find them under the government and administration of one man. And I am also apt to believe, that where a family was numerous enough to subsist by itself, and

continued entire together, without mixing with others, as it often happens, where there is much land, and few people, the government commonly began in the father: for the father having, by the law of nature, the same power with every man else to punish, as he thought fit, any offences against that law, might thereby punish his **transgressing** children, even when they were men, and out of their pupil age; and they were very likely to submit to his punishment, and all join with him against the offender, in their turns, giving him thereby power to execute his sentence against any transgression, and so in effect make him the lawmaker, and governor over all that remained in conjunction with his family. He was fittest to be trusted; paternal affection secured their property and interest under his care; and the custom of obeying him, in their childhood, made it easier to submit to him, rather than to any other. If therefore they must have one to rule them, as government is hardly to be avoided amongst men that live together; who so likely to be the man as he that was their common father; unless **negligence**, cruelty, or any other defect of mind or body made him unfit for it? But when either the father died, and left his next heir, for want of age, wisdom, courage, or any other qualities, less fit for rule; or where several families met, and consented to continue together; there, it is not to be doubted, but they used their natural freedom, to set up him, whom they judged the ablest, and most likely, to rule well over them. **Conformable** hereunto we find the people of America, who (living out of the reach of the conquering swords, and spreading domination of the two great empires of Peru and Mexico) enjoyed their own natural freedom, though, caeteris paribus, they commonly prefer the heir of their deceased king; yet if they find him any way weak, or uncapable, they pass him by, and set up the **stoutest** and bravest man for their ruler.

§ 106. Thus, though looking back as far as records give us any account of peopling the world, and the history of nations, we commonly find the government to be in one hand; yet it destroys not that which I affirm, viz. that the beginning of politic society depends upon the consent of the individuals, to join into, and make one society; who, when they are thus incorporated, might set up what form of government they thought fit. But this having given occasion to men to mistake, and think, that by nature government was **monarchical**, and belonged to the father, it may not be amiss here to consider, why people in the beginning generally pitched upon this form, which though perhaps the father's **pre-eminency** might, in the first institution of some commonwealths, give a rise to, and place in the beginning, the power in one hand; yet it is plain that the reason, that continued the form of government in a single person, was not any regard, or respect to paternal authority; since all petty monarchies, that is, almost all monarchies, near their original, have been commonly, at least upon occasion, elective.

14 §107. First then, in the beginning of things, the father's government of the childhood of those sprung from him, having accustomed them to the rule of one man, and taught them that where it was exercised with care and skill, with affection and love to those under it, it was sufficient to **procure** and preserve to men all the political happiness they sought for in society. It was no wonder that they should pitch upon, and naturally run into that form of government, which from their infancy they had been all accustomed to; and which, by experience, they had found both easy and safe. To which, if we add, that monarchy being simple, and most obvious to men, whom neither experience had instructed in forms of government, nor the ambition or **insolence** of empire had taught to beware of the **encroachments** of **prerogative**, or the inconveniencies of absolute power, which monarchy in succession was apt to lay claim to, and bring upon them; it was not at all strange, that they should not much trouble themselves to think of methods

of restraining any **exorbitances** of those to whom they had given the authority over them, and of balancing the power of government, by placing several parts of it in different hands. They had neither felt the oppression of **tyrannical dominion**, nor did the fashion of the age, nor their possessions, or way of living, (which afforded little matter for **covetousness** or ambition) give them any reason to **apprehend** or provide against it; and therefore it is no wonder they put themselves into such a frame of government, as was not only, as I said, most obvious and simple, but also best suited to their present state and condition; which stood more in need of defence against foreign invasions and injuries, than of **multiplicity** of laws. The equality of a simple poor way of living, confining their desires within the narrow bounds of each man's small property, made few controversies, and so no need of many laws to decide them, or variety of officers to **superintend** the process, or look after the execution of justice, where there were but few trespasses, and few offenders. Since then those, who liked one another so well as to join into society, cannot but be supposed to have some acquaintance and friendship together, and some trust one in another; they could not but have greater apprehensions of others, than of one another: and therefore their first care and thought cannot but be supposed to be, how to secure themselves against foreign force. It was natural for them to put themselves under a frame of government which might best serve to that end, and **chuse** the wisest and bravest man to conduct them in their wars, and lead them out against their enemies, and in this chiefly be their ruler.

§ 108. Thus we see, that the kings of the Indians in America, which is still a pattern of the first ages in Asia and Europe, whilst the inhabitants were too few for the country, and want of people and money gave men no temptation to enlarge their possessions of land, or contest for wider extent of ground, are little more than generals of their armies; and though they command absolutely in war, yet at home and in time of peace they exercise very little dominion, and have but a very moderate **sovereignty**, the resolutions of peace and war being ordinarily either in the people, or in a council. Tho' the war itself, which admits not of **plurality** of governors, naturally **devolves** the command into the king's sole authority.

Vocabulary

divest [dai'vest] v.	to take something away from somebody/something 使解除,使摆脱
incorporate [in'kɔːpəreit] v.	to include something so that it forms a part of something 包含,吸收,使并入
impower [im'pauə] v.	等于 empower, (formal) to give somebody the power or authority to do something 给(某人)……的权力,授权
submit to	to accept the authority, control or greater strength of somebody/something, to agree to something because of this 顺从,屈服,投降,不得已接受
decree [di'kriː] n.	an official order from a ruler or a government that becomes the law 法令,政令
infirmity [in'fəːməti] n.	weakness or illness over a long period (长期的)体弱,生病
avocation [ˌævəu'keiʃn] n.	(formal) a hobby or other activity that you do for interest and enjoyment 业余爱好
contrariety [ˌkɔntrə'raiəti] n.	the relation between contraries 反对,矛盾,相反物
feeble ['fiːbl] a.	very weak 虚弱的,衰弱的
inconvenience [ˌinkən'viːniəns] n.	trouble or problems, especially concerning what you need or would like yourself 不便,麻烦,困难
imbody [im'bɔdi] v.	同 embody, to express or represent an idea or a quality 具体表现,体现,代表(思想或品质)
interpose [ˌintə'pəuz] v.	to place something between two people or things 将……置于(二者)之间,插入,夹进
paternal dominion	父亲的统治权
conjecture [kən'dʒektʃə(r)] n.	an opinion or idea that is not based on definite knowledge and is formed by guessing 猜测,推测
voluntary ['vɔləntri] a.	done willingly, not because you are forced 自愿的,志愿的
contender [kən'tendə(r)] a.	a person who takes part in a competition or tries to win something 竞争者,角逐者,争夺者

favourable [ˌfeivərəbl] a.	good for something and making it likely to be successful or have an advantage 有利的,有助于……的
erect [iˈrekt] v.	(formal) to establish or create something 建立
transgress [trænzˈgres] v.	(formal) to go beyond the limit of what is morally or legally acceptable 越轨,违背(道德),违反(法律)
negligence [ˈneglidʒəns] n.	(formal or law) the failure to give somebody/something enough care or attention 疏忽,失职,失误,过失
conformable [kənˈfɔːməbl] a.	quick to comply 适合的,一致的
stout [staut] a.	(formal) brave and determined 顽强的,坚毅的,不屈不挠的
monarchical [məˈnɑːkikl] a.	(formal) connected with a ruler such as a king or a queen or with the system of government by a king or queen 君主的,帝王的,君主制的
pre-eminency [priːˈeminənsi] n.	high status importance owing to marked superiority 卓越,杰出
procure [prəˈkjuə(r)] v.	(formal) to obtain something, especially with difficulty (设法)获得,取得
insolence [ˈinsələns] n.	the trait of being rude and impertinent, inclined to take liberties 傲慢,无礼,厚颜
encroachment [inˈkrəutʃmənt] n.	(disapproving) to begin to affect or use up too much of somebody's time, rights, personal life, etc. 侵占(某人的时间),侵犯(某人的权利),扰乱(某人的生活等)
prerogative [priˈrɔgətiv] a.	(formal) a right or advantage belonging to a particular person or group because of their importance or social position 特权,优先权
exorbitance [igˈzɔːbitəns] n.	being excessive 过度,不当
tyrannical dominion	残暴的统治
covetousness [ˈkʌvətəsnəs] n.	(formal) having a strong desire for the things that other people have 贪婪
apprehend [ˌæpriˈhend] v.	to understand or recognize something 理解,认识到,领会
multiplicity [ˌmʌltiˈplisəti] n.	(formal) a great number and variety of something 多样性,多种多样
superintend [ˌsuːpərinˈtend] v.	(formal) to be in charge of something and make sure that everything is working, being done, etc. as it should be 主管,监督,监管
chuse [tʃuːz] v.	同 choose 〈古〉选择,选定
sovereignty [ˈsɔvrənti] n.	complete power to govern a country 主权,最高统治权,最高权威

plurality [pluə'ræləti] n.   (formal) a large number 众多,大量
devolve [di'vɔlv] v.   pass on or delegate to another 移交,转移

Text C

The Declaration of Independence①

Thomas Jefferson, et al.

IN CONGRESS, July 4, 1776

The **Unanimous** Declaration of the Thirteen United States of America

1   When in the Course of human events, it becomes necessary for one people to **dissolve** the political bands which have connected them with another, and to assume among the powers of the earth, the separate and equal station to which the Laws of Nature and of Nature's God **entitle** them, a decent respect to the opinions of mankind requires that they should declare the causes which **impel** them to the separation.

2   We hold these truths to be **self-evident**, that all men are created equal, that they are **endowed** by their Creator with certain **unalienable** Rights, that among these are Life, Liberty and the pursuit of Happiness.—That to secure these rights, Governments are instituted among Men, **deriving** their just powers from the **consent** of the governed,—That whenever any Form of Government becomes **destructive** of these ends, it is the Right of the People to alter or to **abolish** it, and to institute new Government, laying its foundation on such principles and organizing its powers in such form, as to

---

① *The Declaration of Independence* is the statement adopted by the Second Continental Congress meeting at the Pennsylvania State House (Independence Hall) in Philadelphia on July 4, 1776. It was John Adams, as a leader in pushing for independence, who persuaded the committee to select Thomas Jefferson to compose the original draft of the document and Congress would then edit it to produce the final version.

them shall seem most likely to effect their Safety and Happiness. **Prudence**, indeed, will dictate that Governments long established should not be changed for light and **transient** causes; and **accordingly** all experience hath shewn, that mankind are more **disposed to** suffer, while evils are **sufferable**, than to **right** themselves by abolishing the forms to which they **are accustomed**. But when a long **train** of **abuses** and **usurpations**, pursuing invariably the same Object **evinces** a design to reduce them under absolute **Despotism**, it is their right, it is their duty, to throw off such Government, and to provide new Guards for their future security. —Such has been the patient **sufferance** of these Colonies; and such is now the necessity which **constrains** them to alter their former Systems of Government. The history of the present King of Great Britain is a history of repeated injuries and usurpations, all having in direct object the establishment of an absolute **Tyranny** over these States. To prove this, let Facts be submitted to a **candid** world.

<u>3</u>   He has refused his **Assent** to Laws, the most **wholesome** and necessary for the public good.

<u>4</u>   He has forbidden his Governors to pass Laws of immediate and **pressing** importance, unless **suspended** in their operation till his Assent should be obtained; and when so suspended, he has utterly neglected to **attend to** them.

<u>5</u>   He has refused to pass other Laws for the **accommodation** of large districts of people, unless those people would **relinquish** the right of **Representation** in the **Legislature**, a right **inestimable** to them and **formidable** to tyrants only.

<u>6</u>   He has called together legislative bodies at places unusual, uncomfortable, and distant from the **depository** of their public Records, for the sole purpose of **fatiguing** them into **compliance** with his measures.

<u>7</u>   He has dissolved Representative Houses repeatedly, for opposing with manly firmness his invasions on the rights of the people.

_8_	He has refused for a long time, after such **dissolutions**, to cause others to be elected; whereby the Legislative powers, incapable of **Annihilation**, have returned to the People **at large** for their exercise; the State remaining in the mean time exposed to all the dangers of invasion from without, and **convulsions** within.

_9_	He has **endeavoured to** prevent the population of these States; for that purpose obstructing the Laws for Naturalization of Foreigners; refusing to pass others to encourage their migrations hither, and raising the conditions of new Appropriations of Lands.

_10_	He has **obstructed** the Administration of Justice, by refusing his Assent to Laws for establishing **Judiciary** powers.

_11_	He has made Judges dependent on his Will alone, for the **tenure** of their offices, and the amount and payment of their salaries.

_12_	He has erected a multitude of New Offices, and sent hither swarms of Officers to **harass** our people, and eat out their substance.

_13_	He has kept among us, in times of peace, **Standing Armies** without the Consent of our legislatures.

_14_	He has affected to **render** the Military independent of and superior to the Civil power.

_15_	He has combined with others to subject us to a jurisdiction foreign to our constitution, and unacknowledged by our laws; giving his Assent to their Acts of pretended Legislation:

_16_	For **Quartering** large bodies of armed troops among us:

_17_	For protecting them, by a **mock Trial**, from punishment for any Murders which they should commit on the Inhabitants of these States:

_18_	For cutting off our Trade with all parts of the world:

_19_	For **imposing** Taxes **on** us without our Consent:

_20_	For **depriving** us in many cases, **of** the benefits of Trial by **Jury**:

_21_	For transporting us beyond Seas to be tried for pretended offences:

22   For abolishing the free System of English Laws in a neighbouring Province, establishing therein an **Arbitrary** government, and enlarging its Boundaries so as to render it at once an example and fit instrument for introducing the same absolute rule into these Colonies:

23   For taking away our **Charters**, abolishing our most valuable Laws, and altering fundamentally the Forms of our Governments:

24   For suspending our own Legislatures, and declaring themselves invested with power to legislate for us in all cases whatsoever.

25   He has **abdicated** Government here, by declaring us out of his Protection and **waging** War against us.

26   He has plundered our seas, ravaged our Coasts, burnt our towns, and destroyed the lives of our people.

27   He is at this time transporting large Armies of foreign **Mercenaries** to **complete** the works of death, **desolation** and tyranny, already begun with circumstances of Cruelty & **perfidy** scarcely paralleled in the most barbarous ages, and totally unworthy the Head of a civilized nation.

28   He has constrained our fellow Citizens taken **Captive** on the high Seas to bear Arms against their Country, to become the executioners of their friends and **Brethren**, or to fall themselves by their Hands.

29   He has excited **domestic insurrections** amongst us, and has endeavoured to bring on the inhabitants of our frontiers, the merciless Indian Savages, whose known rule of warfare, is an undistinguished destruction of all ages, sexes and conditions.

30   In every stage of these Oppressions We have **Petitioned** for Redress in the most humble terms: Our repeated Petitions have been answered only by repeated injury. A Prince whose character is thus marked by every act which may define a Tyrant, is unfit to be the ruler of a free people.

31   Nor have We been wanting in attentions to our British brethren. We have warned them from time to time of attempts by their legislature to

extend an **unwarrantable** jurisdiction over us. We have reminded them of the circumstances of our emigration and settlement here. We have **appealed to** their native justice and **magnanimity**, and we have conjured them by the ties of our common kindred to **disavow** these usurpations, which, would inevitably interrupt our connections and correspondence. They too have been deaf to the voice of justice and of **consanguinity**. We must, therefore, **acquiesce** in the necessity, which **denounces** our Separation, and hold them, as we hold the rest of mankind, Enemies in War, in Peace Friends.

32   We, therefore, the Representatives of the united States of America, in General Congress, Assembled, appealing to the Supreme Judge of the world for the **rectitude** of our intentions, do, in the Name, and by Authority of the good People of these Colonies, solemnly publish and declare, That these United Colonies are, and of Right ought to be Free and Independent States; that they are **Absolved** from all **Allegiance** to the British Crown, and that all political connection between them and the State of Great Britain, is and ought to be totally dissolved; and that as Free and Independent States, they have full Power to **levy War**, conclude Peace, contract Alliances, establish Commerce, and to do all other Acts and Things which Independent States may of right do. And for the support of this Declaration, with a firm reliance on the protection of divine Providence, we mutually pledge to each other our Lives, our Fortunes and our sacred Honor.

Vocabulary

unanimous [juˈnænəməs] a.	in complete agreement 全体一致的
dissolve [diˈzɔlv] v.	stop functioning as a unit （使）解散
entitle [inˈtaitl] v.	give the right to 给予……权力
impel [imˈpel] v.	cause to move forward with force 推动
self-evident [selfˈevidənt] a.	evident without proof or argument 不言而喻的
endow [inˈdau] v.	give qualities or abilities to 赋予
unalienable [ʌnˈeiliənəbl] a.	incapable of being repudiated or transferred to another 不能剥夺的，不能让与的

derive [di'raiv] v.	obtain, come from 获得，源于
consent [kən'sent] n.	permission to do something 准许，同意
destructive [di'strʌktiv] a.	causing destruction or much damage 破坏性的
abolish [ə'bɔliʃ] v.	do away with 废除
prudence ['pruːdns] n.	discretion in practical affairs 谨慎
transient ['trænziənt] a.	enduring a very short time 转瞬即逝的
accordingly [ə'kɔːdiŋli] ad.	because of the reason given, in accordance with 因此，相应地
be disposed to	be willing or prepared to do something 有意于
right [rait] v.	to do justice to 正确对待，恰当对待
be accustomed to	make oneself familiar with something or become used to it 使习惯于
train [trein] n.	a series of events or actions that are connected 一系列相关的事情（或行动）
abuse [ə'bjuz] n.	the use of something in a way that is wrong or harmful 滥用，妄用
usurpation [ˌjuːzəː'peiʃn] n.	(formal) to take somebody's position and/or power without having the right to do this 篡夺，侵权
evince [i'vins] v.	(formal) to show clearly that you have a feeling or quality 表明，表现，显示（感情或品质）
despotism ['despətizəm] n.	the rule of a despot 专制统治，独裁制，暴政
sufferance ['sʌfərəns] n.	patient endurance especially of pain or distress 忍耐
constrain [kən'strein] v.	to force somebody to do something or behave in a particular way 强迫，强制，迫使
tyranny ['tirəni] n.	unfair or cruel use of power or authority 暴虐，专政
candid ['kændid] a.	saying what you think openly and honestly, not hiding your thoughts 坦率的，坦诚的，直言不讳的
assent [ə'sent] n.	(formal) official agreement to or approval of something 同意，赞成
wholesome ['həulsəm] a.	morally good, having a good moral influence 有道德的，有良好道德影响的
pressing ['presiŋ] a.	needing to be dealt with immediately 紧急的，急迫的
suspend [sə'spend] v.	to officially stop something for a time, to prevent something from being active, used, etc. for a time 暂停，中止，使暂停发挥作用（或使用等）
attend to	to deal with somebody/something, to take care of somebody/something 处理，照料

accommodation [əˌkɔməˈdeiʃn] n.	the act of accommodating someone or something 安置
relinquish [riˈliŋkwiʃ] v.	(formal) to stop having something, especially when this happens unwillingly(尤指不情愿地)放弃
representation [ˌreprizenˈteiʃn] n.	the fact of having representatives who will speak or vote for you or on your behalf 代表,维护,支持
legislature [ˈledʒisleitʃə(r)] n.	(formal) a group of people who have the power to make and change laws 立法机关
inestimable [inˈestiməbl] a.	(formal) too great to calculate(大得)难以估量的,无法估计的
formidable [ˈfɔːmidəbl] a.	extremely impressive in strength or excellence, inspiring fear 令人敬畏的,可怕的
depository [diˈpɔzitri] n.	a place where things can be stored 贮藏室,存放处
fatigue [fəˈtiːg] v.	exhaust somebody through overuse or great strain or stress 使疲劳
compliance with	the practice of obeying rules or requests made by people in authority 服从,遵从
dissolution [ˌdisəˈluːʃn] n.	the act of officially ending a parliament 议会的解散
annihilation [əˌnaiəˈleiʃn] n.	to destroy somebody/something completely, to defeat somebody/something completely 彻底消灭,彻底击败
at large	as a whole, in general 全部,总地,一般来说
convulsion [kənˈvʌlʃn] n.	a sudden important change that happens to a country or an organization 动乱,骚动
endeavour [inˈdevə] v.	attempt by employing effort 尽力,竭力
obstruct [əbˈstrʌkt] v.	to prevent somebody from doing something, especially when this is done deliberately(故意)妨碍,阻挠,阻碍
judiciary [dʒuˈdiʃəri] a.	relating to the legal system 司法的
tenure [ˈtenjə(r)] n.	the period of time when somebody holds an important job, especially a political one(尤指重要政治职务的)任期,任职
harass [həˈræs] v.	to annoy or worry somebody by putting pressure on them or saying or doing unpleasant things to them 侵扰,骚扰
Standing Armies	常备军
render [ˈrendə(r)] v.	(formal) to cause somebody/something to be in a particular state or condition;使成为,使处于某状态
quarter [ˈkwɔːtə(r)] v.	(formal) to provide somebody with a place to eat and sleep 给……提供食宿
mock trial	模拟审判,假审判

impose on	to introduce a new law, rule, tax, etc.; to order that a rule, punishment, etc. be used 推行，采用（规章制度），强制实行
deprive of	to prevent somebody from having or doing something, especially something important 剥夺，使不能享有
jury ['dʒuəri] n.	a group of members of the public who listen to the facts of a case in a court and decide whether or not somebody is guilty of a crime 陪审团
arbitrary ['ɑːbitrəri] a.	(formal) using power without restriction and without considering other people 专横的，专制的
charter ['tʃɑːtə(r)] n.	a written statement describing the rights that a particular group of people should have（说明某部分民众应有权利的）宪章
abdicate ['æbdikeit] v.	to fail or refuse to perform a duty 失（职），放弃（职责）
wage [weidʒ] v.	to begin and continue a war, a battle, etc. 开始，继续（战争、战斗等）
mercenary ['mɜːsənəri] n.	a soldier who will fight for any country or group that offers payment 雇佣兵
desolation [ˌdesə'leiʃn] n.	the state of a place that is ruined or destroyed and offers no joy or hope to people 废墟，荒芜，凄凉
perfidy ['pɜːfədi] n.	betrayal of a trust 背叛，背信弃义
captive ['kæptiv] a.	kept as a prisoner or in a confined space; unable to escape 被监禁的，被关起来的，被困住的
brethren ['breðrən] n.	(old-fashioned) used to talk to people in church or to talk about the members of a male religious group（称呼教友或男修会等的成员）弟兄们
domestic [də'mestik] a.	of or inside a particular country, not foreign or international 本国的，国内的
insurrection [ˌinsə'rekʃn] n.	a situation in which a large group of people try to take political control of their own country with violence 起义，叛乱，暴动
petition [pə'tiʃn] n.	a written document signed by a large number of people that asks somebody in a position of authority to do or change something 请愿书
unwarrantable [ʌn'wɒrəntəbl] a.	incapable of being justified or explained 无正当理由的
appeal to	to make a formal request to a court or to somebody in authority for a judgement or a decision to be changed 上诉，申诉

magnanimity[ˌmæɡnəˈnimətɪ] n.	extremely liberal and generous of spirit 宽宏大量
disavow [ˌdisəˈvau] v.	(formal) to state publicly that you have no knowledge of something or that you are not responsible for something/somebody 不承认,否认,拒绝对……承担责任
consanguinity [ˌkɔnsæŋˈgwinəti] n.	(formal) relationship by birth in the same family 同宗,血缘,血亲关系
acquiesce [ˌækwiˈes] v.	(formal) to accept something without arguing, even if you do not really agree with it 默然接受,默许
denounce [diˈnauns] v.	to strongly criticize somebody/something that you think is wrong, illegal, etc. 谴责,指责
rectitude [ˈrektitjuːd] n.	(formal) the quality of thinking or behaving in a correct and honest way 公正,正直,诚实
absolve [əbˈzɔlv] v.	to state formally that somebody is not guilty or responsible for something 宣告……无罪,判定……无责
allegiance [əˈliːdʒəns] n.	a person's continued support for a political party, religion, ruler, etc. (对政党、宗教、统治者的)忠诚,效忠,拥戴
levy war	宣战

Unit 4

Education

Text A A Liberal Education
Text B Importance of Education
Text C Education and Discipline

Text A

A Liberal Education①

Thomas Henry Huxley

<u>1</u>   By way of a beginning, let us ask ourselves—What is education? Above all things, what is our ideal of a thoroughly liberal education? —of that education which, if we could begin life again, we would give ourselves—of that education which, if we could **mould** the fates to our own will, we would give our children? Well, I know not what may be your **conceptions** upon this matter, but I will tell you mine, and I hope I shall find that our views are not very **discrepant.**

<u>2</u>   Suppose it were perfectly certain that the life and fortune of every one of us would, one day or other, depend upon his winning or losing a game at chess. Don't you think that we should all consider it to be a primary duty to learn at least the names and the moves of the pieces; to have a **notion** of a

---

① Excerpted from Thomas Henry Huxley's *A Liberal Education and Where to Find It*.

gambit, and a keen eye for all the means of giving and getting out of **check**? Do you not think that we should look with a **disapprobation** amounting to scorn upon the father who allowed his son, or the state which allowed its members, to grow up without knowing a **pawn** from a **knight**?

<u>3</u>   Yet, it is a very plain and elementary truth that the life, the fortune, and the happiness of every one of us, and, more or less, of those who are connected with us, do depend upon our knowing something of the rules of a game **infinitely** more difficult and complicated than chess. It is a game which has been played for **untold** ages, every man and woman of us being one of the two players in a game of his or her own. The chess-board is the world, the pieces are the phenomena of the universe, the rules of the game are what we call the laws of Nature. The player on the other side is hidden from us. We know that his play is always fair, just and patient. But also we **know, to our cost**, that he never **overlooks** a mistake, or makes the smallest allowance for ignorance. To the man who plays well, the highest **stakes** are paid, with that sort of **overflowing generosity** with which the strong shows delight in strength. And one who plays ill is **checkmated**—without haste, but without **remorse**.

<u>4</u>   My **metaphor** will **remind** some of you of the famous picture in which Retzsch has depicted Satan playing at chess with man for his soul. **Substitute** for the mocking **fiend** in that picture a calm, strong angel who is playing for love, as we say, and would rather lose than win—and I should accept it as an image of human life.

<u>5</u>   Well, what I mean by Education is learning the rules of this **mighty** game. In other words, education is the instruction of the intellect in the laws of Nature, under which name I include not merely things and their forces, but men and their ways; and the **fashioning** of the affections and of the will into an **earnest** and loving desire to move **in harmony with** those laws. For me, education means neither more nor less than this. Anything, which

professes to call itself education must be tried by this standard, and if it fails to **stand the test**, I will not call it education, whatever may be the force of **authority** or of numbers upon the other side.

<u>6</u>   It is important to remember that, in strictness, there is no such thing as an uneducated man. Take an extreme case. Suppose that an adult man, in the full **vigour** of his **faculties**, could be suddenly placed in the world, as Adam is said to have been, and then left to do as he best might. How long would he be left uneducated? Not five minutes. Nature would begin to teach him, through the eye, the ear, the touch, the **properties** of objects. Pain and pleasure would be at his elbow telling him to do this and avoid that; and by slow degrees the man would receive an education which, if narrow, would be thorough, real, and adequate to his circumstances, though there would be no extras and very few accomplishments.

<u>7</u>   And if to this **solitary** man entered a second Adam or, better still, an Eve, a new and greater world, that of social and moral phenomena, would be **revealed**. Joys and **woes**, compared with which all others might seem but faint shadows, would spring from the new relations. Happiness and sorrow would take the place of the coarser monitors, pleasure and pain; but conduct would still be shaped by the observation of the natural consequences of actions; or, in other words, by the laws of the nature of man.

<u>8</u>   To every one of us the world was once as fresh and new as to Adam. And then, long before we were **susceptible** of any other mode of instruction, Nature took us in hand, and every minute of waking life brought its educational influence, shaping our actions **into** rough **accordance with** Nature's laws, so that we might not be ended untimely by too gross disobedience. Nor should I speak of this process of education as past for anyone, be he as old as he may. For every man the world is as fresh as it was at the first day, and as full of untold **novelties** for him who has the eyes to see them. And Nature is still continuing her patient education of us in that great

university, the universe, of which we are all members—Nature having no Test-Acts.

9 Those who take honours in Nature's university, who learn the laws which govern men and things and obey them, are the really great and successful men in this world. The great mass of mankind are the "**Poll**," who pick up just enough to get through without much **discredit**. Those who won't learn at all are **plucked**; and then you can't come up again. Nature's pluck means **extermination**.

10 Thus the question of **compulsory** education is settled so far as Nature is concerned. Her bill on that question was framed and passed long ago. But, like all compulsory legislation, that of Nature is harsh and wasteful in its operation. Ignorance is visited as sharply as willful disobedience—incapacity **meets with** the same punishment as crime. Nature's discipline is not even a word and a blow, and the blow first; but the blow without the word. It is left to you to find out why your ears are boxed.

11 The object of what we commonly call education—that education in which man **intervenes** and which I shall **distinguish** as artificial education—is to make good these **defects** in Nature's methods; to prepare the child to receive Nature's education, neither incapably nor ignorantly, nor with willful disobedience; and to understand the preliminary **symptoms** of her pleasure, without waiting for **the box on the ear**. In short, all artificial education ought to be an **anticipation** of natural education. And a liberal education is an artificial education which has not only prepared a man to escape the great evils of disobedience to natural laws, but has trained him to appreciate and to seize upon the rewards which Nature scatters with as free a hand as her **penalties**.

12 That man, I think, has had a liberal education who has been so trained in youth that his body is the ready servant of his will, and does with ease and pleasure all the work that, as a mechanism, it is capable of; whose intellect

is a clear, cold, logic engine, with all its parts of equal strength, and in smooth working order; ready, like a steam engine, to be turned to any kind of work, and **spin** the **gossamers** as well as forge the anchors of the mind; whose mind is stored with a knowledge of the great and fundamental truths of Nature and of the laws of her operations; one who, no **stunted ascetic**, is full of life and fire, but whose passions are trained to **come to heel** by a vigorous will, the servant of a tender **conscience**; who has learned to love all beauty, whether of Nature or of art, to hate all **vileness**, and to respect others as himself.

13   Such a one and no other, I **conceive**, has had a liberal education; for he is, as completely as a man can be, in harmony with Nature. He will make the best of her, and she of him. They will get on together rarely; she as his ever **beneficent** mother; he as her **mouthpiece**, her conscious self, her minister and interpreter.

Vocabulary

mould [məuld] v.	to influence the way someone's character or attitudes develop 影响(性格和态度)的形成,塑造
conception [kən'sepʃən] n.	a general idea about what something is like, or a general understanding of something 概念,观念,思想
discrepant [di'skrepənt] a.	different in amounts, details, reports, etc. 不同的,不一致的
notion ['nəuʃən] n.	an idea, belief or opinion, especially one that is false or not very clear 概念,观点,看法
gambit ['gæmbit] n.	a planned series of moves at the beginning of a game of chess (国际象棋中)开局时的布局
check [tʃek] n.	the position of the king in chess when it can be directly attacked by the opponent's pieces (国际象棋中)被"将军"的局面
disapprobation [disæprə'beiʃən] n.	disapproval of someone or something because you think they are morally wrong 反对,不赞成;责难
pawn [pɔ:n] n.	one of the eight smallest and least valuable pieces in the game of chess (国际象棋中的)兵,卒
knight [nait] n.	the chess piece with a horse's head on it (国际象棋中的)马

infinitely [ˈinfənətli] ad.	very much 极多地
untold [ʌnˈtəuld] a.	too much or too many to be measured 数不清的
know to one's cost	to realize something is true because you have had a very unpleasant experience 从不愉快的经历中得知
overlook [əuvəˈluk] v.	to not notice something 没有注意到,忽视
stake [steik] n.	money that people risk on the result of a game, race, etc., all of which is taken by the winner 赌金,赌注
overflow [əuvəˈfləu] v.	to flow over the edges of the container or place 溢出,泛滥
generosity [dʒenəˈrɔsəti] n.	willingness to give money, time etc. in order to help or please someone 慷慨,大方
remorse [riˈmɔːs] n.	a strong feeling of being sorry that you have done something very bad 懊悔,悔恨
metaphor [ˈmetəfə] n.	a way of describing something by comparing it to something else that has similar qualities, without using the words "like" or "as" 隐喻,暗喻
remind [riˈmaind] v.	to make someone think about something again 使(某人)想起
substitute [ˈsʌbstitjuːt] v.	to use something new or different instead of something else 代替
fiend [fiːnd] n.	an evil spirit 恶魔,魔鬼
mighty [ˈmaiti] a.	very strong and powerful, or very big and impressive 强大的,雄伟的
fashion [ˈfæʃən] v.	to influence and form someone's ideas and opinions 影响,形成,塑造
earnest [ˈəːnist] a.	very serious and believing that what you say is very important 认真的,郑重其事的
in harmony with	to agree with another idea, feeling etc., or look good with other things 融洽,和谐
profess [prəˈfes] v.	to make a claim about something, especially a false one 自称,伪称,妄称
stand the test	to be done or made well enough to be successful, strong, or useful 经得起考验
authority [ɔːˈθɔriti] n.	the power you have because of your official position or because people respect your knowledge and experience 权力,权威,威信
vigour [ˈvigə] n.	physical and mental energy and determination 活力,精力,气势

faculty ['fækəlti] n.	a natural ability, such as the ability to see, hear, or think clearly 天赋,能力
property ['prɔpəti] n.	a quality or power that belongs naturally to something 特性,性质,性能
solitary ['sɔlətəri] a.	without anyone or anything else; not involving or including anyone or anything else 单个的,唯一的
reveal [ri'vi:l] v.	to make known something that was previously secret or unknown 揭示,揭露,显示
woe [wəu] n.	great sadness 悲伤,悲哀
susceptible [sə'septəbl] a.	able to be changed, instructed etc. 可以改变、教导等
in accordance with	according to a rule, system etc. 按照,依照
novelty ['nɔvəlti] n.	something new and unusual which attracts people's attention and interest 新奇的事物
poll [pəul] n.	an election 选举
discredit [dis'kredit] n.	loss of other people's respect or trust 丧失名誉,丧失信用;不光彩
pluck [plʌk] v.	to take hold of something and remove it from somewhere by pulling it 拔下,扯下
extermination [ik,stə:mi'neiʃən] n.	killing large numbers of people or animals of a particular type so that they no longer exist 灭绝,根除
compulsory [kəm'pʌlsəri] a.	something that is compulsory must be done because it is the law or because someone in authority orders you to 强制的,义务的
meet with	to get a particular reaction or result 遭到,获得
intervene [intə'vi:n] v.	to deal with a problem that you are not directly involved in 干涉,干预
distinguish [dis'tiŋgwiʃ] v.	to recognize and understand the difference between two similar things or people 辨别,区分
defect [di'fekt] n.	a fault or a lack of something that means that something is not perfect 缺陷,瑕疵
symptom ['simptəm] n.	a sign that something exists 征兆,征候
a box on the ear	一耳光;打在脸侧的一拳
anticipation [,æntisə'peiʃən] n.	the act of expecting something to happen 预期,期望
penalty ['penlti] n.	a punishment for breaking a law, rule, or legal agreement 惩罚,处罚
spin [spin] v.	to produce thread to make a web or cocoon 吐丝

gossamer ['gɔsəmə] n.	light silky thread which spiders leave on grass and bushes 蛛丝，游丝
stunt [stʌnt] v.	to stop something or someone from growing to their full size or developing properly 抑制，阻碍……的成长或发育
ascetic [ə'setik] n.	a person who lives without any physical pleasures or comforts, especially for religious reasons 苦行者，禁欲者
come to heel	（狗听到主人唤声）回到主人身边
conscience ['kɔnʃəns] n.	the part of your mind that tells you whether what you are doing is morally right or wrong 良知，良心
vile [vail] a.	evil or immoral 邪恶的，不道德的
conceive [kən'siːv] v.	to imagine a particular situation 想象
beneficent [bi'nefisənt] a.	doing things to help people; generous 仁慈的，宽厚的
mouthpiece ['mauθpiːs] n.	a person, newspaper etc. that expresses the opinions of a government or a political organization 代言人，喉舌，传声筒

I. Vocabulary Building

in/im-: inward

e.g., import, imprison, indoor, inpatient, inject, inland, inlet, inmate, input, intake

ex-: outward

e.g., export, external, excavate, exclude, expatriate, expel, exclaim, exodus, excommunicate, exculpate

out-: outward

e.g., output, outlet, outside, outline, outstanding, outflow, outdoor, outcry, outbreak, outcome, outsource

out-: surpassing

e.g., outdo, outdate, outwit, outsmart, outweigh, outlive, outnumber, outsize, outbid, outlaw

circum-: surrounding

e.g., circumscribe, circumlocution, circumvent, circumnavigate, circumstantial, circumference, circumstance

II. Discussion

Discuss the following questions with your own words.

1. What does the author compare life and education to respectively?
2. What is the image of life in the author's opinion?
3. What is the definition of education given by the author?
4. What would happen to people who won't learn in Nature's university?
5. What is the relation between Nature and a man who receives a liberal education?

III. Translation A

Translate the following sentences selected from the text into Chinese.

1. By way of a beginning, let us ask ourselves—What is education? Above all things, what is our ideal of a thoroughly liberal education? —of that education which, if we could begin life again, we would give ourselves—of that education which, if we could mould the fates to our own will, we would give our children? (Para. 1)

2. For me, education means neither more nor less than this. Anything, which professes to call itself education must be tried by this standard, and if it fails to stand the test, I will not call it education, whatever may be the force of authority or of numbers upon the other side. (Para. 5)

3. And then, long before we were susceptible of any other mode of instruction, Nature took us in hand, and every minute of waking life brought its educational influence, shaping our actions into rough accordance with Nature's laws, so that we might not be ended untimely by too gross disobedience. (Para. 8)

4. The object of what we commonly call education—that education in which man intervenes and which I shall distinguish as artificial education—is to make good these defects in Nature's methods; to prepare the child to

receive Nature's education, neither incapably nor ignorantly, nor with willful disobedience; and to understand the preliminary symptoms of her pleasure, without waiting for the box on the ear. (Para. 11)

5. He will make the best of her, and she of him. They will get on together rarely; she as his ever beneficent mother; he as her mouthpiece, her conscious self, her minister and interpreter. (Para. 13)

IV. Translation B
Translate the following passage into Chinese.

For my part, I hold that where they differ, Christianity is preferable, but where they agree, both are mistaken. The conception which I should substitute as the purpose of education is civilization, a term which, as I meant it, has a definition which is partly individual, partly social. It consists, in the individual, of both intellectual and moral qualities: intellectually, a certain minimum of general knowledge, technical skill in one's own profession, and a habit of forming opinions on evidence; morally, of impartiality, kindliness, and a modicum of self-control. I should add a quality which is neither moral nor intellectual, but perhaps physiological: zest and joy of life. In communities, civilization demands respect for law, justice as between man and man, purposes not involving permanent injury to any section of the human race, and intelligent adaptation of means to ends. (Excerpted from Text C)

V. Writing Exercise

You are probably a college student now. What is the purpose of your college education? Please write an essay with at least 300 words.

Text B

Importance of Education①

Plato

SOCRATES: Well, then, Adeimantus, don't you think that a single boxer who has had the best possible training could easily fight two non-boxers who are rich and fat?

ADEIMANTUS: Maybe not at the same time.

SOCRATES: Not even if he could start to run away and then turn and hit the one who caught up with him first, and could do this often, out in the **stifling** heat of the sun? Couldn't a man like that overcome even more than two such enemies?

ADEIMANTUS: It certainly would not be surprising if he could.

SOCRATES: Well, don't you think that rich people have more knowledge and experience of boxing than of how to fight a war?

ADEIMANTUS: I do.

SOCRATES: **In all likelihood**, then, our athletes will easily be able to fight two or three times their number.

ADEIMANTUS: I will have to grant you that, since I think what you say is right.

SOCRATES: Well, then, what if they sent an **envoy** to another city with the following true message: "We use no gold or silver. It is against divine law for us to do so, but not for you. So join us in this war and you can have the property of our enemy." Do you think that anyone who heard this message would choose to fight hard, **lean hounds**, rather than to join the

---

① Selected from Plato's *The Republic*.

hounds in fighting fat and tender sheep?

ADEIMANTUS: No, I do not. But if the wealth of all other cities were **amassed** by a single one, don't you think that would endanger your non-wealthy city?

SOCRATES: You are happily innocent if you think that any city besides the one we are constructing deserves to be called a city.

ADEIMANTUS: What should we call them, then?

SOCRATES: We will have to find a "greater" title for the others because each of them is a great many cities, but not a city, as they say in the game. They contain two, **at any rate**, which are at war with one another: the city of the poor and that of the rich. And within each of these, there are a great many more. So if you treat them as one city, you will be making a big mistake. But if you treat them as many and offer one the money, power, and the very **inhabitants** of another, you will always find many allies and few enemies. And as long as your own city is **temperately** governed in the way we just arranged, it will be the greatest one—not in reputation; I do not mean that; but the greatest in fact—even if it has only a thousand soldiers to defend it. For you won't easily find one city so great among either Greeks or **barbarians**, though you will find many that are **reputed** to be many times greater. Or do you disagree?

ADEIMANTUS: No, by Zeus, I do not.

SOCRATES: This, then, would also provide our rulers with the best limit for determining the proper size of the city, and how much land they should mark off for a city that size, letting the rest go.

ADEIMANTUS: What limit is that?

SOCRATES: I think it is this: as long as it is willing to remain one city, it may continue to grow, but not beyond that point.

ADEIMANTUS: And it is a good one.

SOCRATES: Then we will also give our guardians this further order, that they are to guard in every possible way against the city's being either small in size or great in reputation, rather than adequate in size and one in number.

ADEIMANTUS: No doubt, that will be a **trivial** instruction for them to follow!

SOCRATES: Here is another that is even more trivial. We mentioned it earlier as well. We said that if an **offspring** of the guardians is inferior, he must be sent off to join the other citizens, and that if the others have an excellent offspring, he must join the guardians. This was meant to make clear that every other citizen, too, must be assigned to what naturally suits him, with one person assigned to one job so that, practicing his own pursuit, each of them will become not many but one, and the entire city thereby naturally grow to be one, not many.

ADEIMANTUS: Oh, yes, that is a more minor one!

SOCRATES: Really, my good Adeimantus, the orders we are giving them are neither as numerous nor as difficult as one would think. Indeed, they are all insignificant provided, as the saying goes, they safeguard the one great thing—or rather not great but adequate.

ADEIMANTUS: What's that?

SOCRATES: Their education and upbringing. For if a good education makes them **moderate** men, they will easily discover all this for themselves—and everything else that we are now **omitting**, such as the possession of women, marriages, and the **procreation** of children, and how all these must be governed as far as possible by the old proverb that friends share everything in common.

ADEIMANTUS: Yes, that would be best.

SOCRATES: And surely once our constitution is well started, it will, as it were, go on growing in a circle. For good education and upbringing, if they are kept up, produce good natures; and sound natures, which in turn receive such an education, grow up even better than their **predecessors in every respect**—but particularly **with respect to** their offspring, as in the case of all the other animals.

ADEIMANTUS: Yes, probably so.

SOCRATES: To put it briefly, then, what the **overseers** of our city must **cling to**, not allow to become **corrupted** without their noticing it, and guard against everything, is this: there must be no innovation in musical or physical training that goes against the established order. On the contrary, they must guard against that as much as they can. And they should dread to hear anyone say that "people think most of the song that floats newest from the singer's lips," in case someone happens to suppose that the poet means not new songs, but a new way of singing, and praises that. We should not praise such a claim, however, or take it to be what the poet meant. You see, a change to a new kind of musical training is something to beware of as wholly dangerous. For one can never change the ways of training people in music without affecting the greatest political laws. That is what Damon says, and I am convinced he is right.

ADEIMANTUS: You can also count me among those who are convinced.

SOCRATES: It seems, then, that it is in musical training that the guardhouse of our guardians must surely be built.

ADEIMANTUS: At any rate, this sort of lawlessness easily **inserts** itself undetected.

SOCRATES: Yes, because it is supposed to be only part of a game that, as such, can do no harm.

ADEIMANTUS: And it does not do any—except, of course, that when it has established itself there, it slowly and silently flows over into people's habits and practices. From these it travels forth with greater vigor into private contracts, and then from private contracts it advances with the utmost **insolence** into the laws and constitution, Socrates, until in the end it overthrows everything public and private.

SOCRATES: Well, is that so?

ADEIMANTUS: I think it is.

SOCRATES: Then, as we were saying at the beginning, our children must take part in games that are more law-abiding right from the start, since, if their games become lawless and the children **follow suit**, isn't it impossible for them to grow up into excellent and law-abiding men?

ADEIMANTUS: Of course.

SOCRATES: So whenever children play in a good way right from the start and absorb lawfulness from musical training, there is the opposite result: lawfulness follows them in everything and **fosters** their growth, correcting anything in the city that may have been neglected before.

ADEIMANTUS: That's true.

SOCRATES: And so such people rediscover the seemingly insignificant conventional views their predecessors had destroyed.

ADEIMANTUS: Which sort?

SOCRATES: Those dealing with things like this: the silence appropriate for younger people in the presence of their elders; the giving up of seats for them and standing up in their presence; the care of parents; hairstyles; clothing; shoes; the general appearance of the body; and everything else of that sort. Don't you agree?

ADEIMANTUS: I do.

SOCRATES: To **legislate** about such things is naive, in my view, since verbal or written **decrees** will never make them **come about** or last.

ADEIMANTUS: How could they?

SOCRATES: At any rate, Adeimantus, it looks as though the start of someone's education determines what follows. Or doesn't like always encourage like?

ADEIMANTUS: It does.

SOCRATES: And the final outcome of education, I imagine we would say, is a single, complete, and fresh product that is either good or the opposite.

ADEIMANTUS: Of course.

SOCRATES: That is why I, for my part, would not try to legislate about such things.

ADEIMANTUS: And with good reason.

SOCRATES: Then, by the gods, what about all that marketplace business, the contracts people make with one another in the marketplace, for example, and contracts with handicraftsmen, and **slanders**, injuries, **indictments**, establishing juries, paying or collecting whatever dues are necessary in marketplace and harbors, and, in a word, the entire regulation of marketplace, city, harbor, or what have you—dare we legislate about any of these?

ADEIMANTUS: No, it would not be appropriate to dictate to men who are fine and good. For they will easily find out for themselves whatever needs to be legislated about such things.

SOCRATES: Yes, my friend, provided that a god grants that the laws we have already described are preserved intact.

ADEIMANTUS: If not, they will spend their lives continually enacting and amending such laws in the hope of finding what is best.

SOCRATES: You mean they will live like those sick people who, because they are **intemperate**, are not willing to abandon their bad way of life.

ADEIMANTUS: That's right.

SOCRATES: Such people really do lead a charming life! Their medical treatment achieves nothing, except to make their illnesses worse and more complex, and they are always hoping that someone will recommend some new drug that will make them healthy.

ADEIMANTUS: Yes, that's exactly what happens to invalids of this sort.

SOCRATES: And isn't it another charming feature of theirs that they think their worst enemy of all is the one who tells them the truth—that until they give up drunkenness, overeating, sexual **indulgence**, and idleness, then no drug, **cautery**, or surgery, no charms, **amulets**, or anything else of that sort will do them any good?

ADEIMANTUS: It is not charming at all. Being harsh to someone who tells the truth is not charming.

SOCRATES: You do not approve of such men, apparently.

ADEIMANTUS: No, by Zeus, I do not.

SOCRATES: Then nor will you approve of an entire city that behaves in the way we were just describing. Or don't you think that such invalids behave in the very same way as cities where the following occurs? Because they are badly governed politically, the citizens are warned not to change the city's whole political system, and the one who does is threatened with the death penalty. But the one who serves these cities most pleasantly, while they remain politically governed in that way; who indulges them, flatters them, **anticipates** their wishes, and is clever at fulfilling them; isn't he, on that account, honored by them as a good man who is wise in the most important matters?

ADEIMANTUS: Yes, I think their behavior is the same and I do not approve of it at all.

Vocabulary

stifling [ˈstaɪflɪŋ] a.	very hot and difficult to breathe 闷热的, 令人窒息的
in all likelihood	almost certainly 几乎肯定地, 极可能地
envoy [ˈenvɔɪ] n.	someone who is sent to another country as an official representative 使者, 代表, 外交官

lean [liːn] a.	thin in a healthy and attractive way 清瘦的，精瘦的
hound [haund] n.	a dog 狗
amass [əˈmæs] v.	to gradually collect a large amount of money, knowledge, or information 积聚，积累，大量收集
at any rate	used when you are stating one definite fact in a situation that is uncertain or unsatisfactory 无论如何，不管怎样
inhabitant [inˈhæbitənt] n.	one of the people who live in a particular place 居民
temperately [ˈtempərətli] ad.	calmly and sensibly 温和地，心平气和地，节制地
barbarian [baːˈbeəriən] n.	someone from a different tribe or land, who people believe to be wild and not civilized 野蛮人，未开化的人
reputed [riˈpjuːtid] a.	according to what most people say or think 据说，一般认为
trivial [ˈtriviəl] a.	unimportant or of little value 微不足道的，没有价值的
offspring [ˈɔfˌspriŋ] n.	someone's child or children 子女，子孙
moderate [ˈmɔdərit] a.	having opinions, or beliefs especially about politics, that are not extreme and that most people consider reasonable or sensible 不极端的，温和的，稳健的
omit [əuˈmit] v.	to not include someone or something, either deliberately or because you forget to do it 省去，略去；遗漏
procreation [ˌprəukriˈeiʃən] n.	producing children or offspring 生育，生殖
predecessor [ˈpriːdisesə] n.	someone who had a job or position before someone else 前任，前辈
in every respect	在所有方面
with respect to	used to introduce a new subject, or to return to one that has already been mentioned 关于，谈到
overseer [ˈəuvəsiə] n.	someone in charge of a group of workers, who checks that their work is done properly 监工，监督人
cling to	坚持，忠于
corrupt [kəˈrʌpt] v.	cause someone to become dishonest and unjust and unable to be trusted 使道德败坏，使腐败
insert [inˈzəːt] v.	to put something inside or into something else 插入，放进
insolence [ˈinsələns] n.	being rude and not showing any respect 粗鲁无礼，傲慢
follow suit	to do the same as someone else has just done 仿效，跟着做
foster [ˈfɔstə] v.	to help a skill, feeling, idea etc. develop over a period of time 促进，培养
legislate [ˈledʒəsleit] v.	to make a law about something 立法

decree [diˈkriː] n.	an official command or decision, especially one made by the ruler of a country 命令, 法令
come about	to happen, especially in a way that seems impossible to control 发生, 产生
slander [ˈslaːndə] n.	the legal offence of making a false spoken statement about someone that is intended to damage the good opinion that people have 诽谤罪
indictment [inˈdaitmənt] n.	the act of officially charging someone with a criminal offence 起诉, 指控, 控告
intemperate [inˈtempərit] a.	not having enough control over your feelings so that you behave in a way that is unacceptable to other people 无节制的, 放纵的
indulgence [inˈdʌldʒəns] n.	the habit of eating too much, drinking too much, etc. 放纵
cautery [ˈkɔːtəri] n.	the act or effect of cauterizing 烧灼术, 烧灼剂
amulet [ˈæmjulit] n.	a small piece of jewellery worn to protect against bad luck, disease etc. 护身符, 驱邪物
anticipate [ænˈtisiˌpeit] v.	to meet (an obligation) before a due date 提前完成, 提前履行

Text C

Education and Discipline①

Bertrand Russell

<u>1</u> Any serious educational theory must consist of two parts: a conception of the ends of life, and a science of psychological **dynamics**, i.e., of the laws of mental change. Two men who differ **as to** the ends of life cannot hope to agree about education. The educational machine, throughout Western civilization, is **dominated** by two **ethical** theories: that of Christianity, and

---

① Excerpted from Bertrand Russell's *In Praise of Idleness: And Other Essays*.

that of nationalism. These two, when taken seriously, are **incompatible**, as is becoming evident in Germany. **For my part**, I hold that where they differ, Christianity is preferable, but where they agree, both are mistaken. The conception which I should substitute as the purpose of education is civilization, a term which, as I meant it, has a definition which is partly individual, partly social. It consists, in the individual, of both intellectual and moral qualities: intellectually, a certain minimum of general knowledge, technical skill in one's own profession, and a habit of forming opinions on evidence; morally, of **impartiality**, kindliness, and a **modicum** of self-control. I should add a quality which is neither moral nor intellectual, but perhaps **physiological**: **zest** and joy of life. In communities, civilization demands respect for law, justice as between man and man, purposes not involving permanent injury to any section of the human race, and intelligent adaptation of means to ends.

<u>2</u>　If these are to be the purpose of education, it is a question for the science of psychology to consider what can be done towards realizing them, and, in particular, what degree of freedom is likely to prove most effective.

<u>3</u>　On the question of freedom in education there are at present three main schools of thought, **deriving** partly from differences as to ends and partly from differences in psychological theory. There are those who say that children should be completely free, however bad they may be; there are those who say they should be completely **subject to** authority, however good they may be; and there are those who say they should be free, but in spite of freedom they should be always good. This last party is larger than it has any logical right to be; Children, like adults, will not all be virtuous if they are all free. The belief that liberty will insure moral perfection is a relic of Rousseauism, and would not survive a study of animals and babies. Those who hold this belief think that education should have no positive purpose,

but should merely offer an environment suitable for **spontaneous** development. I cannot agree with this school, which seems too individualistic, and **unduly indifferent** to the importance of knowledge. We live in communities which require cooperation, and it would be **utopian** to expect all the necessary cooperation to result from spontaneous impulse. The existence of a large population on a limited area is only possible owing to science and technique; education must, therefore, hand on the necessary minimum of these. The educators who allow most freedom are men whose success depends upon a degree of **benevolence**, self-control, and trained intelligence which can hardly be generated where every impulse is left unchecked; their **merits**, therefore, are not likely to be **perpetuated** if their methods are **undiluted**. Education, viewed from a social standpoint, must be something more positive than a mere opportunity for growth. It must, of course, provide this, but it must also provide a mental and moral equipment which children cannot acquire entirely for themselves.

4 The arguments in favor of a great degree of freedom in education are derived not from man's natural goodness, but from the effects of authority, both on those who suffer it and on those who exercise it. Those who are subject to authority become either **submissive** or **rebellious**, and each attitude has its drawbacks.

5 The submissive lose **initiative**, both in thought and action; moreover, the anger generated by the feeling of being **thwarted** tends to find an outlet in bullying those who are weaker. That is why **tyrannical** institutions are self-perpetuating: what a man has suffered from his father he **inflicts** upon his son, and the **humiliations** which he remembers having endured at his public school he passes on to "natives" when he becomes an empire-builder. Thus an unduly authoritative education turns the pupils into timid tyrants, incapable of either claiming or tolerating originality in word or deed. The

effect upon the educators is even worse: they tend to become **sadistic disciplinarians**, glad to inspire terror, and content to inspire nothing else. As these men represent knowledge, the pupils acquire a horror of knowledge, which, among the English upper class, is supposed to be part of human nature, but is really part of the well-grounded hatred of the authoritarian **pedagogue**.

<u>6</u>   Rebels, on the other hand, though they may be necessary, can hardly be just to what exists. Moreover, there are many ways of rebelling, and only a small minority of these are wise. Galileo was a rebel and was wise; believers in the flat-earth theory are equally rebels, but are foolish. There is a great danger in the tendency to suppose that opposition to authority is essentially **meritorious** and that unconventional opinions are bound to be correct: no useful purpose is served by **smashing** lamp-posts or maintaining Shakespeare to be no poet. Yet this excessive rebelliousness is often the effect that too much authority has on spirited pupils. And when rebels become educators, they sometimes encourage defiance in their pupils, for whom at the same time they are trying to produce a perfect environment, although these two aims are scarcely compatible.

<u>7</u>   What is wanted is neither submissiveness nor rebellion, but good nature, and general friendliness both to people and to new ideas. These qualities are due in part to physical causes, to which old-fashioned educators paid too little attention; but they are due still more to freedom from the feeling of **baffled impotence** which arises when vital impulses are thwarted. If the young are to grow into friendly adults, it is necessary, in most cases, that they should feel their environment friendly. This requires that there should be a certain sympathy with the child's important desires, and not merely an attempt to use him for some abstract end such as the glory of God or the greatness of one's country. And, in teaching, every attempt should be

made to cause the pupil to feel that it is worth his while to know what is being taught—at least when this is true. When the pupil cooperates willingly, he learns twice as fast and with half the **fatigue**. All these are valid reasons for a very great degree of freedom.

<u>8</u> It is easy, however, to carry the argument too far. It is not desirable that children, in avoiding the vices of the slave, should acquire those of the **aristocrat**. Consideration for others, not only in great matters, but also in little everyday things, is an essential element in civilization, without which social life would be intolerable. I am not thinking of mere forms of politeness, such as saying "please" and "thank you": formal manners are most fully developed among barbarians, and diminish with every advance in culture. I am thinking rather of willingness to take a fair share of necessary work, to be **obliging** in small ways that save trouble on the balance. It is not desirable to give a child a sense of **omnipotence**, or a belief that adults exist only to **minister to** the pleasures of the young. And those who disapprove of the existence of the idle rich are hardly consistent if they bring up their children without any sense that work is necessary, and without the habits that make continuous application possible.

<u>9</u> There is another consideration to which some advocates of freedom attach too little importance. In a community of children which is left without adult **interference** there is a tyranny of the stronger, which is likely to be far more brutal than most adult tyranny. If two children of two or three years old are left to play together, they will, after a few fights, discover which is bound to be the victor, and the other will then become a slave. Where the number of children is larger, one or two acquire complete mastery, and the others have far less liberty than they would have if the adults interfered to protect the weaker and less **pugnacious**. Consideration for others does not, with most children, arise spontaneously, but has to be taught, and can

hardly be taught except by the exercise of authority. This is perhaps the most important argument against the **abdication** of the adults.

<u>10</u>　　I do not think that educators have yet solved the problem of combining the desirable forms of freedom with the necessary minimum of moral training. The right solution, it must be admitted, is often made impossible by parents before the child is brought to an enlightened school. Just as psychoanalysts, from their clinical experience, conclude that we are all mad, so the authorities in modern schools, from their contact with pupils whose parents have made them unmanageable, **are disposed to** conclude that all children are "difficult" and all parents utterly foolish. Children who have been driven wild by parental tyranny (which often takes the form of solicitous affection) may require a longer or shorter period of complete liberty before they can view any adult without suspicion. But children who have been sensibly handled at home can bear to be checked in minor ways, so long as they feel that they are being helped in the ways that they themselves regard as important. Adults who like children, and are not reduced to a condition of nervous exhaustion by their company, can achieve a great deal in the way of discipline without ceasing to be regarded with friendly feelings by their pupils.

<u>11</u>　　I think modern educational theorists are **inclined** to attach too much importance to the negative virtue of not interfering with children, and too little to the positive merit of enjoying their company. If you have the sort of liking for children that many people have for horse or dogs, they will **be apt to** respond to your suggestions, and to accept prohibitions, perhaps with some good-humoured **grumbling**, but without **resentment.** It is no use to have the sort of liking that consists in regarding them as a field for valuable social endeavor, or—what amounts to the same thing—as an outlet for power-impulses. No child will be grateful for an interest in him that springs from

the thought that he will have a vote to be secured for your party or a body to be sacrificed to king and country. The desirable sort of interest is that which consists in spontaneous pleasure in the presence of children, without any **ulterior** purpose. Teachers who have this quality will seldom need to interfere with children's freedom, but will be able to do so, when necessary, without causing psychological damage.

12 Unfortunately, it is **utterly** impossible for overworked teachers to preserve an instinctive liking for children; they are bound to come to feel towards them as the **proverbial confectioner's apprentice** does toward **macaroons**. I do not think that education ought to be any one's whole profession: it should be undertaken for at most two hours a day by people whose remaining hours are spent away with children. The society of the young is fatiguing, especially when strict discipline is avoided. Fatigue, in the end, produces **irritation**, which is likely to express itself somehow, whatever theories the **harassed** teacher may have taught himself or herself to believe. The necessary friendliness cannot be preserved by self-control alone. But where it exists, it should be unnecessary to have rules in advance as to how "naughty" children are to be treated, since impulse is likely to lead to the right decision, and almost any decision will be right if the child feels that you like him. No rules, however wise, are a substitute for affection and **tact**.

Vocabulary

dynamics [dai'næmiks] n.	the way in which things or people behave, react, and affect each other 动态
as to	according to a particular standard or principle 根据, 依照
dominate ['dɔmi,neit] vt.	to have power and control over someone or something 支配, 控制
ethical ['eθikəl] a.	connected with principles of what is right and wrong 关于伦理的, 道德的
incompatible [,inkəm'pætəbl] a.	not able to exist together without trouble or conflict 不相容的, 不能共存的

for my part	used to say what someone's opinions are, when compared to someone else's opinions 就我而言,对我来说
impartial [ˈimpɑːʃəl] a.	not giving special favour or support to any one person or group; fair 不偏不倚的,公正的
modicum [ˈmɔdikəm] n.	a modicum of; a small amount of something, especially a good quality 少量,一点点
physiological [ˌfiziəˈlɔdʒikl] a.	of the way the body of a person or an animal works and looks 生理的
zest [zest] n.	eager interest and enjoyment 热心,热情,快乐
derive [diˈraiv] v.	to develop or come from something else 源自,源于
subject to	dependent on something else 取决于,有待于
spontaneous [spɔnˈteiniəs] a.	happening or done without being planned or organized, but because you suddenly feel you would like to do it 自动的,自发的
unduly [ʌnˈdjuːli] ad.	too extreme or too much 过度地,过分地
indifferent [inˈdifərənt] a.	not caring about what is happening, especially about other people's problems or feelings 不关心的,不在乎的
utopian [juːˈtəupiən] a.	unrealistic; impossibly ideal 不现实的,过于理想化的
benevolence [biˈnevələns] n.	being kind and generous 仁慈,乐善好施
merit [ˈmerit] n.	one of the good features 优点,长处
perpetuate [pəˈpetʃueit] vt.	to make something continue to exist for a long time 使长存,使永恒
undiluted [ˌʌndaiˈluːtid] a.	very strong and not mixed with other things 没有掺杂的,纯正的
submissive [səbˈmisiv] a.	always willing to obey someone even if they are unkind to you 顺从的,恭顺的
rebellious [riˈbeljəs] a.	deliberately disobeying 叛逆的,反抗的
initiative [iˈniʃətiv] n.	the ability to make decisions and take action without waiting for someone to tell you what to do 主动能力
thwart [θwɔːt] vt.	to prevent someone from doing what they are trying to do 阻挠,阻碍
tyrannical [təˈrænikl] a.	using power over people in a way that is cruel and unfair 专制的,专横的
inflict [inˈflikt] vt.	to make someone suffer something unpleasant 使遭受,使承受
humiliation [hjuːˌmiliˈeiʃən] n.	a feeling of shame and great embarrassment, because you have been made to look stupid or weak 羞辱,丢脸

sadistic [sə'dıstık] a.	cruel and enjoying making other people suffer 施虐狂的
disciplinarian [ˌdɪsəplɪn'eərɪən] n.	someone who believes people should obey orders and rules, and who makes them do this 严格执行纪律者
pedagogue ['pedəgɒg] n.	a teacher who cares too much about rules 刻板的老师,过分拘泥于条条框框的老师
meritorious [ˌmerɪ'tɔːrɪəs] a.	very good and deserving praise 极好而值得称赞的
smash [smæʃ] v.	to break into small pieces violently or noisily, or to make something do this by dropping, throwing, or hitting it 打破,打碎,使粉碎
baffle ['bæfl] vt.	to confuse someone completely 使困惑,使难倒
impotence ['ɪmpətəns] n.	the quality or state of being unable to take effective action because you do not have enough power, strength, or control 无能为力,没有能力
fatigue [fə'tiːg] n.	very great tiredness 疲劳,劳累
aristocrat ['ærɪstəkræt] n.	someone who belongs to the highest social class 贵族(成员)
obliging [ə'blaɪdʒɪŋ] a.	willing and eager to help 乐于助人的,热心相助的
omnipotence [ɒm'nɪpətəns] n.	the quality or state of being able to do everything 全能,无所不能
minister to	to give help to someone who needs it 给以……帮助
pugnacious [pʌg'neɪʃəs] a.	very eager to quarrel or fight with people 爱争吵的,好斗的
abdication [ˌæbdɪ'keɪʃ(ə)n] n.	failing to do what is required by a duty or responsibility 放弃责任
be disposed to do sth	feel willing to do something or behave in a particular way 愿意做某事
inclined [ɪn'klaɪnd] a.	wanting to do sth 想要做某事
be apt to do sth	having a natural tendency to do something 有做某事倾向的,易于做某事的
grumble ['grʌmbl] v.	to keep complaining in an unhappy way 发牢骚,抱怨
resentment [rɪ'zentmənt] n.	a feeling of anger because something has happened that you think is unfair 愤恨,不满,憎恶
ulterior [ʌl'tɪərɪə] **purpose**	reasons for doing something that you deliberately hide in order to get an advantage for yourself 不可告人的目的
proverbial [prə'vɜːbɪəl] a.	commonly spoken of; widely known 俗话说的,众所周知的
confectioner [kən'fekʃənə] n.	someone who makes or sells sweets, cakes etc. 甜食商

apprentice [ə'prentis] n.   someone who agrees to work for an employer for a fixed period of time in order to learn a particular skill or job 学徒

macaroon [mækə'ruːn] n.   a small round cake made of sugar, eggs, and crushed almonds or coconut 蛋白杏仁饼,蛋白椰子饼

irritation [iri'teiʃən] n.   the feeling of being annoyed about something 烦恼,不快

harassed ['hærəst] a.   anxious and tired because you have too many problems or things to do 烦恼的,疲惫的

tact [tækt] n.   the ability to be polite and careful about what you say or do so that you do not upset or embarrass other people 得体,乖巧,机敏

Unit 5

Women

Text A Professions for Women
Text B Beauty
Text C The Tragedy of Woman's Emancipation

Text A

Professions for Women[①]

Virginia Woolf

<u>1</u> When your secretary invited me to come here, she told me that your Society is concerned with the employment of women and she suggested that I might tell you something about my own professional experiences. It is true I am a woman; it is true I am employed; but what professional experiences have I had? It is difficult to say. My profession is literature; and in that profession there are fewer experiences for women than in any other, with the exception of the stage—fewer, I mean, that **are peculiar to** women. For the road was cut many years ago—by Fanny Burney, by Aphra Behn, by Harriet Martineau, by Jane Austen, by George Eliot—many famous women, and many more unknown and forgotten, have been before me, making the path smooth, and regulating my steps. Thus, when I came to write, there were

---

① Virginia Woolf delivered the speech before the Women's Service League on January 21, 1931.

very few material obstacles in my way. Writing was a **reputable** and harmless occupation. The family peace was not broken by the scratching of a pen. No demand was made upon the family purse. For ten and sixpence one can buy paper enough to write all the plays of Shakespeare—if one has a mind that way. Pianos and models, Paris, Vienna and Berlin, masters and mistresses, are not needed by a writer. The cheapness of writing paper is, of course, the reason why women have succeeded as writers before they have succeeded in the other professions.

<u>2</u>　　But to tell you my story—it is a simple one. You have only got to figure to yourselves a girl in a bedroom with a pen in her hand. She had only to move that pen from left to right—from ten o'clock to one. Then it occurred to her to do what is simple and cheap enough after all—to slip a few of those pages into an envelope, fix a penny stamp in the corner, and drop the envelope into the red box at the corner. It was thus that I became a journalist; and my effort was rewarded on the first day of the following month—a very glorious day it was for me—by a letter from an editor containing a cheque for one pound ten shillings and sixpence. But to show you how little I deserve to be called a professional woman, how little I know of the struggles and difficulties of such lives, I have to admit that instead of spending that sum upon bread and butter, rent, shoes and stockings, or butcher's bills, I went out and bought a cat—a beautiful cat, a Persian cat, which very soon involved me in bitter disputes with my neighbours.

<u>3</u>　　What could be easier than to write articles and to buy Persian cats with the profits? But wait a moment. Articles have to be about something. Mine, I seem to remember, was about a novel by a famous man. And while I was writing this review, I discovered that if I were going to review books I should need to do battle with a certain **phantom**. And the phantom was a woman, and when I came to know her better I called her after the **heroine** of a famous poem, *The Angel in the House*. It was she who used to come between me

and my paper when I was writing reviews. It was she who bothered me and wasted my time and so **tormented** me that at last I killed her. You who **come of** a younger and happier generation may not have heard of her—you may not know what I mean by the Angel in the House. I will describe her as shortly as I can. She was intensely sympathetic. She was immensely charming. She was utterly unselfish. She **excelled in** the difficult arts of family life. She sacrificed herself daily. If there was chicken, she took the leg; if there was a **draught** she sat in it—in short she was so **constituted** that she never had a mind or a wish of her own, but preferred to sympathize always with the minds and wishes of others. Above all—I need not say it—she was pure. Her purity was supposed to be her chief beauty—her **blushes**, her great grace. In those days—the last of Queen Victoria—every house had its Angel. And when I came to write I encountered her with the very first words. The shadow of her wings fell on my page; I heard the **rustling** of her skirts in the room. Directly, that is to say, I took my pen in my hand to review that novel by a famous man, she slipped behind me and whispered: "My dear, you are a young woman. You are writing about a book that has been written by a man. Be sympathetic; be tender; flatter; deceive; use all the arts and **wiles** of our sex. Never let anybody guess that you have a mind of your own. Above all, be pure." And she made as if to guide my pen. I now record the one act for which I take some **credit** to myself, though the credit rightly belongs to some excellent ancestors of mine who left me a certain sum of money—shall we say five hundred pounds a year? —so that it was not necessary for me to depend solely on charm for my living. I turned upon her and caught her by the throat. I did my best to kill her. My excuse, if I were to be **had up** in a court of law, would be that I acted in self-defence. Had I not killed her she would have killed me. She would have plucked the heart out of my writing. For, as I found, directly I put pen to paper, you cannot review even a novel without having a mind of your own, without expressing what you think to be the truth about human relations, morality, sex. And all these questions, according to the Angel of the House, cannot be dealt with freely and openly by women; they must charm, they must **conciliate**, they must—to put it bluntly—tell lies if they are to succeed. Thus, whenever I felt the shadow of her wing or the **radiance** of her **halo** upon my page, I took up the inkpot and flung it at her. She died hard. Her **fictitious** nature was of great assistance to her. It is far harder to kill a phantom than a reality. She was always creeping back when I thought I had **dispatched** her. Though I flatter myself that I killed her in the end, the struggle was severe; it took much time that had better have been spent upon learning Greek grammar; or in **roaming** the world in search of adventures. But it was a real experience; it was an experience that was bound to **befall** all women writers at that time. Killing the Angel in the House was part of the occupation of a woman writer.

4   But to continue my story. The Angel was dead; what then remained? You may say that what remained was a simple and common object—a young woman in a bedroom with an inkpot. In other words, now that she had rid herself of falsehood, that young woman had only to be herself. Ah, but what is "herself"? I mean, what is a woman? I **assure** you, I do not know. I do not believe that you know. I do not believe that anybody can know until she has expressed herself in all the arts and professions open to human skill. That indeed is one of the reasons why I have come here out of respect for you, who are in process of showing us by your experiments what a woman is, who are in process of providing us, by your failures and successes, with that extremely important piece of information.

5   But to continue the story of my professional experiences. I made one pound ten and six by my first review; and I bought a Persian cat with the **proceeds**. Then I grew ambitious. A Persian cat is all very well, I said; but a Persian cat is not enough. I must have a motor car. And it was thus that I became a novelist—for it is a very strange thing that people will give you a

motor car if you will tell them a story. It is a still stranger thing that there is nothing so delightful in the world as telling stories. It is far pleasanter than writing reviews of famous novels. And yet, if I am to obey your secretary and tell you my professional experiences as a novelist, I must tell you about a very strange experience that befell me as a novelist. And to understand it you must try first to imagine a novelist's state of mind. I hope I am not giving away professional secrets if I say that a novelist's chief desire is to be as **unconscious** as possible. He has to **induce** in himself a state of **perpetual lethargy.** He wants life to proceed with the utmost quiet and regularity. He wants to see the same faces, to read the same books, to do the same things day after day, month after month, while he is writing, so that nothing may break the illusion in which he is living—so that nothing may disturb or disquiet the mysterious nosings about, feelings round, **darts, dashes** and sudden discoveries of that very shy and **illusive** spirit, the imagination. I suspect that this state is the same both for men and women. Be that as it may, I want you to imagine me writing a novel in a state of **trance.** I want you to figure to yourselves a girl sitting with a pen in her hand, which for minutes, and indeed for hours, she never dips into the inkpot. The image that comes to my mind when I think of this girl is the image of a fisherman lying sunk in dreams **on the verge of** a deep lake with a **rod** held out over the water. She was letting her imagination sweep unchecked round every rock and **cranny** of the world that lies **submerged** in the depths of our unconscious being. Now came the experience that I believe to be far commoner with women writers than with men. The line raced through the girl's fingers. Her imagination had rushed away. It had sought the pools, the depths, the dark places where the largest fish **slumber.** And then there was a smash. There was an explosion. There was foam and confusion. The imagination had dashed itself against something hard. The girl was roused from her dream. She was indeed in a state of the most acute and difficult distress. To speak without **figure**, she had thought of something, something about the body, about the passions which it was unfitting for her as a woman to say. Men, her reason told her, would be shocked. The consciousness of what men will say of a woman who speaks the truth about her passions had roused her from her artist's state of unconsciousness. She could write no more. The trance was over. Her imagination could work no longer. This I believe to be a very common experience with women writers—they are **impeded** by the extreme conventionality of the other sex. For though men sensibly allow themselves great freedom in these respects, I doubt that they realize or can control the extreme severity with which they condemn such freedom in women.

6 These then were two very genuine experiences of my own. These were two of the adventures of my professional life. The first—killing the Angel in the House—I think I solved. She died. But the second, telling the truth about my own experiences as a body, I do not think I solved. I doubt that any woman has solved it yet. The obstacles against her are still immensely powerful—and yet they are very difficult to define. Outwardly, what is simpler than to write books? Outwardly, what obstacles are there for a woman rather than for a man? Inwardly, I think, the case is very different; she has still many ghosts to fight, many prejudices to overcome. Indeed it will be a long time still, I think, before a woman can sit down to write a book without finding a phantom to be **slain**, a rock to be dashed against. And if this is so in literature, the freest of all professions for women, how is it in the new professions which you are now for the first time entering?

7 Those are the questions that I should like, had I time, to ask you. And indeed, if I have **laid stress upon** these professional experiences of mine, it is because I believe that they are, though in different forms, yours also. Even when the path is **nominally** open—when there is nothing to prevent a woman from being a doctor, a lawyer, a civil servant—there are many phantoms and obstacles, as I believe, **looming** in her way. To discuss and define them is I

think of great value and importance; for thus only can the labour be shared, the difficulties be solved. But besides this, it is necessary also to discuss the ends and the aims for which we are fighting, for which we are doing battle with these **formidable** obstacles. Those aims cannot be taken for granted; they must be perpetually questioned and examined. The whole position, as I see it—here in this hall surrounded by women practising for the first time in history I know not how many different professions—is one of extraordinary interest and importance. You have won rooms of your own in the house **hitherto** exclusively owned by men. You are able, though not without great labour and effort, to pay the rent. You are earning your five hundred pounds a year. But this freedom is only a beginning; the room is your own, but it is still bare. It has to be furnished; it has to be decorated; it has to be shared. How are you going to furnish it, how are you going to decorate it? With whom are you going to share it, and upon what terms? These, I think are questions of the utmost importance and interest. For the first time in history you are able to ask them; for the first time you are able to decide for yourselves what the answers should be. Willingly would I stay and discuss those questions and answers—but not tonight. My time is up; and I must **cease**.

Vocabulary

be peculiar to	to be a feature that only belongs to someone or something 为……所特有
reputable ['repjutəbl] a.	respected for being honest or for doing good work 声誉好的, 有声望的
phantom ['fæntəm] n.	something that is not real and exists only in a person's mind 幻影, 幻象
heroine ['herəuin] n.	the chief female character in a story, play, movie, etc. 女主角
torment [tɔː'mənt] vt.	to cause someone or something to feel extreme physical or mental pain 折磨, 使痛苦
come of	to result from something 来自; 是……的结果

Unit 5 Women

excel in	to do something very well, or much better than most people 擅长, 优于
draught [drɑːft] n.	a current of cold air flowing through a room 一股冷风, 穿堂风
constitute ['kɔnstitjuːt] v.	to make up or form something 构成
blush [blʌʃ] n.	the red colour on your face that appears when you are embarrassed 脸红
rustle ['rʌsl] vi.	to make a soft, light sound because parts of something are touching or rubbing against each other 沙沙作响, 发出窸窣声
wiles [wailz] n.	clever talk or tricks used to persuade someone to do what you want 花言巧语
credit ['kredit] n.	approval or praise that you give someone for something they have done 赞扬, 赞许
have up	to take someone to court, especially to prove they are guilty of a crime 传讯某人, 控告某人
conciliate [kən'silieit] v.	to do something to make people more likely to stop arguing, especially by giving them something they want 安抚, 调停
radiance ['reidiəns] n.	a soft light that shines from or onto something 光彩
halo ['heiləu] n.	a bright circle of light 光环, 光晕
fictitious [fik'tiʃəs] a.	invented by someone and not real 虚构的, 杜撰的
dispatch [dis'pætʃ] vt.	to deliberately kill a person or animal 故意杀死
roam [rəum] vt.	to walk or travel, usually for a long time, with no clear purpose or direction 闲逛, 漫游
befall [bi'fɔːl] vt.	happen to someone 降临到某人身上
assure [ə'ʃuə] vt.	to tell someone that something will definitely happen or is definitely true so that they are less worried 保证, 使确信
proceeds ['prəusiːdz] n.	the money that has been gained from doing something or selling something 收入, 收益
unconscious [ʌn'kɔnʃəs] a.	a feeling or thought that is unconscious is one that you have without realizing it 无意识的, 不自觉的
induce [in'djuːs] vt.	to make someone decide to do something, especially something that seems unwise 劝诱, 诱导
perpetual [pə'petʃuəl] a.	permanent 永久的, 无休止的
lethargy ['leθədʒi] n.	a lack of energy or a lack of interest in doing things 无精打采, 懒洋洋

dart [dɑːt] n.	a sudden, quick movement in a particular direction 投掷,迅速移动
dash [dæʃ] n.	the act of running or moving quickly or suddenly in a particular direction or to a particular place 猛冲,飞奔
illusive [iˈluːsiv] a.	false but seeming to be real or true 虚假的,貌似真实的
trance [trɑːns] n.	a state in which you behave as if you were asleep but are still able to hear and understand what is said to you 恍惚状态
on the verge of	濒临,接近
rod [rɔd] n.	a long thin pole or bar 竿,棒
cranny [ˈkræni] n.	a small narrow hole in a wall or rock 裂缝,缝隙
submerge [səbˈməːdʒ] vt.	to go under the surface of water, or to put something under water or another liquid 淹没,浸没
slumber [ˈslʌmbə] v.	to sleep 睡眠
figure [ˈfigə] n.	a word or expression that is used in a different way from the normal one, to give you a picture in your mind 比喻
impede [imˈpiːd] vt.	to prevent something from happening in the normal way, or make it happen more slowly 阻碍,延缓
slay [slei] vt.	to kill someone 杀害,谋杀
lay stress on/upon	强调
nominally [ˈnɔminəli] ad.	officially described as something when this is not really true 名义上
loom [luːm] v.	to appear as a large, unclear shape, especially in a threatening way 隐约出现,耸现
formidable [ˈfɔmidəbəl] a.	difficult to deal with and needing a lot of effort or skill 难对付的
hitherto [hiðəˈtuː] ad.	up to this time 至今
cease [siːs] v.	to stop doing something or stop happening 停止,结束

I. Vocabulary Building

inter-: between

e. g., internet, intermission, intersection, interwar, interlock, intertwine, intermarry, interpose, international, interpersonal

co-/col-/cor-/com-: doing something at the same time

e. g., cooperation, coincidence, colleague, coordination, compassion, combine, correlate, collude, collocate, collaborate

intra-: within

e. g., intramural, intravenous, intrastate, intranet, intraday, intrapersonal, intracellular, intracranial, intrauterine, intraocular

extra-: outside

e. g., extraordinary, extraterrestrial, extraterritorial, extracurricular, extraneous, extradite, extract, extrapolate

II. Discussion

Discuss the following questions with your own words.

1. What was the phantom that emerged when the author was going to review books?

2. What kind of woman is "the angel in the house"?

3. Why did the author kill "the angel in the house"?

4. In which state was the author when she was writing?

5. What are the obstacles for the author in her writing? Has she solved them?

III. Translation A

Translate the following sentences selected from the text into Chinese.

1. Writing was a reputable and harmless occupation. The family peace was not broken by the scratching of a pen. No demand was made upon the family purse. For ten and sixpence one can buy paper enough to write all the plays of Shakespeare—if one has a mind that way. (Para. 1)

2. And while I was writing this review, I discovered that if I were going to review books I should need to do battle with a certain phantom. And the phantom was a woman, and when I came to know her better I called her after the heroine of a famous poem, *The Angel in the House*. It was she who used to come between me and my paper when I was writing reviews. It was she

who bothered me and wasted my time and so tormented me that at last I killed her. (Para. 2)

3. Thus, whenever I felt the shadow of her wing or the radiance of her halo upon my page, I took up the inkpot and flung it at her. She died hard. Her fictitious nature was of great assistance to her. It is far harder to kill a phantom than a reality. She was always creeping back when I thought I had dispatched her. (Para. 3)

4. I hope I am not giving away professional secrets if I say that a novelist's chief desire is to be as unconscious as possible. He has to induce in himself a state of perpetual lethargy. He wants life to proceed with the utmost quiet and regularity. He wants to see the same faces, to read the same books, to do the same things day after day, month after month, while he is writing, so that nothing may break the illusion in which he is living—so that nothing may disturb or disquiet the mysterious nosings about, feelings round, darts, dashes and sudden discoveries of that very shy and illusive spirit, the imagination. (Para. 5)

5. The line raced through the girl's fingers. Her imagination had rushed away. It had sought the pools, the depths, the dark places where the largest fish slumber. And then there was a smash. There was an explosion. There was foam and confusion. The imagination had dashed itself against something hard. The girl was roused from her dream. She was indeed in a state of the most acute and difficult distress. (Para. 5)

IV. Translation B

Translate the following passage into Chinese.

One could hardly ask for more important evidence of the dangers of considering persons as split between what is "inside" and what is "outside" than that interminable half-comic half-tragic tale, the oppression of women.

How easy it is to start off by defining women as caretakers of their surfaces, and then to disparage them (or find them adorable) for being "superficial". It is a crude trap, and it has worked for too long. But to get out of the trap requires that women get some critical distance from the excellence and privilege which is beauty, enough distance to see how much beauty itself has been abridged in order to prop up the mythology of the "feminine". There should be a way of saving beauty from women, and for them. (Excerpted from Text B)

V. Writing Exercise

Have women achieved equality with men in China? If not, how can they achieve equality? Please write an essay with at least 300 words.

Text B

Beauty[①]

Susan Sontag

1 For the Greeks, beauty was a virtue: a kind of excellence. Persons then were assumed to be what we now have to call—**lamely**, enviously—*whole* persons. If it did occur to the Greeks to distinguish between a person's "inside" and "outside", they still expected that inner beauty would be matched by beauty of the other kind. The well-born young Athenians who gathered around Socrates found it quite **paradoxical** that their hero was so intelligent, so brave, so honorable, so **seductive**—and so ugly. One of Socrates' main **pedagogical** acts was to be ugly—and teach those innocent, no

---

① Excerpted from Susan Sontag's A Woman's Beauty: Put-Down or Power Source?, *Vogue*, April. 1975.

doubt splendid-looking **disciples** of his how full of **paradoxes** life really was.

2   They may have resisted Socrates' lesson. We do not. Several thousand years later, we are more **wary** of the **enchantments** of beauty. We not only split off—with the greatest **facility**—the "inside" (character, intellect) from the "outside" (looks); but we are actually surprised when someone who is beautiful is also intelligent, talented, good.

3   It was principally the influence of Christianity that **deprived** beauty of the central place it had in classical ideals of human excellence. By limiting excellence (*virtus* in Latin) to *moral* virtue only, Christianity set beauty **adrift**—as an **alienated**, arbitrary, **superficial** enchantment. And beauty has continued to lose prestige. For close to two centuries it has become a convention to **attribute** beauty **to** only one of the two sexes: the sex which, however Fair, is always Second. Associating beauty with women has put beauty even further on the defensive, morally.

4   A beautiful woman, we say in English. But a handsome man. "Handsome" is the **masculine** equivalent of—and refusal of—a compliment which has accumulated certain **demeaning overtones**, by being reserved for women only. That one can call a man "beautiful" in French and in Italian suggests that Catholic countries—unlike those countries shaped by the Protestant version of Christianity—still retain some **vestiges** of the **pagan** admiration for beauty. But the difference, if one exists, is of degree only. In every modern country that is Christian or post-Christian, women *are* the beautiful sex—to the **detriment** of the notion of beauty as well as of women.

5   To be called beautiful is thought to name something essential to women's character and concerns. (In contrast to men—whose essence is to be strong, or effective, or competent.) It does not take someone **in the throes of** advanced feminist awareness to perceive that the way women are taught to be involved with beauty encourages **narcissism**, reinforces dependence and

immaturity. Everybody (women and men) knows that. For it is "everybody", a whole society, that has identified being feminine with caring about how one *looks*. (In contrast to being masculine—which is identified with caring about what one *is* and *does* and only secondarily, if at all, about how one looks.) Given these **stereotypes**, it is no wonder that beauty enjoys, at best, a rather mixed reputation.

<u>6</u>   It is not, of course, the desire to be beautiful that is wrong but the obligation to be—or to try. What is accepted by most women as a flattering idealization of their sex is a way of making women feel inferior to what they actually are—or normally grow to be. For the ideal of beauty is administered as a form of self-oppression. Women are taught to see their bodies in *parts*, and to evaluate each part separately. Breasts, feet, hips, waistline, neck, eyes, nose, **complexion**, hair, and so on—each in turn is **submitted** to an anxious, **fretful**, often despairing **scrutiny**. Even if some **pass muster**, some will always be found wanting. Nothing less than perfection will do.

<u>7</u>   In men, good looks is a whole, something taken in at a glance. It does not need to be confirmed by giving measurements of different regions of the body, nobody encourages a man to **dissect** his appearance, feature by feature. As for perfection, that is considered trivial—almost unmanly. Indeed, in the ideally good-looking man a small imperfection or **blemish** is considered positively desirable. According to one movie critic (a woman) who is a declared Robert Redford[①] fan, it is having that cluster of skin-colored **moles** on one cheek that saves Redford from being merely a "pretty face." Think of the **depreciation** of women—as well as of beauty—that is implied in that judgment.

<u>8</u>   "The privileges of beauty are immense," said Cocteau. To be sure,

---

① Charles Robert Redford Jr. (born in 1936) is an American actor, director, producer, businessman, environmentalist, and philanthropist.

beauty is a form of power. And deservedly so. What is **lamentable** is that it is the only form of power that most women are encouraged to seek. This power is always conceived in relation to men; it is not the power to do but the power to attract. It is a power that **negates** itself. For this power is not one that can be chosen freely—at least, not by women—or **renounced** without social **censure.**

9 To **preen**, for a woman, can never be just a pleasure. It is also a duty. It is her work. If a woman does real work—and even if she has **clambered** up to a leading position in politics, law, medicine, business, or whatever—she is always under pressure to confess that she still works at being attractive. But in so far as she is keeping up as one of the Fair Sex she brings under suspicion her very capacity to be objective, professional, authoritative, thoughtful. Damned if they do—women are. And damned if they don't.

10 One could hardly ask for more important evidence of the dangers of considering persons as split between what is "inside" and what is "outside" than that **interminable** half-comic half-tragic tale, the oppression of women. How easy it is to start off by defining women as caretakers of their surfaces, and then to **disparage** them (or find them **adorable**) for being "superficial". It is a crude trap, and it has worked for too long. But to get out of the trap requires that women get some critical distance from that excellence and privilege which is beauty, enough distance to see how much beauty itself has been **abridged** in order to **prop up** the **mythology** of the "feminine". There should be a way of saving beauty *from* women—and *for* them.

Vocabulary

lamely [ˈleimli] ad.	not strong, good, or effective 软弱无力地
paradox [ˈpærədɔks] n.	something that is made up of two opposite things and that seems impossible but is actually true or possible 悖论，自相矛盾
paradoxical [ˌpærəˈdɔksikəl] a.	of the nature of a paradox 自相矛盾的

seductive [sɪˈdʌktɪv] a.	very attractive 有魅力的，吸引人的
pedagogical [ˌpedəˈɡɒdʒɪkl] a.	of or relating to teachers or education 教学的，教师的
disciple [dɪˈsaɪpl] n.	someone who believes in the ideas of a great teacher, especially a religious one, and tries to follow them 追随者，信徒
wary [ˈweəri] a.	not having or showing complete trust in someone or something that could be dangerous or cause trouble 小心翼翼的，谨慎的
enchantment [ɪnˈtʃɑːntmənt] n.	a quality that attracts and holds your attention by being interesting, pretty, etc. 迷人之处，魅力
facility [fəˈsɪlɪti] a.	a natural ability to do something easily and well 天赋，才能
deprive [dɪˈpraɪv] vt.	to take something from someone or something else 剥夺
adrift [əˈdrɪft] a.	without ties, guidance, or security 散开，分离
alienated [ˈeɪliəneɪtɪd] a.	separated from society or people 疏远的
superficial [ˌsuːpəˈfɪʃəl] a.	concerned only with what is obvious or apparent, not thorough or complete 表面的，浅薄的
attribute to	to regard as a characteristic of a person or thing 归于
masculine [ˈmæskjulɪn] a.	belonging to men, done by men, or considered to be typical of men 男性的，男子气概的
demean [dɪˈmiːn] vt.	to do something that you think you are too good for 降低身份，贬低
overtone [ˈəʊvətəʊn] n.	a sign of an emotion or attitude that is not expressed directly 含蓄的表示，弦外之音
vestige [ˈvestɪdʒ] n.	a small part or amount of something that still remains when most of it no longer exists 痕迹，遗迹，残余
pagan [ˈpeɪɡən] a.	pagan religious beliefs and customs do not belong to any of the main religions of the world, and may come from a time before these religions 异教徒的
detriment [ˈdetrɪmənt] n.	the state of being harmed or damaged by something 损害，伤害
in the throes of	in the middle of a very difficult situation 处于……的困境之中
narcissism [ˈnɑːsɪsɪzəm] n.	a tendency to admire your own physical appearance or abilities 自恋，自我陶醉
stereotype [ˈsteriətaɪp] n.	a fixed idea or image of what a particular type of person or thing is like 刻板印象

complexion [kəmˈplekʃən] n.	the natural color or appearance of the skin on your face 面容，皮肤
submit [səbˈmit] vt.	to accept the authority, control or greater strength of someone or something 顺从，不得已接受
fretful [ˈfretfəl] a.	upset and worried 焦躁的，不安的
scrutiny [ˈskruːtəni] n.	careful and thorough examination of someone or something 仔细审视
pass muster	to be accepted as good enough 被认为合格，通过检查
dissect [diˈsekt] vt.	to examine something in great detail so that you discover its faults or understand it better 剖析
blemish [ˈblemiʃ] n.	a small mark, especially a mark on someone's skin or on the surface of an object, that spoils its appearance 瑕疵，污点
mole [məul] n.	a small dark brown mark on the skin that is slightly higher than the skin around it （色素）痣
depreciation [diˌpriːʃiˈeiʃən] n.	a reduction in the value or price of something 贬值，跌价
lamentable [ˈlæməntəbl] a.	very unsatisfactory or disappointing 可叹的，令人惋惜的
negate [niˈgeit] vt.	to deny the existence or truth of 否定
renounce [riˈnauns] vt.	to refuse to follow, obey, or recognize any further 宣布放弃
censure [ˈsenʃə] n.	the act of expressing strong disapproval and criticism 严厉谴责，声讨
preen [priːn] vi.	to spend a lot of time in front of a mirror making yourself look tidier and more attractive 精心打扮
clamber [ˈklæmbə] v.	to climb slowly, using your hands and feet 攀登，爬
interminable [inˈtəːminəbəl] a.	very long and boring 冗长乏味的
disparage [diˈspæridʒ] vt.	to criticize someone or something in a way that shows you do not think they are very good or important 贬低，诋毁
abridged [əˈbridʒd] a.	an abridged book, play etc. has been made shorter but keeps its basic structure and meaning 删节的，节略的
prop up	to prevent something from falling by putting something against it or under it 支撑，撑住
mythology [miˈθɔlədʒi] n.	ideas that are believed by many people but that are not true 神话

Text C

The Tragedy of Woman's Emancipation[1]

Emma Goldman

<u>1</u>   I begin with an admission: Regardless of all political and economic theories, treating of the fundamental differences between various groups within the human race, regardless of class and race distinctions, regardless of all artificial boundary lines between woman's rights and man's rights, I hold that there is a point where these differentiations may meet and grow into one perfect whole.

<u>2</u>   With this I do not mean to propose a peace treaty. The general social **antagonism** which has taken hold of our entire public life today, brought about through the force of opposing and contradictory interests, will crumble to pieces when the reorganization of our social life, based upon the principles of economic justice, shall have become a reality.

<u>3</u>   Peace or harmony between the sexes and individuals does not necessarily depend on a superficial equalization of human beings; nor does it call for the elimination of individual traits and peculiarities. The problem that confronts us today, and which the nearest future is to solve, is how to be one's self and yet in oneness with others, to feel deeply with all human beings and still retain one's own characteristic qualities. This seems to me to be the basis upon which the mass and the individual, the true democrat and the true individuality, man and woman, can meet without antagonism and opposition. The motto should not be: Forgive one another; rather, Understand one another. The oft-quoted sentence of Madame de Staël: "To understand

---

[1] Excerpted from Emma Goldman's *Anarchism and Other Essays*.

everything means to forgive everything," has never particularly appealed to me; it has the **odor** of the **confessional**; to forgive one's fellow-being conveys the idea of **pharisaical** superiority. To understand one's fellow-being **suffices**. The admission partly represents the fundamental aspect of my views on the emancipation of woman and its effect upon the entire sex.

4   Emancipation should make it possible for woman to be human in the truest sense. Everything within her that **craves** assertion and activity should reach its fullest expression; all artificial barriers should be broken, and the road towards greater freedom cleared of every trace of centuries of **submission** and slavery.

5   This was the original aim of the movement for woman's emancipation. But the results so far achieved have isolated woman and have robbed her of the fountain springs of that happiness which is so essential to her. Merely external emancipation has made of the modern woman an artificial being, who reminds one of the products of French **arboriculture** with its **arabesque** trees and shrubs, pyramids, wheels, and **wreaths**; anything, except the forms which would be reached by the expression of her own inner qualities. Such artificially grown plants of the female sex are to be found in large numbers, especially in the so-called intellectual sphere of our life.

6   Liberty and equality for woman! What hopes and aspirations these words awakened when they were first uttered by some of the noblest and bravest souls of those days. The sun in all his light and glory was to rise upon a new world; in this world woman was to be free to direct her own destiny—an aim certainly worthy of the great enthusiasm, courage, **perseverance**, and ceaseless effort of the tremendous host of pioneer men and women, who staked everything against a world of prejudice and ignorance.

7   My hopes also move towards that goal, but I hold that the emancipation of woman, as interpreted and practically applied today, has failed to reach that great end. Now, woman is confronted with the necessity of

emancipating herself from emancipation, if she really desires to be free. This may sound paradoxical, but is, nevertheless, only too true.

8   What has she achieved through her emancipation? Equal **suffrage** in a few States. Has that purified our political life, as many well-meaning advocates predicted? Certainly not. Incidentally, it is really time that persons with plain, sound judgment should cease to talk about corruption in politics in a boarding school tone. Corruption of politics has nothing to do with the morals, or the **laxity** of morals, of various political personalities. Its cause is altogether a material one. Politics is the **reflex** of the business and industrial world, the mottos of which are: "To take is more blessed than to give"; "buy cheap and sell dear"; "one soiled hand washes the other." There is no hope even that woman, with her right to vote, will ever purify politics.

9   Emancipation has brought woman economic equality with man; that is, she can choose her own profession and trade; but as her past and present physical training has not equipped her with the necessary strength to compete with man, she is often compelled to exhaust all her energy, use up her **vitality**, and **strain** every nerve in order to reach the market value. Very few ever succeed, for it is a fact that women teachers, doctors, lawyers, architects, and engineers are neither met with the same confidence as their male colleagues, nor receive equal **remuneration.** And those that do reach that **enticing** equality, generally do so **at the expense of** their physical and psychical well-being. As to the great mass of working girls and women, how much independence is gained if the narrowness and lack of freedom of the home is exchanged for the narrowness and lack of freedom of the factory, sweat-shop, department store, or office? In addition is the burden which is laid on many women of looking after a "home, sweet home"—cold, dreary, disorderly, **uninviting**—after a day's hard work. Glorious independence! No wonder that hundreds of girls are so willing to accept the first offer of marriage, sick and tired of their "independence" behind the counter, at the

sewing or typewriting machine. They are just as ready to marry as girls of the middle class, who long to throw off the **yoke** of parental **supremacy**. A so-called independence which leads only to earning the merest subsistence is not so enticing, not so ideal, that one could expect woman to sacrifice everything for it. Our highly praised independence is, after all, but a slow process of dulling and stifling woman's nature, her love instinct, and her mother instinct.

10   Nevertheless, the position of the working girl is far more natural and human than that of her seemingly more fortunate sister in the more cultured professional walks of life—teachers, physicians, lawyers, engineers, etc., who have to make a dignified, proper appearance, while the inner life is growing empty and dead.

11   The narrowness of the existing conception of woman's independence and emancipation; the dread of love for a man who is not her social equal; the fear that love will rob her of her freedom and independence; the horror that love or the joy of motherhood will only hinder her in the full exercise of her profession—all these together make of the emancipated modern woman a compulsory **vestal**, before whom life, with its great clarifying sorrows and its deep, **entrancing** joys, rolls on without touching or gripping her soul.

12   Emancipation, as understood by the majority of its adherents and **exponents**, is of too narrow a scope to permit the boundless love and **ecstasy** contained in the deep emotion of the true woman, sweetheart, mother, in freedom.

13   The tragedy of the self-supporting or economically free woman does not lie in too many, but in too few experiences. True, she surpasses her sister of past generations in knowledge of the world and human nature; it is just because of this that she feels deeply the lack of life's essence, which alone can enrich the human soul, and without which the majority of women have become mere professional **automatons**.

__14__   That such a state of affairs was bound to come was **foreseen** by those who realized that, in the domain of ethics, there still remained many decaying ruins of the time of the undisputed superiority of man; ruins that are still considered useful. And, what is more important, a goodly number of the emancipated are unable to get along without them. Every movement that aims at the destruction of existing institutions and the replacement thereof with something more advanced, more perfect, has followers who in theory stand for the most radical ideas, but who, nevertheless, in their every-day practice, are like the average **Philistine, feigning** respectability and **clamoring for** the good opinion of their opponents. There are, for example, Socialists, and even **Anarchists**, who stand for the idea that property is robbery, yet who will grow indignant if anyone owe them the value of a half-dozen pins.

__15__   The same Philistine can be found in the movement for woman's emancipation. Yellow journalists and **milk-and-water** litterateurs have painted pictures of the emancipated woman that make the hair of the good citizen and his dull companion stand up on end. Every member of the woman's rights movement was pictured as a George Sand[①] in her absolute disregard of morality. Nothing was sacred to her. She had no respect for the ideal relation between man and woman. In short, emancipation stood only for a reckless life of lust and sin; regardless of society, religion, and morality. The exponents of woman's rights were highly indignant at such misrepresentation, and, lacking humor, they **exerted** all their energy to prove that they were not at all as bad as they were painted, but the very **reverse**. Of course, as long as woman was the slave of man, she could not be good and pure, but now that she was free and independent she would prove how good she could be and that her influence would have a purifying effect on all institutions in society. True, the movement for woman's rights has broken

---

① Pseudonym of Amantine-Lucile-Aurore Dupin (1804—1876), a French novelist and memoirist.

many old **fetters**, but it has also forged new ones. The great movement of true emancipation has not met with a great race of women who could look liberty in the face. Their narrow, **Puritanical** vision **banished** man, as a disturber and doubtful character, out of their emotional life. Man was not to be tolerated at any price, except perhaps as the father of a child, since a child could not very well come to life without a father. Fortunately, the most rigid Puritans never will be strong enough to kill the **innate** craving for motherhood. But woman's freedom is closely allied with man's freedom, and many of my so-called emancipated sisters seem to overlook the fact that a child born in freedom needs the love and devotion of each human being about him, man as well as woman. Unfortunately, it is this narrow conception of human relations that has brought about a great tragedy in the lives of the modern man and woman.

16   About fifteen years ago appeared a work from the pen of the brilliant Norwegian Laura Marholm, called *Woman, a Character Study*. She was one of the first to call attention to the emptiness and narrowness of the existing conception of woman's emancipation, and its tragic effect upon the inner life of woman. In her work Laura Marholm speaks of the fate of several gifted women of international fame: the genius Eleonora Duse; the great mathematician and writer Sonya Kovalevskaia; the artist and poet-nature Marie Bashkirtzeff, who died so young. Through each description of the lives of these women of such extraordinary mentality runs a marked trail of unsatisfied craving for a full, rounded, complete, and beautiful life, and the unrest and loneliness resulting from the lack of it. Through these masterly psychological sketches one cannot help but see that the higher the mental development of woman, the less possible it is for her to meet a **congenial** mate who will see in her, not only sex, but also the human being, the friend, the comrade and strong individuality, who cannot and ought not lose a single trait of her character.

<u>17</u>　　The average man with his self-sufficiency, his ridiculously superior airs of patronage towards the female sex, is an impossibility for woman as depicted in the Character Study by Laura Marholm. Equally impossible for her is the man who can see in her nothing more than her mentality and her genius, and who fails to awaken her woman nature.

<u>18</u>　　A rich intellect and a fine soul are usually considered necessary attributes of a deep and beautiful personality. In the case of the modern woman, these attributes serve as a hindrance to the complete assertion of her being. For over a hundred years the old form of marriage, based on the Bible, "till death doth part," has been denounced as an institution that stands for the sovereignty of the man over the woman, of her complete submission to his **whims** and commands, and absolute dependence on his name and support. Time and again it has been conclusively proved that the old **matrimonial** relation restricted woman to the function of man's servant and the bearer of his children. And yet we find many emancipated women who prefer marriage, with all its deficiencies, to the narrowness of an unmarried life: narrow and unendurable because of the chains of moral and social prejudice that cramp and bind her nature.

<u>19</u>　　The explanation of such inconsistency on the part of many advanced women is to be found in the fact that they never truly understood the meaning of emancipation. They thought that all that was needed was independence from external tyrannies; the internal tyrants, far more harmful to life and growth—ethical and social conventions—were left to take care of themselves; and they have taken care of themselves. They seem to get along as beautifully in the heads and hearts of the most active exponents of woman's emancipation, as in the heads and hearts of our grandmothers.

<u>20</u>　　These internal tyrants, whether they be in the form of public opinion or what will mother say, or brother, father, aunt, or relative of any sort; what will Mrs. Grundy, the employer, the Board of Education say? All these busybodies, moral detectives, jailers of the human spirit, what will they say?

Until woman has learned to defy them all, to stand firmly on her own ground and to insist upon her own unrestricted freedom, to listen to the voice of her nature, whether it call for life's greatest treasure, love for a man, or her most glorious privilege, the right to give birth to a child, she cannot call herself emancipated. How many emancipated women are brave enough to acknowledge that the voice of love is calling, wildly beating against their breasts, demanding to be heard, to be satisfied.

21 The French writer Jean Reibrach, in one of his novels, *New Beauty*, attempts to picture the ideal, beautiful, emancipated woman. This ideal is embodied in a young girl, a physician. She talks very cleverly and wisely of how to feed infants; she is kind, and administers medicines free to poor mothers. She converses with a young man of her acquaintance about the **sanitary** conditions of the future, and how various **bacilli** and germs shall be exterminated by the use of stone walls and floors, and by the doing away with rugs and hangings. She is, of course, very plainly and practically dressed, mostly in black. The young man, who, at their first meeting, was **overawed** by the wisdom of his emancipated friend, gradually learns to understand her, and recognizes one fine day that he loves her. They are young, and she is kind and beautiful, and though always in rigid **attire**, her appearance is softened by a spotlessly clean white collar and cuffs. One would expect that he would tell her of his love, but he is not one to commit romantic absurdities. Poetry and the enthusiasm of love cover their blushing faces before the pure beauty of the lady. He silences the voice of his nature, and remains correct. She, too, is always exact, always rational, always well behaved. I fear if they had formed a union, the young man would have risked freezing to death. I must confess that I can see nothing beautiful in this new beauty, who is as cold as the stone walls and floors she dreams of. Rather would I have the love songs of romantic ages, rather Don Juan and Madame Venus, rather an elopement by ladder and rope on a moonlight night, followed by the father's curse, mother's moans, and the moral comments of

neighbors, than correctness and propriety measured by yardsticks. If love does not know how to give and take without restrictions, it is not love, but a transaction that never fails to lay stress on a plus and a minus.

<u>22</u>   The greatest shortcoming of the emancipation of the present day lies in its artificial stiffness and its narrow respectabilities, which produce an emptiness in woman's soul that will not let her drink from the fountain of life. I once remarked that there seemed to be a deeper relationship between the old-fashioned mother and hostess, ever on the alert for the happiness of her little ones and the comfort of those she loved, and the truly new woman, than between the latter and her average emancipated sister. The disciples of emancipation pure and simple declared me a **heathen**, fit only for the **stake.** Their blind zeal did not let them see that my comparison between the old and the new was merely to prove that a goodly number of our grandmothers had more blood in their veins, far more humor and wit, and certainly a greater amount of naturalness, kind-heartedness, and simplicity, than the majority of our emancipated professional women who fill the colleges, halls of learning, and various offices. This does not mean a wish to return to the past, nor does it condemn woman to her old sphere, the kitchen and the nursery.

<u>23</u>   Salvation lies in an energetic march onward towards a brighter and clearer future. We are in need of unhampered growth out of old traditions and habits. The movement for woman's emancipation has so far made but the first step in that direction. It is to be hoped that it will gather strength to make another. The right to vote, or equal civil rights, may be good demands, but true emancipation begins neither at the polls nor in courts. It begins in woman's soul. History tells us that every oppressed class gained true liberation from its masters through its own efforts. It is necessary that woman learn that lesson, that she realize that her freedom will reach as far as her power to achieve her freedom reaches. It is, therefore, far more important for her to begin with her inner **regeneration**, to cut loose from the

weight of prejudices, traditions, and customs. The demand for equal rights in every vocation of life is just and fair; but, after all, the most vital right is the right to love and be loved. Indeed, if partial emancipation is to become a complete and true emancipation of woman, it will have to do away with the ridiculous notion that to be loved, to be sweetheart and mother, is synonymous with being slave or **subordinate**. It will have to do away with the absurd notion of the **dualism** of the sexes, or that man and woman represent two antagonistic worlds.

<u>24</u>   Pettiness separates; breadth unites. Let us be broad and big. Let us not overlook vital things because of the bulk of trifles confronting us. A true conception of the relation of the sexes will not admit of conqueror and conquered; it knows of but one great thing: to give of one's self boundlessly, in order to find one's self richer, deeper, better. That alone can fill the emptiness, and transform the tragedy of woman's emancipation into joy, limitless joy.

Vocabulary

emancipation [iˈmænsiˈpeiʃən] n.	the act or process of freeing someone from someone else's control or power 解放
antagonism [ænˈtægənizəm] n.	hatred between people or groups of people 对抗，敌对
odor [ˈəudə] n.	a smell, especially an unpleasant one 气味
confessional [kənˈfeʃənəl] n.	a place in a church, usually an enclosed room, where a priest hears people make their confessions 忏悔室
pharisaical [færiˈseiikəl] a.	marked by hypocritical censorious self-righteousness 拘泥于形式的，伪善的
suffice [səˈfais] v.	to be enough 足够，满足
crave [kreiv] v.	to have a very strong desire for 渴望
submission [səbˈmiʃən] n.	the act of accepting the authority or control of someone else 服从，顺从
arboriculture [ˈɑːbəriˌkʌltʃə] n.	the study or practice of growing trees and shrubs 树木栽培
arabesque [ærəˈbesk] n.	a type of design where lines wind around each other 蔓藤花纹

wreath [ri:θ] n.		an arrangement of flowers and/or leaves in the shape of a circle, traditionally hung on doors as a decoration at Christmas 花环
perseverance [ˌpəːsiˈviərəns] n.		the quality of continuing to try to achieve a particular aim despite difficulties 毅力,不屈不挠的精神
suffrage [ˈsʌfridʒ] n.		the right to vote in political elections 选举权,投票权
laxity [ˈlæksəti] n.		being not strict or careful enough about standards of behaviour, work, safety, etc. 松懈,不严格
reflex [ˈriːfleks] a.		a copy exact in essential or peculiar features 反映,体现
vitality [vaiˈtæləti] n.		great energy and cheerfulness 生命力,生气
strain [strein] n.		to try very hard to do something using all your physical or mental strength 使劲,竭力
remuneration [riˌmjuːnəˈreiʃən] n.		an amount of money paid to someone for the work that person has done 报酬
enticing [inˈtaisiŋ] a.		very pleasant or interesting so that you feel strongly attracted 有吸引力的,迷人的
at the expense of		if something is done at the expense of something else, it is only achieved by harming the other thing 以损害……为代价
uninviting [ˌʌninˈvaitiŋ] a.		unattractive or unpleasant 无吸引力的,令人反感的
yoke [jəuk] n.		something that restricts your freedom, making life hard or unpleasant 束缚,羁绊
supremacy [suˈpreməsi] n.		the position in which you are more powerful and advanced than anyone else 至高无上,最高地位
vestal [ˈvestəl] n.		a chaste woman 修女,贞洁的女子
entrancing [inˈtrɑːnsiŋ] a.		very interesting and attractive 使人着迷的
exponent [ikˈspəunənt] n.		someone who supports an idea, belief etc. and who tries to explain it and persuade others that it is good or useful 倡导者,鼓吹者
ecstasy [ˈekstəsi] n.		a feeling of extreme happiness 狂喜,欣喜若狂
automaton [ɔːˈtɔmətən] n.		someone who seems to be unable to feel emotions 没有感情的人
foresee [fɔːˈsiː] vt.		to know that something is going to happen before it actually happens 预见,预知
philistine [ˈfiləstain] n.		a person who is guided by materialism and is usually disdainful of intellectual or artistic values 不喜欢文化艺术的人,庸俗的人
feign [fein] vt.		to pretend to feel or be affected by something 假装

clamor ['klæmə] vi.	to demand something loudly 大声疾呼,强烈要求
anarchist ['ænəkist] n.	a person who believes that government and laws are not necessary 无政府主义者
milk-and-water	weak, insipid 无力的,动辄伤感的
exert [ig'zə:t] vt.	put to use 施加,运用
reverse [ri'və:s] n.	the exact opposite of what has just been mentioned 相反
fetter ['fetə] n.	the thing that prevents someone from being free 桎梏
puritanical [ˌpjuəri'tænikəl] a.	having extreme attitudes about religion and moral behavior 清教徒式的,道德极严格的
banish ['bæniʃ] vt.	to send someone or something away 驱逐,放逐
innate ['ineit] a.	existing from the time a person or animal is born 与生俱来的
congenial [kən'dʒi:niəl] a.	pleasant to spend time with because their interests and character are similar to your own 志趣相投的,合得来的
whim [wim] n.	a sudden feeling that you would like to do something or have something, especially when there is no particularly important or good reason 突发的念头,一时的兴致
matrimonial [ˌmætri'məuniəl] a.	connected with marriage or with being married 婚姻的
sanitary ['sænətəri] a.	relating to the ways that dirt, infection, and waste are removed, so that places are clean and healthy for people to live in 有关卫生的,与健康有关的
bacillus [bə'siləs] n. (pl.) bacilli [bə'silai]	a straight rod-shaped bacterium that requires oxygen for growth 杆菌
overawe [ˌəuvər'ɔ:] vt.	to make someone feel respect or fear, so that they are nervous or unable to say or do anything 使敬畏,使慑服
attire [ə'taiə] n.	clothes 服装
heathen ['hi:ðən] n.	an unconverted member of a people or nation that does not acknowledge the God of the Bible 异教徒
stake [steik] n.	a post that a person was tied to and burned on in the past as a form of punishment 火刑柱
regeneration [riˌdʒenə'reiʃən] n.	spiritual renewal or revival 重生,新生
subordinate [sə'bɔ:dineit] n.	a person who has a position with less authority and power than someone else in an organization 下级,部属
dualism ['dju:əlizəm] n.	the state of having two parts 双重性,二元性

Unit 6

Methodology

Text A The Demarcation Between Science and Pseudo-Science
Text B Discourse on Method
Text C The Myths of Objectivism and Subjectivism

Text A

The Demarcation Between Science and Pseudo-Science[①]

Karl R. Popper

1   When I received the list of participants in this course and realized that I had been asked to speak to philosophical colleagues I thought, after some hesitation and **consultation**, that you would probably prefer me to speak about those problems which interest me most, and about those developments with which I am most intimately **acquainted.** I therefore decided to do what I have never done before: to give you a report on my own work in the philosophy of science, since the autumn of 1919 when I first began to **grapple with** the problem, *"When should a theory be **ranked** as scientific?"* or *"Is there a **criterion** for the scientific character or **status** of a theory?"*

2   The problem which troubled me at the time was neither, "When is a

---

① Excerpted from Karl R. Popper's *Conjectures and Refutations*.

theory true?" nor, "When is a theory acceptable?" My problem was different. I *wished to distinguish between science and pseudo-science*; knowing very well that science often **errs**, and that pseudo-science may happen to **stumble on** the truth.

3   I knew, of course, the most widely accepted answer to my problem: that science is distinguished from pseudo-science—or from **"metaphysics"**—by its *empirical method*, which is essentially *inductive*, proceeding from observation or experiment. But this did not satisfy me. On the contrary, I often **formulated** my problem as one of distinguishing between a genuinely empirical method and a non-empirical or even a pseudo-empirical method—that is to say, a method which, although it appeals to observation and experiment, nevertheless does not **come up to** scientific standards. The latter method may be exemplified by **astrology**, with its **stupendous** mass of empirical evidence based on observation—on **horoscopes** and on biographies.

4   But as it was not the example of astrology which led me to my problem I should perhaps briefly describe the atmosphere in which my problem arose and the examples by which it was stimulated. After the **collapse** of the Austrian Empire there had been a revolution in Austria: the air was full of revolutionary **slogans** and ideas, and new and often wild theories. Among the theories which interested me Einstein's theory of relativity was no doubt by far the most important. Three others were Marx's theory of history, Freud's psychoanalysis, and Alfred Adler's so-called "individual psychology".

5   There was a lot of popular nonsense talked about these theories, and especially about relativity (as still happens even today), but I was fortunate in those who introduced me to the study of this theory. We all—the small circle of students to which I belonged—were **thrilled** with the result of Eddington's **eclipse** observations which in 1919 brought the first important confirmation of Einstein's theory of gravitation. It was a great experience for us, and one which had a lasting influence on my intellectual development.

6 The three other theories I have mentioned were also widely discussed among students at that time. I myself happened to come into personal contact with Alfred Adler, and even to co-operate with him in his social work among the children and young people in the working-class districts of Vienna where he had established social guidance clinics.

7 It was during the summer of 1919 that I began to feel more and more dissatisfied with these three theories—the Marxist theory of history, psychoanalysis, and individual psychology; and I began to feel **dubious** about their **claims** to scientific status. My problem perhaps first took the simple form, "What is wrong with Marxism, psychoanalysis, and individual psychology? Why are they so different from physical theories, from Newton's theory, and especially from the theory of relativity?"

8 To make this contrast clear I should explain that few of us at the time would have said that we believed in the *truth* of Einstein's theory of gravitation. This shows that it was not my doubting the *truth* of those other three theories which **bothered** me, but something else. Yet neither was it that I merely felt mathematical physics to be more *exact* than the sociological or psychological type of theory. Thus what worried me was neither the problem of truth, at that stage at least, nor the problem of exactness or measurability. It was rather that I felt that these other three theories, though **posing** as sciences, had in fact more in common with primitive myths than with science; that they resembled astrology rather than astronomy.

9 I found that those of my friends who were admirers of Marx, Freud, and Adler, were impressed by a number of points common to these theories, and especially by their apparent *explanatory power*. These theories appeared to be able to explain **practically** everything that happened within the fields to which they **referred**. The study of any of them seemed to have the effect of an intellectual **conversion** or **revelation**, opening your eyes to a new truth hidden from those not yet initiated. Once your eyes were thus opened you saw

confirming instances everywhere: the world was full of **verifications** of the theory. Whatever happened always confirmed it. Thus its truth appeared manifest; and unbelievers were clearly people who did not want to see the manifest truth; who refused to see it, either because it was against their class interest, or because of their **repressions** which were still "un-analyzed" and crying aloud for **treatment.**

10 The most characteristic element in this situation seemed to me the **incessant** stream of confirmations, of observations which "verified" the theories **in question**; and this point was constantly emphasized by their **adherents**. A Marxist could not open a newspaper without finding on every page confirming evidence for his interpretation of history; not only in the news, but also in its presentation—which revealed the class bias of the paper—and especially of course in what the paper did *not* say. The Freudian analysts emphasized that their theories were constantly verified by their "clinical observations". As for Adler, I was much impressed by a personal experience. Once, in 1919, I reported to him a case which to me did not seem particularly Adlerian, but which he found no difficulty in analyzing in terms of his theory of **inferiority** feelings, although he had not even seen the child. Slightly shocked, I asked him how he could be so sure. "Because of my thousandfold experience," he replied; whereupon I could not help saying: "And with this new case, I suppose, your experience has become thousand-and-one-fold."

11 What I had in mind was that his previous observations may not have been much **sounder** than this new one; that each in its turn had been interpreted **in the light of** "previous experience", and at the same time **counted as** additional confirmation. What, I asked myself, did it confirm? No more than that a case could be interpreted in the light of the theory. But this meant very little, I **reflected**, since every conceivable case could be interpreted in the light of Adler's theory, or equally of Freud's. I may

illustrate this by two very different examples of human behavior: that of a man who pushes a child into the water with the intention of drowning it; and that of a man who sacrifices his life in an attempt to save the child. Each of these two cases can be explained with equal ease in Freudian and in Adlerian terms. According to Freud the first man suffered from repression (**say**, of some component of his Oedipus complex), while the second man had achieved **sublimation**. According to Adler the first man suffered from feelings of inferiority (producing perhaps the need to prove to himself that he dared to commit some crime), and so did the second man (whose need was to prove to himself that he dared to rescue the child). I could not think of any human behavior which could not be interpreted in terms of either theory. It was precisely this fact—that they always fitted, that they were always confirmed—which in the eyes of their admirers constituted the strongest argument in favor of these theories. **It began to dawn on me that** this apparent strength was in fact their weakness.

<u>12</u>　　With Einstein's theory the situation was **strikingly** different. Take one typical instance—Einstein's prediction, just then confirmed by the findings of Eddington's expedition. Einstein's gravitational theory had led to the result that light must be attracted by heavy bodies (such as the sun), precisely as material bodies were attracted. As a consequence it could be calculated that light from a distant fixed star whose apparent position was close to the sun would reach the earth from such a direction that the star would seem to be slightly shifted away from the sun; or, in other words, that stars close to the sun would look as if they had moved a little away from the sun, and from one another. This is a thing which cannot normally be observed since such stars are **rendered** invisible in daytime by the sun's **overwhelming** brightness; but during an eclipse it is possible to take photographs of them. If the same **constellation** is photographed at night one can measure the distances on the two photographs, and check the predicted effect. Now the impressive thing

about this case is the *risk* involved in a prediction of this kind. If observation shows that the predicted effect is definitely absent, then the theory is simply refuted. The theory is *incompatible with certain possible results of observation*—in fact with results which everybody before Einstein would have expected.① This is quite different from the situation I have previously described, when it turned out that the theories in question were compatible with the most divergent human behavior, so that it was practically impossible to describe any human behavior that might not be claimed to be a verification of these theories. These considerations led me in the winter of 1919-20 to conclusions which I may now reformulate as follows.

13 It is easy to obtain confirmations, or verifications, for nearly every theory—if we look for confirmations.

14 Confirmations should count only if they are the result of *risky predictions*; that is to say, if, unenlightened by the theory in question, we should have expected an event which was incompatible with the theory—an event which would have refuted the theory.

15 Every "good" scientific theory is a prohibition: it forbids certain things to happen. The more a theory forbids, the better it is.

16 A theory which is not refutable by any conceivable event is nonscientific. Irrefutability is not a virtue of a theory (as people often think) but a vice.

17 Every genuine *test* of a theory is an attempt to falsify it, or to refute it. Testability is **falsifiability**; but there are degrees of testability: some theories are more testable, more exposed to refutation, than others; they take, as it were, greater risks.

18 Confirming evidence should not count *except when it is the result of a genuine test of the theory*; and this means that it can be presented as a serious but unsuccessful attempt to falsify the theory. (I now speak in such

---

① This is a slight oversimplification, for about half of the Einstein effect may be derived from the classical theory, provided we assume a ballistic theory of light. (Footnote by the author)

cases of "corroborating evidence".)

19　　Some genuinely testable theories, when found to be false, are still **upheld** by their admirers—for example by introducing *ad hoc* some auxiliary assumption, or by re-interpreting the theory *ad hoc* in such a way that it escapes refutation. Such a procedure is always possible, but it rescues the theory from refutation only at the price of destroying, or at least lowering, its scientific status. (I later described such a rescuing operation as a "*conventionalist twist*" or a "*conventionalist **stratagem**".)

20　　One can sum up all this by saying that *the criterion of the scientific status of a theory is its falsifiability, or refutability, or testability.*

Vocabulary

demarcation [diməˈkeiʃən] n.	establishment of boundaries or limits separating two groups, areas, or things 划界,分界
pseudo-science n.	伪科学
consultation [kɔnsəlˈteiʃən] n.	the process of getting advice from someone 咨询
be acquainted with	熟悉,熟知
grapple with	应对,处理
rank [ræŋk] vi.	to occupy a certain position in a list or scale 排名
criterion [kraiˈtiəriən] n.	a factor on which you judge or decide something 标准
status [ˈsteitəs] n.	a formal classification of something 地位,身份
err [əː] vi.	to make a mistake 犯错
stumble on	偶然发现
metaphysics [metəˈfiziks] n.	a part of philosophy which is concerned with understanding reality and developing theories about what exists and how we know that it exists 形而上学
empirical [imˈpirikəl] a.	empirical evidence or study relies on practical experience rather than theories 凭经验的,经验的
inductive [inˈdʌktiv] a.	using particular facts and examples to form general rules and principles 归纳法的,归纳的
formulate [ˈfɔːmjuleit] vt.	to express or describe a thought, opinion, or idea using particular words 清晰地表达
come up to	达到、接近(要求、标准)

astrology [əs'trɒlədʒi] n.	the study of the movements of the planets, sun, moon, and stars in the belief that these movements can have an influence on people's lives 占星术
stupendous [stju:'pendəs] a.	surprisingly impressive or large 惊人的,巨大的
horoscope ['hɒrəskəup] n.	a description of your character and the things that will happen to you, based on the position of the stars and planets at the time of your birth 星象,占星术
collapse [kə'læps] n.	to fail or come to an end completely and suddenly 崩溃,瓦解
slogan ['sləugən] n.	a memorable saying of a particular group or organization 口号,标语
thrill [θril] v.	to feel a great pleasure or excitement 狂喜,激动
eclipse [i'klips] n.	日食
dubious ['djubiəs] a.	unsure, uncertain about something 有疑虑的
claim [kleim] n.	something which someone says which cannot be proved and can be false 断言
bother ['bɒðə] v.	to trouble, to annoy 使烦恼
pose as	假扮
practically ['præktikəli] ad.	almost 几乎
refer to	关系到,适用于
conversion [kən'və:ʃən] n.	a change of religion or belief 皈依
revelation [revə'leiʃən] n.	communication of knowledge of a man by a divine or supernatural source 启示
verification [verifi'keiʃən] n.	providing proof that something, especially a theory or hypothesis, is correct 证实
repression [ri'preʃən] n.	repression of feelings, especially sexual ones, is a person's unwillingness to allow themselves to have natural feeling and desires 压抑
treatment ['tri:mənt] n.	medical care 治疗
incessant [in'sesənt] a.	continuing without stopping 连续不断的
in question	在讨论中的,在考虑中的
adherent [əd'hiərənt] n.	someone who holds a particular belief or supports a particular person or group 追随者,信徒
inferiority [in,fiəri'ɒriti] n.	the feeling of being not as good as others 自卑
sound [saund] a.	reliable, sensible, reasonable 可靠的,有理的
in the light of	鉴于,根据,按照
count as	算作

reflect [ri'flekt] v.	to think deeply about 深思
say	比如说
sublimation [sʌbli'meiʃən] n.	the diversion of psychic energy derived from sexual impulses into nonsexual activity, especially of a creative nature 升华
it dawns on sb. that …	意识到……
strikingly ['straikiŋli] ad.	in a way that is easy to notice 引人注目地
render ['rendə] v.	to cause someone or something to be in a particular condition 使成为,使变得
overwhelming [əuvə'welmiŋ] a.	very large or greater, more important etc. than any other 压倒性的
constellation [kɔnstə'leiʃən] n.	a particular pattern formed by a group of stars 星座
falsifiability [fɔlsifaiə'biliti] n.	the property of a statement, theory or hypothesis that can be shown to be false 可证伪性
uphold [ʌp'həuld] vt.	to defend or support 支持,鼓励
ad hoc	特别的,专设的,专门的
stratagem ['strætədʒəm] n.	a plan that is intended to achieve a particular effect, usu. by deceiving people 计谋,诡计

I. Vocabulary Building

pseudo-: false

e.g., pseudonym, pseudonymous, pseudograph, pseudoclassic, pseudo-Aristotle

homo-: same, similar

e.g., homogeneous, homosexual, homophony, homocentric, homomorphic

hetero-: different

e.g., heterosexual, heterogeneous, heterogeneity, heterodoxy, heteronomy

matri-/mater-: related to mother

e.g., matriarch, matriarchal, maternal, maternity, matricide

patri-/pater-: related to father

e.g., patriarch, patriarchal, paternal, paternity, patricide

II. Discussion

Discuss the following questions with your own words.

1. Do you believe in astrology? Why or why not?

2. What are your understandings of the features of natural sciences?

3. What are your understandings of the features of pseudo-science?

4. What makes Einstein's theory of relativity unique according to the author?

5. What are the demarcations of science and pseudo-science according to the author?

III. Translation A

Translate the following sentences selected from the text into Chinese.

1. On the contrary, I often formulated my problem as one of distinguishing between a genuinely empirical method and a non-empirical or even a pseudo-empirical method—that is to say, a method which, although it appeals to observation and experiment, nevertheless does not come up to scientific standards. (Para. 3)

2. These theories appeared to be able to explain practically everything that happened within the fields to which they referred. The study of any of them seemed to have the effect of an intellectual conversion or revelation, opening your eyes to a new truth hidden from those not yet initiated. (Para. 9)

3. A Marxist could not open a newspaper without finding on every page confirming evidence for his interpretation of history; not only in the news, but also in its presentation—which revealed the class bias of the paper—and especially of course in what the paper did *not* say. (Para. 10)

4. It was precisely this fact—that they always fitted, that they were always confirmed—which in the eyes of their admirers constituted the strongest argument in favor of these theories. It began to dawn on me that this apparent strength was in fact their weakness. (Para. 11)

5. As a consequence it could be calculated that light from a distant fixed star whose apparent position was close to the sun would reach the earth from such a direction that the star would seem to be slightly shifted away from the sun; or, in other words, that stars close to the sun would look as if they had moved a little away from the sun, and from one another. (Para. 12)

IV. Translation B
Translate the following passage into Chinese.

From my childhood, I have been familiar with letters; and as I was given to believe that by their help a clear and certain knowledge of all that is useful in life might be acquired, I was ardently desirous of instruction. But as soon as I had finished the entire course of study, at the close of which it is customary to be admitted into the order of the learned, I completely changed my opinion. For I found myself involved in so many doubts and errors, that I was convinced I had advanced no farther in all my attempts at learning, than the discovery at every turn of my own ignorance. And yet I was studying in one of the most celebrated schools in Europe, in which I thought there must be learned men, if such were anywhere to be found. I had been taught all that others learned there; and not contented with the sciences actually taught us, I had, in addition, read all the books that had fallen into my hands, treating of such branches as are esteemed the most curious and rare. I knew the judgment which others had formed of me; and I did not find that I was considered inferior to my fellows, although there were among them some who were already marked out to fill the places of our instructors. And, in fine, our age appeared to me as flourishing, and as fertile in powerful minds as any preceding one. I was thus led to take the liberty of judging of all other men by myself, and of concluding that there was no science in existence that was of such a nature as I had previously been given to believe. (Excerpted from Text B)

V. Writing Exercise

Read Text C and summarize the major points of objectivism and subjectivism respectively.

Text B

Discourse on Method①

René Descartes

Chapter 1

<u>1</u> Good sense is, of all things among men, the most equally **distributed**; for everyone thinks himself so **abundantly** provided with it, that those even who are the most difficult to satisfy in everything else, do not usually desire a larger **measure** of this quality than they already possess. And in this it is not likely that all are mistaken the **conviction** is rather to be held as **testifying** that the power of judging aright and of distinguishing truth from error, which is properly what is called good sense or reason, is **by nature** equal in all men; and that the diversity of our opinions, consequently, does not arise from some being endowed with a larger share of reason than others, but solely from this, that we conduct our thoughts along different ways, and do

---

① Excerpted from René Descartes' *Discourse on the Method of Rightly Conducting the Reason, and Seeking Truth in the Sciences*, translated by Donald A. Cress.

not fix our attention on the same objects. For to be possessed of a **vigorous** mind is not enough; the prime **requisite** is rightly to apply it. The greatest minds, as they are capable of the highest excellences, are open likewise to the greatest **aberrations**; and those who travel very slowly may yet make far greater progress, **provided** they keep always to the straight road, than those who, while they run, forsake it.

...

<u>2</u>   My present design, then, is not to teach the method which each ought to follow for the right conduct of his reason, but solely to describe the way in which I have endeavored to conduct my own.

...

<u>3</u>   From my childhood, I have been familiar with letters; and as **I was given to** believe that by their help a clear and certain knowledge of all that is useful in life might be **acquired**, I was **ardently** desirous of instruction. But as soon as I had finished the entire course of study, at the close of which it is customary to be admitted into the order of the **learned**, I completely changed my opinion. For I found myself involved in so many doubts and errors, that I was convinced I had advanced no farther in all my attempts at learning, than the discovery at every turn of my own ignorance. And yet I was studying in one of the most celebrated schools in Europe, in which I thought there must be learned men, if such were anywhere to be found. I had been taught all that others learned there; and not contented with the sciences actually taught us, I had, in addition, read all the books that had fallen into my hands, treating of such branches as are esteemed the most curious and rare. I knew the judgment which others had formed of me; and I did not find that I was considered inferior to my fellows, although there were among them some who were already marked out to fill the places of our instructors. And, **in fine**, our age appeared to me as flourishing, and as fertile in powerful minds as any preceding one. I was thus led to **take the liberty of** judging of all other

men by myself, and of concluding that there was no science in existence that was of such a nature as I had previously been given to believe.

4 I still continued, however, to **hold in esteem** the studies of the schools. I was aware that the languages taught in them are necessary to the understanding of the writings of the ancients; that the grace of fable stirs the mind; that the memorable deeds of history elevate it; and, if read with **discretion**, aid in forming the judgment; that the **perusal** of all excellent books is, as it were, to interview with the noblest men of past ages, who have written them, and even a studied interview, in which are discovered to us only their choicest thoughts; that eloquence has incomparable force and beauty; that poesy has its ravishing graces and delights; that in the mathematics there are many refined discoveries eminently suited to gratify the **inquisitive**, as well as further all the arts and lessen the labor of man; that numerous highly useful **precepts** and **exhortations** to virtue are contained in treatises on morals; that theology points out the path to heaven; that philosophy affords the means of discoursing with an appearance of truth on all matters, and commands the admiration of the more simple; that **jurisprudence**, medicine, and the other sciences, secure for their cultivators honors and riches; and, in fine, that it is useful to **bestow** some attention upon all, even upon those **abounding** the most in **superstition** and error, that we may be in a position to determine their real value, and guard against being deceived.

5 But I believed that I had already given sufficient time to languages, and **likewise** to the reading of the writings of the ancients, to their histories and fables. For to hold converse with those of other ages and to travel, are almost the same thing. It is useful to know something of the manners of different nations, that we may be enabled to form a more correct judgment regarding our own, and be prevented from thinking that everything contrary to our customs is ridiculous and irrational, a conclusion usually come to by

those whose experience has been limited to their own country. On the other hand, when too much time is occupied in traveling, we become strangers to our native country; and the over curious in the customs of the past are generally ignorant of those of the present. Besides, fictitious narratives lead us to imagine the possibility of many events that are impossible; and even the most faithful histories, if they do not wholly misrepresent matters, or exaggerate their importance to render the account of them more worthy of perusal, omit, at least, almost always the meanest and least striking of the attendant circumstances; hence it happens that the remainder does not represent the truth, and that such as regulate their conduct by examples drawn from this source, are apt to fall into the extravagances of the knight-errants of romance, and to **entertain** projects that exceed their powers.

<u>6</u>　　I esteemed eloquence highly, and was in **raptures** with poesy; but I thought that both were gifts of nature rather than fruits of study. Those in whom the faculty of reason is **predominant**, and who most skillfully dispose their thoughts **with a view to** render them clear and intelligible, are always the best able to **persuade others of** the truth of what they lay down, though they should speak only in the language of Lower Brittany, and be wholly ignorant of the rules of rhetoric; and those whose minds are stored with the most agreeable fancies, and who can give expression to them with the greatest **embellishment** and harmony, are still the best poets, though unacquainted with the art of poetry.

<u>7</u>　　I was especially delighted with the mathematics, **on account of** the certitude and evidence of their reasonings; but I had not as yet a precise knowledge of their true use; and thinking that they but contributed to the advancement of the mechanical arts, I was astonished that foundations, so strong and solid, should have had no loftier superstructure reared on them. On the other hand, I compared the **disquisitions** of the ancient moralists to very **towering** and magnificent palaces with no better foundation than sand

and mud; they **laud** the virtues very highly, and exhibit them as estimable far above anything on earth; but they give us no adequate criterion of virtue, and frequently that which they designate with so fine a name is but **apathy**, or pride, or despair, or **parricide**.

8   I **revered** our theology, and aspired as much as anyone to reach heaven: but being given assuredly to understand that the way is not less open to the most ignorant than to the most learned, and that the revealed truths which lead to heaven are above our comprehension, I did not presume to subject them to the impotency of my reason; and I thought that in order competently to undertake their examination, there was need of some special help from heaven, and of being more than man.

9   Of philosophy I will say nothing, except that when I saw that it had been cultivated for many ages by the most distinguished men, and that yet there is not a single matter within its sphere which is not still in dispute, and nothing, therefore, which is above doubt, I did not presume to anticipate that my success would be greater in it than that of others; and further, when I considered the number of conflicting opinions touching a single matter that may be upheld by learned men, while there can be but one true, I reckoned as well-nigh false all that was only probable.

10   As to the other sciences, **inasmuch as** these borrow their principles from philosophy, I judged that no solid superstructures could be reared on foundations so infirm; and neither the honor nor the gain held out by them was sufficient to determine me to their cultivation. ...

Chapter 2

11   I was then in Germany, attracted **thither** by the wars in that country, which have not yet been brought to a **termination**; and as I was returning to the army from the **coronation** of the emperor, the setting in of winter **arrested** me in a locality where, as I found no society to interest me, and was besides

fortunately undisturbed by any cares or passions, I remained the whole day in **seclusion**, with full opportunity to occupy my attention with my own thoughts. Of these one of the very first that occurred to me was, that there is seldom so much perfection in works composed of many separate parts, upon which different hands had been employed, as in those completed by a single master. Thus it is observable that the buildings which a single architect has planned and executed, are generally more elegant and **commodious** than those which several have attempted to improve, by making old walls serve for purposes for which they were not originally built. Thus also, those ancient cities which, from being at first only villages, have become, in course of time, large towns, are usually but ill laid out compared with the regularity constructed towns which a professional architect has freely planned on an open plain; so that although the several buildings of the former may often equal or surpass in beauty those of the latter, yet when one observes their indiscriminate **juxtaposition**, there a large one and here a small, and the consequent crookedness and irregularity of the streets, one **is disposed to** allege that chance rather than any human will guided by reason must have led to such an arrangement. And if we consider that nevertheless there have been at all times certain officers whose duty it was to see that private buildings contributed to public **ornament**, the difficulty of reaching high perfection with but the materials of others to operate on, will be readily acknowledged. In the same way I fancied that those nations which, starting from a semi-barbarous state and advancing to civilization by slow degrees, have had their laws successively determined, and, **as it were**, forced upon them simply by experience of the hurtfulness of particular crimes and disputes, would by this process come to be possessed of less perfect institutions than those which, from the **commencement** of their association as communities, have followed the appointments of some wise legislator. It is thus quite certain that the **constitution** of the true religion, the **ordinances** of which are **derived from** God, must be incomparably superior to that of every other. And, to speak of human affairs, I believe that the pre-eminence of Sparta was due not to the goodness of each of its laws in particular, for many of these were very strange, and even opposed to good morals, but to the circumstance that, originated by a single individual, they all tended to a single **end**. In the same way I thought that the sciences contained in books (such of them at least as are made up of probable reasonings, without **demonstrations**), composed as they are of the opinions of many different individuals massed together, are farther **removed from** truth than the simple inferences which a man of good sense using his natural and unprejudiced judgment draws respecting the matters of his experience. And because we have all to pass through a state of infancy to manhood, and have been of necessity, for a length of time, governed by our desires and preceptors (whose dictates were frequently conflicting, while neither perhaps always counseled us for the best), I farther concluded that it is almost impossible that our judgments can be so correct or solid as they would have been, had our reason been mature from the moment of our birth, and had we always been guided by it alone.

...

12　　**For my part**, I should doubtless have belonged to the latter class, had I received instruction from but one master, or had I never known the diversities of opinion that **from time immemorial** have prevailed among men of the greatest learning. But I had become aware, even so early as during my college life, that no opinion, however absurd and incredible, can be imagined, which has not been **maintained** by some one of the philosophers; and afterwards in the course of my travels I remarked that all those whose opinions are decidedly **repugnant** to ours are not in that account barbarians and savages, but on the contrary that many of these nations make an equally good, if not better, use of their reason than we do. I took into account also the very different character which a person brought up from infancy in France or Germany exhibits, from that which, with the same mind originally, this individual would have possessed had he lived always among the Chinese or with savages, and the circumstance that in dress itself the fashion which pleased us ten years ago, and which may again, perhaps, be received into favor before ten years have gone, appears to us at this moment extravagant and ridiculous. I was thus led to infer that the ground of our opinions is far more custom and example than any certain knowledge. And, finally, although such be the ground of our opinions, I remarked that a plurality of suffrages is no guarantee of truth where it is at all of difficult discovery, as in such cases it is much more likely that it will be found by one than by many. I could, however, select from the crowd no one whose opinions seemed worthy of preference, and thus I found myself constrained, as it were, to use my own reason in the conduct of my life.

13 ... in like manner, instead of the great number of precepts of which logic is composed, I believed that the four following would prove perfectly sufficient for me, provided I took the firm and **unwavering** resolution never in a single instance to fail in observing them.

14 The first was never to accept anything for true which I did not clearly know to be such; that is to say, carefully to avoid precipitancy and prejudice, and to comprise nothing more in my judgment than what was presented to my mind so clearly and distinctly as to exclude all ground of doubt.

15 The second, to divide each of the difficulties under examination into as many parts as possible, and as might be necessary for its adequate solution.

16 The third, to conduct my thoughts in such order that, by commencing with objects the simplest and easiest to know, I might **ascend** by little and little, and, as it were, step by step, to the knowledge of the more complex; assigning in thought a certain order even to those objects which in their own nature do not stand in a relation of antecedence and sequence.

17 And the last, in every case to make **enumerations** so complete, and reviews so general, that I might be assured that nothing was omitted. ...

Chapter 3

18 And finally, as it is not enough, before commencing to rebuild the house in which we live, that it be pulled down, and materials and builders provided, or that we engage in the work ourselves, according to a plan which we have beforehand carefully drawn out, but as it is likewise necessary that we be furnished with some other house in which we may live commodiously during the operations, so that I might not remain irresolute in my actions, while my reason compelled me to suspend my judgment, and that I might not be prevented from living thenceforward in the greatest possible felicity, I formed a provisory code of morals, composed of three or four **maxims**, with which I am desirous to make you acquainted.

19 The first was to obey the laws and customs of my country, adhering firmly to the faith in which, by the grace of God, I had been educated from my childhood and regulating my conduct in every other matter according to the most **moderate** opinions, and the farthest removed from extremes, which should happen to be adopted in practice with general consent of the most judicious of those among whom I might be living. ...

20 My second maxim was to be as firm and resolute in my actions as I was able, and not to adhere less steadfastly to the most doubtful opinions, when once adopted, than if they had been highly certain; imitating in this the example of travelers who, when they have lost their way in a forest, ought not to wander from side to side, far less remain in one place, but proceed constantly towards the same side in as straight a line as possible, without changing their direction for slight reasons, although perhaps it might be chance alone which at first determined the selection; for in this way, if they do not exactly reach the point they desire, they will come at least in the end

to some place that will probably be preferable to the middle of a forest.

<u>21</u>   My third maxim was to endeavor always to conquer myself rather than fortune, and change my desires rather than the order of the world, and in general, accustom myself to the persuasion that, except our own thoughts, there is nothing absolutely in our power; so that when we have done our best in things external to us, all wherein we fail of success is to be held, as regards us, absolutely impossible: and this single principle seemed to me sufficient to prevent me from desiring for the future anything which I could not obtain, and thus render me contented; ... But I confess there is need of prolonged discipline and frequently repeated meditation to accustom the mind to view all objects in this light; and I believe that in this chiefly consisted the secret of the power of such philosophers as in former times were enabled to rise superior to the influence of fortune, and, amid suffering and poverty, enjoy a happiness which their gods might have envied. ...

<u>22</u>   In fine, to conclude this code of morals, I thought of reviewing the different occupations of men in this life, with the view of making choice of the best. And, without wishing to offer any remarks on the employments of others, I may state that it was my conviction that I could not do better than continue in that in which I was engaged, **viz.**, in devoting my whole life to the culture of my reason, and in making the greatest progress I was able in the knowledge of truth, on the principles of the method which I had prescribed to myself. This method, from the time I had begun to apply it, had been to me the source of satisfaction so intense as to lead me to, believe that more perfect or more innocent could not be enjoyed in this life; and as by its means I daily discovered truths that appeared to me of some importance, and of which other men were generally ignorant, the gratification thence arising so occupied my mind that I was wholly indifferent to every other object. Besides, the three preceding maxims were founded singly on the design of continuing the work of self-instruction.

Vocabulary

distribute [di'stribjut] vt.	to share things among a group of people 分配
abundant [ə'bʌndənt] a.	present in large quantities 丰富的
measure ['meʒə] n.	a particular quantity or amount 一定数量，一定程度
conviction [kən'vikʃən] n.	a very strong belief or opinion 坚定的信仰
testify ['testifai] a.	to show clearly that something is the case 证明
by nature	就其本性而言，天生地
vigorous ['vigərəs] a.	full of energy and enthusiasm 精力充沛的，有力的
requisite ['rekwizit] n.	something that is needed for a particular purpose 必需物
aberration [æbə'reiʃən] n.	an action or event that is very different from what usually happens or what someone usually does 异常，反常
provided [prə'vaidid] conj.	假如，只要
be given to	习惯于
acquire [ə'kwaiə] vt.	to get or gain something 取得，获得
ardent ['ɑːdənt] a.	showing strong positive feelings about an activity and determination to succeed at it 热心的，热切的
learned ['ləːnid] a.	possessing a lot of knowledge 博学的
in fine	最后
take the liberty of	冒昧，擅自
hold … in esteem	尊敬……
discretion [di'skreʃən] n.	the quality of behaving in a quiet and controlled way without drawing attention to yourself or giving away personal or private information 审慎
perusal [pə'ruːsəl] n.	the action of carefully reading 熟读，细读
inquisitive [in'kwizitiv] a.	interested in a lot of different things and wanting to find out more about them 好奇的，爱探究的
precept ['priːsept] n.	a rule on which a way of thinking or behaving is based 训诫，准则
exhortation [egzɔː'teiʃən] n.	a communication intended to urge or persuade the recipients to take some action 训诫，劝告
jurisprudence [dʒuəris'pruːdəns] n.	the study of law 法学
bestow [bes'təu] vt.	to give someone something of great value or importance 授予，赠予，给予
abound in	充满，富于
superstition [suːpə'stiʃən] n.	belief in things that are not real or possible 迷信
likewise ['laikwaiz] ad.	similarly 同样地

entertain [entə'tein] vt.	to main (a though, notion, idea, etc.) 抱有
rapture ['ræptʃə] n.	great excitement and happiness 狂喜
predominant [pri'dɔminənt] a.	more important or noticeable than anything else in a set of people or things 主导性的
with a view to	鉴于
persuade sb. of …	使相信……
embellishment [im'beliʃmənt] n.	a decoration added to something to make it seem more attractive or interesting 装饰
on account of	由于
disquisition [diskwi'ziʃən] n.	a long speech or written report 专题论文
towering ['tauəriŋ] a.	much better than other people of the same kind 超群的, 杰出的
laud [lɔːd] vt.	to praise someone or something 称赞, 赞美
apathy ['æpəθi] n.	do not seem to be interested in or enthusiastic about anything 冷漠, 漠不关心
parricide ['pærisaid] n.	弑亲
revere [ri'viə] vt.	to respect and admire someone or something very much 尊敬
inasmuch as	由于, 因为
thither ['ðiðə] ad.	到那里
termination [təːmi'neiʃən] n.	the act of ending something, or the end of something 终止, 结束
coronation [kɔrə'neiʃən] n.	加冕
arrest [ə'rest] vt.	to stop something happening or to make it happen more slowly 抑制, 阻止
seclusion [si'kluʒən] n.	the state of being private and away from other people 隐居, 与世隔绝
commodious [kə'məudiəs] a.	宽大的, 舒服的
juxtaposition [ˌdʒʌkstəpə'ziʃən] n.	to put two things or objects together (so as to make a comparison) 并列
be disposed to	倾向于
ornament ['ɔːnəmənt] n.	decoration that is added to something 装饰, 点缀
as it were	就好像
commencement [kə'mensmənt] n.	the beginning of something 开始, 开端
constitution [kɔn'stitjuʃən] n.	the parts or structure of something 构成, 组成
ordinance ['ɔːdinəns] n.	an order given by a ruler or governing organization 法令, 法规

be derived from	来自于，源自
end [end] n.	purpose 目的
demonstration [ˌdemənˈstreiʃən] n.	a clear proof of some fact or situation 证明
be removed from	与……不一样，远离……
for one's part	就……来说，依……看
from time immemorial	自古以来
maintain [ˈmeintein] vt.	keep in a certain state, position, or activity 保持，主张
repugnant [riˈpʌgnənt] a.	very unpleasant and offensive 使人厌恶的，使人反感的
unwavering [ʌnˈweivəriŋ] a.	something that it is strong and firm and does not weaken 坚定的，不动摇的
ascend [əˈsend] v.	to move up through the air 上升
enumeration [iˌnjuːməˈreiʃən] n.	a numbered list 列举，列数
maxim [ˈmæksim] n.	a rule for good or sensible behavior, especially one in the form of a saying 准则，格言
moderate [ˈmɔdərit] a.	having opinions or beliefs that are not extreme and that most people consider reasonable 温和的
viz. [viz] ad.	namely 即

Text C

The Myths of Objectivism and Subjectivism[①]

George Lakoff and Mark Johnson

The Choices Our Culture Offers

<u>1</u>   We have given an account of the way in which truth is based on understanding. We have argued that truth is always relative to a conceptual system, that any human conceptual system is mostly metaphorical in nature, and that, therefore, there is no fully **objective**, unconditional, or absolute truth. To many people raised in the culture of science or in other subcultures

---

① Excerpted from George Lakoff and Mark Johnson's *Metaphors We Live By*.

where absolute truth is taken for granted, this will be seen as a surrender to **subjectivity** and **arbitrariness**—to the Humpty-Dumpty notion that something means "just what I choose it to mean—neither more nor less." For the same reason, those who **identify with** the Romantic tradition may see any victory over objectivism as a triumph of imagination over science—a triumph of the view that each individual makes his own reality, free of any constraints.

<u>2</u>   Either of these views would be a misunderstanding based on the mistaken cultural assumption that the only alternative to objectivism is **radical** subjectivity—that is, either you believe in absolute truth or you can make the world in your own image. If you're not being *objective*, you're being *subjective*, and there is no third choice. We see ourselves as offering a third choice to the **myths** of objectivism and subjectivism.

<u>3</u>   **Incidentally**, we are not using the term "myth" in any **derogatory** way. Myths provide ways of comprehending experience; they give order to our lives. Like metaphors, myths are necessary for making sense of what goes on around us. All cultures have myths, and people cannot function without myth any more than they can function without metaphor. And just as we often take the *metaphors* of our own culture as truths, so we often take the *myths* of our own culture as truths. The myth of objectivism is particularly **insidious** in this way. Not only does it purport not to be a myth, but it makes both myths and metaphors objects of belittlement and scorn: according to the objectivist myth, myths and metaphors cannot be taken seriously because they are not objectively true. As we will see, the myth of objectivism is itself not objectively true. But this does not make it something to be scorned or ridiculed. The myth of objectivism is part of the everyday functioning of every member of this culture. It needs to be examined and understood. We also think it needs to be **supplemented**—not by its opposite, the myth of subjectivism, but by a new experientialist myth, which we think better fits the realities of our experience. In order to get clear about what an

experientialist alternative would be like, we first need to examine the myths of objectivism and subjectivism in detail.

The Myth of Objectivism

<u>4</u>　　The myth of objectivism says that:

1) The world is made up of objects. They have properties independent of any people or other beings who experience them. For example, take a rock. It's a separate object and it's hard. Even if no people or other beings existed in the universe, it would still be a separate object and it would still be hard.

2) We get our knowledge of the world by experiencing the objects in it and getting to know what **properties** the objects have and how these objects are related to one another. For example, we find out that a rock is a separate object by looking at it, feeling it, moving it around, etc. We find out that it's hard by touching it, trying to squeeze it, kicking it, banging it against something softer, etc.

3) We understand the objects in our world in terms of **categories** and concepts. These categories and concepts correspond to properties the objects have in themselves (inherently) and to the relationships among the objects. Thus, we have a word "rock", which corresponds to a concept ROCK. Given a rock, we can tell that it is in the category ROCK and that a piano, a tree, or a tiger would not be. Rocks have inherent properties independent of any beings: they're solid, hard, dense, occur in nature, etc. We understand what a "rock" is in terms of these properties.

4) There is an objective reality, and we can say things that are objectively, absolutely, and unconditionally true and false about it. But, as human beings, we are subject to human error, that is, illusions, errors of perception, errors of judgment, emotions, and personal and cultural **biases**. We cannot rely upon the subjective judgments of individual people. Science provides us with a **methodology** that allows us to rise above our subjective

limitations and to achieve understanding from a universally **valid** and unbiased point of view. Science can ultimately give a correct, definitive, and general account of reality, and, through its methodology, it is constantly progressing toward that goal.

5) Words have fixed meanings. That is, our language expresses the concepts and categories that we think in terms of. To describe reality correctly, we need words whose meanings are clear and precise, words that fit reality. These may be words that arise naturally, or they may be technical terms in a scientific theory.

6) People can be objective and can speak objectively, but they can do so only if they use language that is clearly and precisely defined, that is straightforward and direct, and that can fit reality. Only by speaking in this way can people communicate precisely about the external world and make statements that can be judged objectively to be true or false.

7) Metaphor and other kinds of poetic, fanciful, rhetorical, or **figurative** language can always be avoided in speaking objectively, and they should be avoided, since their meanings are not clear and precise and do not fit reality in any obvious way.

8) Being objective is generally a good thing. Only objective knowledge is really knowledge. Only from an objective, unconditional point of view can we really understand ourselves, others, and the external world. Objectivity allows us to rise above personal prejudice and bias, to be fair, and to take an unbiased view of the world.

9) To be objective is to be **rational**; to be subjective is to be irrational and to give in to the emotions.

10) Subjectivity can be dangerous, since it can lead to losing touch with reality. Subjectivity can be unfair, since it takes a personal point of view and can, therefore, be biased. Subjectivity is self-indulgent, since it exaggerates the importance of the individual.

The Myth of Subjectivism

5   The myth of subjectivism says that:

1) In most of our everyday practical activities we rely on our senses and develop intuitions we can trust. When important issues arise, regardless of what others may say, our own senses and intuitions are our best guides for action.

2) The most important things in our lives are our feelings, **aesthetic** sensibilities, moral practices, and spiritual awareness. These are purely subjective. None of these is purely rational or objective.

3) Art and poetry **transcend** rationality and objectivity and put us in touch with the more important reality of our feelings and intuitions. We gain this awareness through imagination rather than reason.

4) The language of the imagination, especially metaphor, is necessary for expressing the unique and most personally significant aspects of our experience. In matters of personal understanding the ordinary agreed-upon meanings that words have will not do.

5) Objectivity can be dangerous, because it misses what is most important and meaningful to individual people. Objectivity can be unfair, since it must ignore the most relevant realms of our experience in favor of the abstract, universal, and impersonal. For the same reason, objectivity can be inhuman. There are no objective and rational means for getting at our feelings, our aesthetic sensibilities, etc. Science is of no use when it comes to the most important things in our lives.

Fear of Metaphor

6   Objectivism and subjectivism need each other in order to exist. Each defines itself in opposition to the other and sees the other as the enemy. Objectivism takes as its allies scientific truth, rationality, precision,

fairness, and **impartiality**. Subjectivism takes as its allies the emotions, intuitive insight, imagination, humaneness, art, and a "higher" truth. Each is master in its own realm and views its realm as the better of the two. They coexist, but in separate domains. Each of us has a realm in his life where it is appropriate to be objective and a realm where it is appropriate to be subjective. The portions of our lives governed by objectivism and subjectivism vary greatly from person to person and from culture to culture. Some of us even attempt to live our entire lives totally by one myth or the other.

7 In Western culture as a whole, objectivism is by far the greater potentate, claiming to rule, at least **nominally**, the realms of science, law, government, journalism, morality, business, economics, and scholarship. But, as we have argued, objectivism is a myth.

8 Since the time of the Greeks, there has been in Western culture a tension between truth, on the one hand, and art, on the other, with art viewed as **illusion** and allied, via its link with poetry and theater, to the tradition of persuasive public oratory. Plato viewed poetry and rhetoric with suspicion and banned poetry from his **utopian** Republic because it gives no truth of its own, stirs up the emotions, and thereby blinds mankind to the real truth. Plato, typical of persuasive writers, stated his view that truth is absolute and art mere illusion by the use of a powerful rhetorical device, his Allegory of the Cave. To this day, his metaphors dominate Western philosophy, providing subtle and elegant expression for his view that truth is absolute. Aristotle, on the other hand, saw poetry as having a positive value: "It is a great thing, indeed, to make proper use of the poetic forms, ... But the greatest thing by far is to be a master of metaphor" (*Poetics* 1459a); "ordinary words convey only what we know already; it is from metaphor that we can best get hold of something fresh" (*Rhetoric* 1410b).

9 But although Aristotle's theory of how metaphors work is *the* classic

view, his praise of metaphor's ability to **induce** insight was never carried over into modern philosophical thought. With the rise of empirical science as a model for truth, the suspicion of poetry and rhetoric became dominant in Western thought, with metaphor and other figurative devices becoming objects of scorn once again. Hobbes, for example, finds metaphors absurd and misleadingly emotional; they are "*ignes fatui*; and reasoning upon them is wandering amongst innumerable absurdities; and their end, **contention** and **sedition**, or contempt" (*Leviathan*, pt. 1, chap. 5). Hobbes finds absurdity in "the use of metaphors, tropes, and other rhetorical figures, instead of words proper. For though it be lawful to say, for example in common speech, *the way goeth, or leadeth hither, or thither; the proverb says this or that*, whereas ways cannot go, nor proverbs speak; yet in reckoning, and seeking of truth, such speeches are not to be admitted" (Ibid.).

<u>10</u>　　Locke, continuing the empiricist tradition, shows the same contempt for figurative speech, which he views as a tool of rhetoric and an enemy of truth:

> ... if we would speak of things as they are, we must allow that all the art of rhetoric, besides order and clearness; all the artificial and figurative application of words eloquence hath invented, are for nothing else but to **insinuate** wrong ideas, move the passions, and thereby mislead the judgment; and so indeed are perfect cheats: and therefore, however laudable or allowable oratory may render them in **harangues** and popular addresses, they are certainly, in all discourses that pretend to inform or instruct, wholly to be avoided; and where truth and knowledge are concerned, cannot but be thought a great fault, either of the language or person that makes use of them.... It is evident how much men love to deceive and be deceived, since rhetoric, that powerful instrument of error and deceit, has its established professors, is publicly taught, and has always been had in great reputation. [*Essay*

Concerning Human Understanding, bk. 3, chap. 10]

11   The fear of metaphor and rhetoric in the empiricist tradition is a fear of subjectivism—a fear of emotion and the imagination. Words are viewed as having "proper senses" in terms of which truths can be expressed. To use words metaphorically is to use them in an improper sense, to stir the imagination and thereby the emotions and thus to lead us away from the truth and toward illusion. The empiricist distrust and fear of metaphor is wonderfully summed up by Samuel Parker:

> All those Theories in Philosophy which are expressed only in metaphorical Termes, are not real Truths, but the meer products of Imagination, dress'd up (like Childrens babies) in a few spangled empty words.... Thus their wanton and luxuriant fancies climbing up into the Bed of Reason, do not only defile it by unchaste and illegitimate Embraces, but instead of real conceptions and notices of Things, impregnate the mind with nothing but Ayerie and Subventaneous Phantasmes. [*Free and Impartial Censure of the Platonick Philosophy* (1666)]

12   As science became more powerful via technology and the Industrial Revolution became a dehumanizing reality, there occurred a reaction among poets, artists, and occasional philosophers: the development of the Romantic tradition. Wordsworth and Coleridge gladly left reason, science, and objectivity to the dehumanized empiricists and **exalted** imagination as a more humane means of achieving a higher truth, with emotion as a natural guide to self-understanding. Science, reason, and technology had **alienated** man from himself and his natural environment, or so the Romantics alleged; they saw poetry, art, and a return to nature as a way for man to recover his lost humanity. Art and poetry were seen, not as products of reason, but as the **spontaneous** overflow of powerful feelings. The result of this Romantic view was the alienation of the artist and poet from mainstream society.

<u>13</u>　　The Romantic tradition, by embracing subjectivism, reinforced the **dichotomy** between truth and reason, on the one hand, and art and imagination, on the other. By giving up on rationality, the Romantics played into the hands of the myth of objectivism, whose power has continued to increase ever since. The Romantics did, however, create a domain for themselves, where subjectivism continues to **hold sway**. It is an **impoverished** domain compared to that of objectivism. In terms of real power in our society—in science, law, government, business, and the media—the myth of objectivism reigns supreme. Subjectivism has **carved out** a domain for itself in art and perhaps in religion. Most people in this culture see it as an **appendage** to the realm of objectivism and a retreat for the emotions and the imagination.

The Third Choice: An Experientialist Synthesis

<u>14</u>　　What we are offering in the experientialist account of understanding and truth is an alternative which denies that subjectivity and objectivity are our only choices. We reject the objectivist view that there is absolute and unconditional truth without adopting the subjectivist alternative of truth as obtainable only through the imagination, unconstrained by external circumstances. The reason we have focused so much on metaphor is that it unites reason and imagination. Reason, at the very least, involves categorization, **entailment**, and inference. Imagination, in one of its many aspects, involves seeing one kind of thing in terms of another kind of thing— what we have called metaphorical thought. Metaphor is thus imaginative rationality. Since the categories of our everyday thought are largely metaphorical and our everyday reasoning involves metaphorical entailments and inferences, ordinary rationality is therefore imaginative by its very nature. Given our understanding of poetic metaphor in terms of metaphorical

entailments and inferences, we can see that the products of the poetic imagination are, for the same reason, partially rational in nature.

15   Metaphor is one of our most important tools for trying to comprehend partially what cannot be comprehended totally: our feelings, aesthetic experiences, moral practices, and spiritual awareness. These endeavors of the imagination are not **devoid of** rationality; since they use metaphor, they employ an imaginative rationality.

16   An experientialist approach also allows us to **bridge the gap** between the objectivist and subjectivist myths about impartiality and the possibility of being fair and objective. The two choices offered by the myths are absolute objectivity, on the one hand, and purely subjective intuition, on the other. We have seen that truth is relative to understanding, which means that there is no absolute standpoint from which to obtain absolute objective truths about the world. This does not mean that there are no truths; it means only that truth is relative to our conceptual system, which is grounded in, and constantly tested by, our experiences and those of other members of our culture in our daily interactions with other people and with our physical and cultural environments.

17   Though there is no absolute objectivity, there can be a kind of objectivity relative to the conceptual system of a culture. The point of impartiality and fairness in social matters is to rise above relevant *individual* biases. The point of objectivity in scientific experimentation is to **factor out** the effects of *individual* illusion and error. This is not to say that we can always, or even ever, be completely successful in factoring out individual biases to achieve complete objectivity relative to a conceptual system and a cultural set of values. It is only to say that pure subjective intuition is not always our only **recourse**. Nor is this to say that the concepts and values of a particular culture constitute the final **arbiter** of fairness within the culture. There may be, and typically are, transcultural concepts and values that

define a standard of fairness very different from that of a particular culture. What was fair in Nazi Germany, for example, was not fair in the eyes of the world community. Closer to home, there are court cases that constantly involve issues of fairness across subcultures with conflicting values. Here the majority culture usually gets to define fairness relative to *its* values, but these mainstream cultural values change over time and are often subject to criticism by other cultures.

18　　What the myths of objectivism and subjectivism both miss is the way we understand the world through our interactions with it. What objectivism misses is the fact that understanding, and therefore truth, is necessarily relative to our cultural conceptual systems and that it cannot be framed in any absolute or neutral conceptual system. Objectivism also misses the fact that human conceptual systems are metaphorical in nature and involve an imaginative understanding of one kind of thing in terms of another. What subjectivism specifically misses is that our understanding, even our most imaginative understanding, is given in terms of a conceptual system that is grounded in our successful functioning in our physical and cultural environments. It also misses the fact that metaphorical understanding involves metaphorical entailment, which is an imaginative form of rationality.

Vocabulary

objective [əbˈdʒektiv] a.	existing outside the mind as something real, not only as an idea 客观的
subjective [sʌbˈdʒektiv] a.	existing only in your mind or imagination 主观的
arbitrary [ˈɑːbitrəri] a.	decided or arranged without any reason or plan, often unfairly 任意的，武断的
identify with	等同于，与……有关
radical [ˈrædikəl] a.	far beyond the norm 极端的，彻底的
myth [miθ] n.	an idea or story that many people believe, but which is not true 错误观念，荒谬的说法

incidentally [ˌinsiˈdentəli] ad.		used to add more information to what you have just said, or to introduce a new subject that you have just thought of 顺便提一下
derogatory [diˈrɔgətəri] a.		derogatory remarks, attitudes etc. are insulting and disapproving 贬低的
insidious [inˈsidiəs] a.		unpleasant or dangerous and develops gradually without being noticed 阴险的
supplement [ˈsʌplimənt] vt.		to add something, especially to what you earn or eat, in order to increase it to an acceptable level 增加,补充
property [ˈprɔpəti] n.		a quality or power that a substance has 属性
category [ˈkætigəri] n.		a group of people or things that are all of the same type 范畴,种类
bias [baiəs] n.		a partiality that prevents objective consideration of an issue or situation 偏见
methodology [ˌmeθəˈdɔlədʒi] n.		a system of methods and principles for doing something 方法论
valid [ˈvælid] a.		something that is based on what is reasonable or sensible 合理的,有效的
figurative [ˈfigərətiv] a.		比喻的
rational [ˈræʃnəl] a.		based on reasons rather than emotions 基于理性的
aesthetics [iːsˈθetiks] n.		the study of beauty 美学
transcend [trænˈsend] vt.		to go beyond the usual limits of something 超越,超出
impartiality [imˌpɑːʃiˈæliti] n.		an inclination to weigh both views or opinions equally 不偏不倚
nominally [ˈnɔminəli] ad.		officially described as being something, when this is not really true 名义上
illusion [iˈluːʒn] n.		an idea or opinion that is wrong, especially about yourself 幻觉
utopian [juːˈtəupiən] a.		related to utopia 乌托邦的
induce [inˈdjuːs] vt.		to cause a particular physical condition 引起,诱发
contention [kənˈtenʃən] n.		argument and disagreement between people 争论,争端
sedition [siˈdiʃən] n.		Sedition is speech, writing, or behavior intended to encourage people to fight against or oppose the government 煽动(言论、文章或活动)
insinuate [inˈsinjueit] v.		to say something which seems to mean something unpleasant without saying it openly 暗示,暗指
harangue [həˈræŋ] n.		a loud bombastic declamation expressed with strong emotion 长篇大论,慷慨激昂的演说

exalt [ig'zɔːlt] vt.	to put someone or something into a high rank or position 提升，提拔
alienate ['eiliəneit] vt.	to make it difficult for someone to belong to a particular group or to feel comfortable with a particular person 使疏远，使异化
spontaneous [spɔn'teiniəs] a.	spontaneous events happen because of processes within something rather than being caused by things outside it 自发的，自然的
dichotomy [dai'kɔtəmi] n.	if there is a dichotomy between two things, there is a very great difference or opposition between them 二分法
hold sway	支配，统治
impoverished [im'pɔvəriʃt] a.	poor 贫乏的
carve out	雕刻出，开拓出
appendage [ə'pendidʒ] n.	something that is connected to a larger or more important thing 附加物，附属物
entailment [in'teilmənt] n.	something that is inferred (deduced or entailed or implied) 蕴含
be devoid of	缺乏
bridge the gap	弥合裂痕
factor out	分析出因素，找到因子
recourse [ri'kɔːs] n.	something or someone turned to for assistance or security 求助，求援
arbiter ['aːbitə] n.	someone or something that settles an argument between two opposing sides 仲裁人

Unit 7

Speeches

Text A　I Have a Dream
Text B　Richard M. Nixon's Resignation Address
Text C　We Shall Fight on the Beaches

Text A

I Have a Dream[①]

Martin Luther King, Jr.

Standing on the steps of the Lincoln Memorial in Washington, D.C., on August 28, 1963, Martin Luther King, Jr., delivered what is regarded today as one of the greatest speeches in American history. King himself seemed to sense the historic importance of the moment as he opened his "I Have a Dream" speech by calling the March on Washington for Jobs and Freedom "the greatest demonstration for freedom in the history of our nation." The landmark protest, which drew more than 200,000 people, announced a turning point in the civil rights movement and set the stage for the movement's two most important legislative achievements, the Civil Rights Act of 1964 and the Voting Rights Act of 1965.

---

① It is a public speech delivered by American civil rights activist Martin Luther King, Jr. during the March on Washington for Jobs and Freedom on August 28, 1963.

1   I am happy to join with you today in what will go down in history as the greatest demonstration for freedom in the history of our nation.

2   Five score years ago, a great American, in whose symbolic shadow we stand today, signed **the Emancipation Proclamation.** This momentous **decree** came as a great **beacon** light of hope to millions of Negro slaves who had been **seared** in the flames of **withering** injustice. It came as a joyous daybreak to end the long night of their **captivity.**

3   But one hundred years later, the Negro still is not free. One hundred years later, the life of the Negro is still sadly crippled by the **manacles** of **segregation** and the chains of **discrimination.** One hundred years later, the Negro lives on a lonely island of poverty **in the midst of** a vast ocean of material prosperity. One hundred years later, the Negro is still **languished** in the corners of American society and finds himself an **exile** in his own land. And so we've come here today to dramatize a shameful condition.

4   **In a sense** we've come to our nation's capital to cash a check. When the architects of our republic wrote the magnificent words of the Constitution and the Declaration of Independence, they were signing a **promissory note** to which every American was to fall **heir.** This note was a promise that all men, yes, black men as well as white men, would be guaranteed the "**unalienable** Rights" of "Life, Liberty and the pursuit of Happiness." It is obvious today that America has **defaulted** on this promissory note, **insofar** as her citizens of color are concerned. Instead of honoring this **sacred** obligation, America has given the Negro people a bad check, a check which has come back marked "insufficient funds."

5   But we refuse to believe that the bank of justice is bankrupt. We refuse to believe that there are insufficient funds in the great **vaults** of opportunity of this nation. And so, we've come to cash this check, a check that will give us upon demand the riches of freedom and the security of justice.

6   We have also come to this **hallowed** spot to remind America of the fierce

urgency of Now. This is no time to engage in the luxury of cooling off or to take the **tranquilizing drug** of **gradualism.** Now is the time to make real the promises of democracy. Now is the time to rise from the dark and **desolate** valley of segregation to the sunlit path of racial justice. Now is the time to lift our nation from the **quicksands** of racial injustice to the solid rock of brotherhood. Now is the time to make justice a reality for all of God's children.

7   It would be fatal for the nation to overlook the urgency of the moment. This **sweltering** summer of the Negro's **legitimate** discontent will not pass until there is an **invigorating** autumn of freedom and equality. Nineteen sixty-three is not an end, but a beginning. And those who hope that the Negro needed to **blow off steam** and will now be content will have a rude awakening if the nation returns to business as usual. And there will be neither rest nor tranquility in America until the Negro is granted his citizenship rights. The **whirlwinds** of revolt will continue to shake the foundations of our nation until the bright day of justice emerges.

8   But there is something that I must say to my people, who stand on the warm **threshold** which leads into the palace of justice: In the process of gaining our rightful place, we must not be guilty of wrongful deeds. Let us not seek to satisfy our thirst for freedom by drinking from the cup of bitterness and hatred. We must forever conduct our struggle on the high plane of dignity and discipline. We must not allow our creative protest to **degenerate** into physical violence. Again and again, we must rise to the **majestic** heights of meeting physical force with soul force.

9   The marvelous new **militancy** which has **engulfed** the Negro community must not lead us to a distrust of all white people, for many of our white brothers, as evidenced by their presence here today, have come to realize that their destiny is tied up with our destiny. And they have come to realize that their freedom is **inextricably** bound to our freedom.

10   We cannot walk alone.

11   And as we walk, we must make the **pledge** that we shall always march ahead.

12   We cannot turn back.

13   There are those who are asking the devotees of civil rights, "When will you be satisfied?" We can never be satisfied as long as the Negro is the victim of the unspeakable horrors of police brutality. We can never be satisfied as long as our bodies, heavy with the **fatigue** of travel, cannot gain lodging in the motels of the highways and the hotels of the cities. We cannot be satisfied as long as a Negro in Mississippi cannot vote and a Negro in New York believes he has nothing for which to vote. No, no, we are not satisfied, and we will not be satisfied until "justice rolls down like waters, and righteousness like a mighty stream."

14   I am not unmindful that some of you have come here out of great **trials and tribulations**. Some of you have come fresh from narrow jail cells. And some of you have come from areas where your quest—quest for freedom left you **battered** by the storms of persecution and **staggered** by the winds of police brutality. You have been the **veterans** of creative suffering. Continue to work with the faith that unearned suffering is **redemptive**. Go back to Mississippi, go back to Alabama, go back to South Carolina, go back to Georgia, go back to Louisiana, go back to the **slums** and **ghettos** of our northern cities, knowing that somehow this situation can and will be changed.

15   Let us not **wallow** in the valley of despair, I say to you today, my friends.

16   And so even though we face the difficulties of today and tomorrow, I still have a dream. It is a dream deeply rooted in the American dream.

17   I have a dream that one day this nation will rise up and live out the true meaning of its creed: "We hold these truths to be self-evident, that all men are created equal."

18   I have a dream that one day on the red hills of Georgia, the sons of former slaves and the sons of former slave owners will be able to sit down together at the table of brotherhood.

19   I have a dream that one day even the state of Mississippi, a state sweltering with the heat of injustice, sweltering with the heat of oppression, will be transformed into an **oasis** of freedom and justice.

20   I have a dream that my four little children will one day live in a nation where they will not be judged by the color of their skin but by the content of their character. I have a dream today.

21   I have a dream that one day, down in Alabama, with its **vicious** racists, with its governor having his lips **dripping** with the words of "**interposition**" and "**nullification**"—one day right there in Alabama little black boys and black girls will be able to join hands with little white boys and white girls as sisters and brothers. I have a dream today!

22   I have a dream that one day every valley shall be **exalted**, and every hill and mountain shall be made low, the rough places will be made plain, and the **crooked** places will be made straight; "and the glory of the Lord shall be revealed and all flesh shall see it together."

23   This is our hope, and this is the faith that I go back to the South with.

24   With this faith, we will be able to **hew out** of the mountain of despair a stone of hope. With this faith, we will be able to transform the **jangling discords** of our nation into a beautiful symphony of brotherhood. With this faith, we will be able to work together, to pray together, to struggle together, to go to jail together, to stand up for freedom together, knowing that we will be free one day.

25   And this will be the day—this will be the day when all of God's children will be able to sing with new meaning:

My country 'tis of thee, sweet land of liberty, of thee I sing.
Land where my fathers died, land of the Pilgrim's pride,

From every mountainside, let freedom ring!

And if America is to be a great nation, this must become true.

And so let freedom ring from the **prodigious** hilltops of New Hampshire.

Let freedom ring from the mighty mountains of New York.

Let freedom ring from the **heightening** Alleghenies of Pennsylvania.

Let freedom ring from the snow-capped Rockies of Colorado.

Let freedom ring from the **curvaceous** slopes of California.

26 But not only that:

Let freedom ring from Stone Mountain of Georgia.

Let freedom ring from Lookout Mountain of Tennessee.

Let freedom ring from every hill and **molehill** of Mississippi.

From every mountainside, let freedom ring.

27 And when this happens, when we allow freedom ring, when we let it ring from every village and every **hamlet**, from every state and every city, we will be able to speed up that day when all of God's children, black men and white men, Jews and **Gentiles**, Protestants and Catholics, will be able to join hands and sing in the words of the old Negro **spiritual**: Free at last! free at last!

28 Thank God Almighty, we are free at last!

Vocabulary

the Emancipation Proclamation	解放宣言
decree [diˈkriː] n.	a legally binding command or decision entered on the court record 法令
beacon [ˈbiːkən] n.	a tower with a light that gives warning of shoals to passing ships 灯塔,信号浮标,烽火,指路明灯
sear [siə] vt.	cause to wither or parch from exposure to heat 烧焦,使枯萎
withering [ˈwiðəriŋ] a.	wreaking or capable of wreaking complete destruction 干枯的,凋零的
captivity [kæpˈtiviti] n.	the state of being imprisoned 囚禁

manacle ['mænəkl] n.		shackle that consists of a metal loop that can be locked around the wrist; usually used in pairs 镣铐，手铐
segregation [ˌsegri'geiʃən] n.		a social system that provides separate facilities for minority groups 隔离
discrimination [diˌskrimi'neiʃən] n.		unfair treatment of a person or group on the basis of prejudice 歧视
in the midst of		在……之中
languish ['læŋgwiʃ] vi		lose vigor, health, or flesh, as through grief 憔悴，凋萎
exile ['eksail] n.		the act of expelling a person from their native land 流放
in a sense		在某种意义上
promissory note		本票，期票
heir [eə] n.		a person who is entitled by law or by the terms of a will to inherit the estate of another 继承人
unalienable [ʌn'eiliənəbəl] a.		incapable of being repudiated or transferred to another 不可剥夺的
default [di'fɔːlt] v.		if a person, company, or country defaults on something that they have legally agreed to do, such as paying some money or doing a piece of work before a particular time, they fail to do it 不履行
insofar [insə(u)'faː] ad.		to the degree or extent that 在……的范围下
sacred ['seikrid] a.		worthy of respect or dedication 神圣的
vault [vɔːlt] n.		地库
hallowed ['hæləud] a.		worthy of religious veneration 神圣的
tranquilizing drug		镇静剂
gradualism ['grædʒuəlizəm] n.		the belief in or the policy of change by gradual, often slow stages 渐进主义
desolate ['desələt] a.		providing no shelter or sustenance 荒凉的
quicksand ['kwiksænd] n.		a treacherous situation that tends to entrap and destroy 流沙
sweltering ['swelt(ə)riŋ] a.		excessively hot and humid or marked by sweating and faintness 闷热的
legitimate [lə'dʒitəmit] a.		authorized, sanctioned by, or in accordance with law 合法的
invigorating [in'vigəreitiŋ] a.		imparting strength and vitality 爽快的，精力充沛的
blow off steam		发泄，释放多余的压力
whirlwind ['wəːlwind] n.		a more or less vertical column of air whirling around itself as it moves over the surface of the Earth 旋风

threshold	[ˈθreʃhold] n.	the sill of a door; a horizontal piece of wood or stone that forms the bottom of a doorway and offers support when passing through a doorway 门槛
degenerate	[diˈdʒenəret] v.	grow worse 退化，恶化
majestic	[məˈdʒestik] a.	having or displaying great dignity or nobility 庄严的，宏伟的
militancy	[ˈmilitənsi] n.	a militant aggressiveness 交战状态
engulf	[inˈgʌlf] v.	flow over or cover completely 吞没
inextricably	[ˌinikˈstrikəbli] ad.	逃不掉地
pledge	[pledʒ] n.	a binding commitment to do or give or refrain from something 保证，誓言
fatigue	[fəˈtiːg] n.	temporary loss of strength and energy resulting from hard physical or mental work 疲劳
trials and tribulations		艰难困苦
battered	[ˈbætəd] a.	damaged by blows or hard usage 破旧的，磨损的，弄垮的，受到虐待的
stagger	[ˈstægə] v.	walk as if unable to control one's movements 蹒跚
veteran	[ˈvetərən] n.	an experienced person who has been through many battles; someone who has given long service 老兵
redemptive	[riˈdemptiv] a.	bringing about salvation or redemption from sin 赎回的
slum	[slʌm] n.	a district of a city marked by poverty and inferior living conditions 贫民窟
ghetto	[ˈgetəu] n.	a poor densely populated city district occupied by a minority ethnic group linked together by economic hardship and social restrictions 贫民区
wallow	[ˈwɔləu] vi.	devote oneself entirely to something; indulge in to an immoderate degree, usually with pleasure 沉迷
oasis	[əuˈeisis] n.	a fertile tract in a desert 绿洲
vicious	[ˈviʃəs] a.	marked by deep ill will; deliberately harmful 恶毒的，品行不端的
drip	[drip] v.	fall in drops 滴落下来
interposition	[intəpəˈziʃən] n.	the action of interjecting or interposing an action or remark that interrupts 干涉，介入
nullification	[ˌnʌlifiˈkeiʃən] n.	the act of nullifying; making null and void; counteracting or overriding the effect or force of something 废除，无效，〔美〕州对联邦法令的拒绝执行或承认
exalt	[igˈzɔlt] vi.	heighten or intensify 提升

crooked ['krukid] a.	having or marked by bends or angles; not straight or aligned 弯曲的
hew out	把……开采出;开辟出
jangling ['dʒæŋgl] a.	like the discordant ringing of nonmusical metallic objects striking together 刺耳的
discord ['diskɔːd] n.	lack of agreement or harmony 不和谐
prodigious [prə'didʒəs] a.	so great in size or force or extent as to elicit awe 巨大的
heightening ['haitniŋ] a.	reaching a higher intensity 升高的
curvaceous [kəː'veiʃəs] a.	曲线美的
molehill ['məulhil] n.	小山,小土堆
hamlet ['hæmlit] n.	a community of people smaller than a village 小村庄
Gentiles ['dʒentailz] n.	外邦人,异教徒,非犹太人(常指基督教徒)
spiritual ['spiritʃuəl] n.	圣歌(尤指美国南部黑人的)

II. Vocabulary Building

pre-: before, in advance

e. g. , preschool, prehistory, prepay, prebuilt, precaution, precedent, predict, predisposition, preoccupation, prerogative

post-: after

e. g. , postwar, postpone, postface, postgraduate, postmodernism, posterior, postmeridian, postliberation, postscript

ante-: before

e. g. , antedate, anterior, antecedent, antecede, antemeridian

II. Discussion

Discuss the following questions with your own words.

1. Why does King mention about Lincoln and the founder of the nation?

2. What is Martin Luther King, Jr. 's dream, and according to Dr. King how could it become a reality?

3. What examples of figurative language can be found in the text? And how do these uses enhance the overall impact of the speech?

4. In what specific ways does King call forth his experience as a preacher to lend persuasive power to the speech?

5. In his speech, how does Dr. King respond to the question, "When will you be satisfied?"

III. Translation A

Translate the following sentences selected from the text into Chinese.

1. Five score years ago, a great American, in whose symbolic shadow we stand today, signed the Emancipation Proclamation. This momentous decree came as a great beacon light of hope to millions of Negro slaves who had been seared in the flames of withering injustice. It came as a joyous daybreak to end the long night of their captivity. (Para. 2)

2. But one hundred years later, the Negro still is not free. One hundred years later, the life of the Negro is still sadly crippled by the manacles of segregation and the chains of discrimination. One hundred years later, the Negro lives on a lonely island of poverty in the midst of a vast ocean of material prosperity. One hundred years later, the Negro is still languished in the corners of American society and finds himself an exile in his own land. And so we've come here today to dramatize a shameful condition. (Para. 3)

3. We have also come to this hallowed spot to remind America of the fierce urgency of Now. This is no time to engage in the luxury of cooling off or to take the tranquilizing drug of gradualism. Now is the time to make real the promises of democracy. Now is the time to rise from the dark and desolate valley of segregation to the sunlit path of racial justice. Now is the time to lift our nation from the quicksands of racial injustice to the solid rock of brotherhood. Now is the time to make justice a reality for all of God's children. (Para. 6)

4. This sweltering summer of the Negro's legitimate discontent will not pass until there is an invigorating autumn of freedom and equality. Nineteen

sixty-three is not an end, but a beginning. And those who hope that the Negro needed to blow off steam and will now be content will have a rude awakening if the nation returns to business as usual. And there will be neither rest nor tranquility in America until the Negro is granted his citizenship rights. The whirlwinds of revolt will continue to shake the foundations of our nation until the bright day of justice emerges. (Para. 7)

5. There are those who are asking the devotees of civil rights, "When will you be satisfied?" We can never be satisfied as long as the Negro is the victim of the unspeakable horrors of police brutality. We can never be satisfied as long as our bodies, heavy with the fatigue of travel, cannot gain lodging in the motels of the highways and the hotels of the cities. We cannot be satisfied as long as a Negro in Mississippi cannot vote and a Negro in New York believes he has nothing for which to vote. No, no, we are not satisfied, and we will not be satisfied until "justice rolls down like waters, and righteousness like a mighty stream." (Para. 13)

IV. Translation B
Translate the following passage into Chinese.

For more than a quarter of a century in public life, I have shared in the turbulent history of this evening. I have fought for what I believe in. I have tried, to the best of my ability, to discharge those duties and meet those responsibilities that were entrusted to me. Sometimes I have succeeded. And sometimes I have failed. But always I have taken heart from what Theodore Roosevelt once said about the man in the arena, whose face is marred by dust and sweat and blood, who strives valiantly, who errs and comes short again and again because there is not effort without error and shortcoming, but who does actually strive to do the deed, who knows the great enthusiasms, the great devotions, who spends himself in a worthy cause, who at the best knows in the end the triumphs of high achievements and with the worst if he fails, at least fails while daring greatly. (Excerpted from Text B)

V. Writing Exercise

Please write a speech with the title "I Have a Dream, Too!"

Text B

Richard M. Nixon's Resignation Address[①]

Richard M. Nixon

Good evening:

1 This is the 37th time I have spoken to you from this office, where so many decisions have been made that shape the history of this nation. Each time I have done so to discuss with you some matter that I believe affected the national interest. In all the decisions I have made in my public life I have always tried to do what was best for the nation.

2 Throughout the long and difficult period of Watergate, I have felt it was my duty to **persevere**—to make every possible effort to complete the term of office to which you elected me. In the past few days, however, it has become evident to me that I no longer have a strong enough political base in the Congress to **justify** continuing that effort. As long as there was such a base, I felt strongly that it was necessary to see the constitutional process through to its conclusion? that to do otherwise would be unfaithful to the spirit of that deliberately difficult process, and a dangerously destabilizing precedent for the future. But with the disappearance of that base, I now believe that the constitutional purpose has been served. And there is no longer a need for the process to be prolonged.

---

① The speech was delivered on August 8, 1974.

3   I would have preferred to carry through to the finish whatever the personal **agony** it would have involved, and my family **unanimously** urged me to do so. But the interests of the nation must always come before any personal considerations.

4   From the discussions I have had with Congressional and other leaders I have concluded that because of the Watergate matter I might not have the support of the Congress that I would consider necessary to back the very difficult decisions and carry out the duties of this office in the way the interests of the nation will require.

5   I have never been a quitter.

6   To leave office before my term is completed is **abhorrent** to every instinct in my body. But as President, I must put the interests of America first.

7   America needs a fulltime President and a fulltime Congress, particularly at this time with problems we face at home and abroad. To continue to fight through the months ahead for my personal **vindication** would almost totally absorb the time and attention of both the President and the Congress in a period when our entire focus should be on the great issues of peace abroad and prosperity without inflation at home.

8   Therefore, I shall resign the Presidency effective at noon tomorrow.

9   Vice President Ford will be sworn in as President at that hour in this office.

10   As I recall the high hopes for America with which we began this second term, I feel a great sadness that I will not be here in this office working on your behalf to achieve those hopes in the next two and a half years. But in turning over direction of the Government to Vice President Ford I know, as I told the nation when I nominated him for that office ten months ago, that the leadership of America would be **in good hands.**

11   In passing this office to the Vice President, I also do so with the profound sense of the weight of responsibility that will fall on his shoulders

tomorrow, and therefore of the understanding, the patience, the cooperation he will need from all Americans. As he assumes that responsibility he will deserve the help and the support of all of us. As we look to the future, the first essential is to begin healing the wounds of this nation. To put the bitterness and divisions of the recent past behind us and to rediscover those shared ideals that lie at the heart of our strength and unity as a great and as a free people.

12   By taking this action, I hope that I will have hastened the start of that process of healing which is so desperately needed in America. I regret deeply any injuries that may have been done in the course of the events that led to this decision. I would say only that if some of my judgments were wrong, and some were wrong, they were made in what I believed at the time **to be the best interests of** the nation.

13   To those who have stood with me during these past difficult months, to my family, my friends, the many others who joined in supporting my cause because they believed it was right, I will be eternally grateful for your support. And to those who have not felt able to give me your support, let me say I leave with no bitterness toward those who have opposed me, because all of us in the final analysis have been concerned with the good of the country, however our judgments might differ.

14   So let us all now join together in affirming that common commitment and in helping our new President succeed for the benefit of all Americans. I shall leave this office with regret at not completing my term but with gratitude for the privilege of serving as your President for the past five and a half years. These years have been a momentous time in the history of our nation and the world. They have been a time of achievement in which we can all be proud, achievements that represent the shared efforts of the administration, the Congress and the people. But the challenges ahead are equally great. And they, too, will require the support and the efforts of the Congress and the

people, working in cooperation with the new Administration.

15   We have ended America's longest war. But in the work of securing a lasting peace in the world, the goals ahead are even more farreaching and more difficult. We must complete a structure of peace, so that it will be said of this generation—our generation of Americans—by the people of all nations, not only that we ended one war but that we prevented future wars.

16   We have unlocked the doors that for a quarter of a century stood between the United States and the People's Republic of China. We must now insure that the one-quarter of the world's people who live in the People's Republic of China will be and remain, not our enemies, but our friends.

17   In the Middle East, 100 million people in the Arab countries, many of whom have considered us their enemy for nearly 20 years, now look on us as their friends. We must continue to build on that friendship so that peace can settle at last over the Middle East and so that the **cradle** of civilization will not become its grave. Together with the Soviet Union we have made the crucial breakthroughs that have begun the process of limiting nuclear arms. But, we must set as our goal, not just limiting, but reducing and finally destroying these terrible weapons, so that they cannot destroy civilization. And so that the threat of nuclear war will no longer hang over the world and the people. We have opened a new relation with the Soviet Union. We must continue to develop and expand that new relationship, so that the two strongest nations of the world will live together in cooperation rather than confrontation.

18   Around the world—in Asia, in Africa, in Latin America, in the Middle East—there are millions of people who live in terrible poverty, even starvation. We must keep as our goal turning away from production for war and expanding production for peace so that people everywhere on this earth can at last look forward, in their children's time, if not in our own time, to having the necessities for a **decent** life. Here, in America, we are fortunate

that most of our people have not only the blessings of liberty but also the means to live full and good, and by the world's standards even abundant lives.

19   We must **press on**, however, toward a goal not only of more and better jobs but of full opportunity for every American, and of what we are striving so hard right now to achieve—prosperity without **inflation.**

20   For more than a quarter of a century in public life, I have shared in the **turbulent** history of this evening. I have fought for what I believe in. I have tried, to the best of my ability, to discharge those duties and meet those responsibilities that were entrusted to me. Sometimes I have succeeded. And sometimes I have failed. But always I have **taken heart from** what Theodore Roosevelt once said about the man in the arena, whose face is **marred** by dust and sweat and blood, who strives **valiantly**, who **errs** and **comes short** again and again because there is not effort without error and shortcoming, but who does actually strive to do the deed, who knows the great enthusiasms, the great devotions, who spends himself in a worthy cause, who at the best knows in the end the triumphs of high achievements and with the worst if he fails, at least fails while daring greatly.

21   I pledge to you tonight that as long as I have a breath of life in my body, I shall continue in that spirit. I shall continue to work for the great causes to which I have been dedicated throughout my years as a Congressman, a Senator, Vice President and President, the cause of peace—not just for America but among all nations—prosperity, justice and opportunity for all of our people.

22   There is one cause above all to which I have been devoted and to which I shall always be devoted for as long as I live.

23   When I first took the **oath** of office as President five and a half years ago, I made this sacred commitment: to **consecrate** my office, my energies, and all the wisdom I can **summon** to the cause of peace among nations. I've

done my very best in all the days since to be true to that pledge. As a result of these efforts, I am confident that the world is a safer place today, not only for the people of America but for the people of all nations, and that all of our children have a better chance than before of living in peace rather than dying in war.

24   This, more than anything, is what I hoped to achieve when I sought the Presidency.

25   This, more than anything, is what I hope will be my legacy to you, to our country, as I leave the Presidency.

26   To have served in this office is to have felt a very personal sense of **kinship** with each and every American.

27   In leaving it, I do so with this prayer: May God's grace be with you in all the days ahead.

Vocabulary

persevere [pə:si'viə] vi.	be persistent, refuse to stop 坚持,不屈不挠
justify ['dʒʌstifai] v.	show to be reasonable or provide adequate ground for 证明合法,证明……是正当的
agony ['ægəni] n.	intense feelings of suffering; acute mental or physical pain 极大的痛苦
unanimously [ju:'næniməsli] ad.	of one mind; without dissent 全体一致地
abhorrent [əb'hɔr(ə)nt] a.	offensive to the mind 厌恶的
vindication [,vindi'keiʃən] n.	the justification for some act or belief 辩护,证明无罪
in good hands	在行内人的手里,被照看得很好
to be the best interests of	最符合……的利益
cradle ['kreid(ə)l] n.	where something originated or was nurtured in its early existence 摇篮,发源地
decent ['di:s(ə)nt] a.	socially or conventionally correct; refined or virtuous 好的,得体的
press on	向前推进
inflation [in'fleiʃ(ə)n] n.	a general and progressive increase in prices 通货膨胀
turbulent ['tə:bjul(ə)nt] n.	characterized by unrest or disorder or insubordination 骚乱的,混乱的,狂暴的

take heart from	获得勇气,获得启发
mar [mɑː] vt.	destroy or injure severely 损毁,损伤
valiantly [ˈvæljəntli] ad.	with valor; in a valiant manner 勇敢地,英勇地
err [əː] vi.	to make a mistake or be incorrect 犯错,做错,犯罪
come short	缺乏,不足
oath [əuθ] n.	a solemn promise, usually invoking a divine witness, regarding your future acts or behavior 誓言
consecrate [ˈkɔnsikreit] vt.	give entirely to a specific person, activity, or cause 奉献,献身于
summon [ˈsʌmən] vt.	ask to come 召唤,召集
kinship [ˈkinʃip] n.	a close connection marked by community of interests or similarity in nature or character 亲属关系,家属关系,亲密关系

Text C

We Shall Fight on the Beaches①

Winston Churchill

House of Commons:

1   The position of the B. E. F② had now become critical As a result of a most skillfully conducted retreat and German errors, the bulk of the British Forces reached the Dunkirk bridgehead. The **peril** facing the British nation was now suddenly and universally perceived. On May 26, "**Operation Dynamo**"—the **evacuation** from Dunkirk began. The seas remained absolutely calm. The Royal Air Force—bitterly **maligned** at the time by the Army—fought **vehemently** to deny the enemy the total air supremacy which would

---

① The speech was delivered on June 4, 1940.
② British Expeditionary Force.

have wrecked the operation. At the outset, it was hoped that 45,000 men might be evacuated; in the event, over 338,000 Allied troops reached England, including 26,000 French soldiers. On June 4, Churchill reported to the House of Commons, seeking to check the mood of national **euphoria** and relief at the unexpected deliverance, and to make a clear appeal to the United States.

2. From the moment that the French defenses at Sedan and on the Meuse were broken at the end of the second week of May, only a rapid retreat to Amiens and the south could have saved the British and French Armies who had entered Belgium at the appeal of the Belgian King; but this strategic fact was not immediately realized. The French High Command hoped they would be able to close the gap, and the Armies of the north were **under their orders**. Moreover, a retirement of this kind would have involved almost certainly the destruction of the fine Belgian Army of over 20 divisions and the abandonment of the whole of Belgium. Therefore, when the force and scope of the German penetration were realized and when a new French **Generalissimo**, General Weygand, assumed command in place of General Gamelin, an effort was made by the French and British Armies in Belgium to keep on holding the right hand of the Belgians and to give their own right hand to a newly created French Army which was to have advanced across the Somme in great strength to grasp it.

3. However, the German eruption swept like a sharp **scythe** around the right and rear of the Armies of the north. Eight or nine armored divisions, each of about four hundred armored vehicles of different kinds, but carefully **assorted** to be complementary and divisible into small self-contained units, cut off all communications between us and the main French Armies. It severed our own communications for food and **ammunition**, which ran first to Amiens and afterwards through Abbeville, and it **shore its way up** the coast to Boulogne and Calais, and almost to Dunkirk. Behind this armored and

mechanized onslaught came a number of German divisions in **lorries**, and behind them again there plodded comparatively slowly the dull brute mass of the ordinary German Army and German people, always so ready to be led to the trampling down in other lands of liberties and comforts which they have never known in their own.

<u>4</u> I have said this armored scythe—stroke almost reached Dunkirk—almost but not quite. Boulogne and Calais were the scenes of desperate fighting. The Guards defended Boulogne for a while and were then withdrawn by orders from this country. The Rifle Brigade, the 60th Rifles, and the Queen Victoria's Rifles, with a **battalion** of British tanks and 1,000 Frenchmen, in all about four thousand strong, defended Calais to the last. The British **Brigadier** was given an hour to surrender. He **spurned** the offer, and four days of intense street fighting passed before silence reigned over Calais, which marked the end of a memorable resistance. Only 30 unwounded survivors were brought off by the Navy, and we do not know the fate of their comrades. Their sacrifice, however, was not in vain. At least two armored divisions, which otherwise would have been turned against the British Expeditionary Force, had to be sent to overcome them. They have added another page to the glories of the light divisions, and the time gained enabled the Graveline water lines to be flooded and to be held by the French troops.

<u>5</u> Thus it was that the port of Dunkirk was kept open. When it was found impossible for the Armies of the north to reopen their communications to Amiens with the main French Armies, only one choice remained. It seemed, indeed, **forlorn**. The Belgian, British and French Armies were almost surrounded. Their sole line of retreat was to a single port and to its neighboring beaches. They were pressed on every side by heavy attacks and far outnumbered in the air.

<u>6</u> When, a week ago today, I asked the House to fix this afternoon as the occasion for a statement, I feared it would be my hard lot to announce the

greatest military disaster in our long history. I thought—and some good judges agreed with me—that perhaps 20,000 or 30,000 men might be re-embarked. But it certainly seemed that the whole of the French First Army and the whole of the British Expeditionary Force north of the Amiens-Abbeville gap would be broken up in the open field or else would have to **capitulate** for lack of food and ammunition. These were the hard and heavy tidings for which I called upon the House and the nation to prepare themselves a week ago. The whole root and core and brain of the British Army, on which and around which we were to build, and are to build, the great British Armies in the later years of the war, seemed about to perish upon the field or to be led into an **ignominious** and starving captivity.

<u>7</u> That was the prospect a week ago. But another blow which might well have proved final was yet to fall upon us. The King of the Belgians had called upon us to come to his aid. Had not this Ruler and his Government severed themselves from the Allies, who rescued their country from extinction in the late war, and had they not sought refuge in what was proved to be a fatal neutrality, the French and British Armies might well at the outset have saved not only Belgium but perhaps even Poland. Yet at the last moment, when Belgium was already invaded, King Leopold called upon us to come to his aid, and even at the last moment we came. He and his brave, efficient Army, nearly half a million strong, guarded our left **flank** and thus kept open our only line of retreat to the sea. Suddenly, without prior consultation, with the least possible notice, without the advice of his Ministers and upon his own personal act, he sent a **plenipotentiary** to the German Command, surrendered his Army, and exposed our whole flank and means of retreat.

<u>8</u> I asked the House a week ago to suspend its judgment because the facts were not clear, but I do not feel that any reason now exists why we should not form our own opinions upon this pitiful episode. The surrender of the Belgian Army compelled the British at the shortest notice to cover a flank to

the sea more than 30 miles in length. Otherwise all would have been cut off, and all would have shared the fate to which King Leopold had condemned the finest Army his country had ever formed. So in doing this and in exposing this flank, as anyone who followed the operations on the map will see, contact was lost between the British and two out of the three corps forming the First French Army, who were still farther from the coast than we were, and it seemed impossible that any large number of Allied troops could reach the coast.

9 The enemy attacked on all sides with great strength and fierceness, and their main power, the power of their far more numerous Air Force, was thrown into the battle or else concentrated upon Dunkirk and the beaches. Pressing in upon the narrow exit, both from the east and from the west, the enemy began to fire with cannon upon the beaches by which alone the shipping could approach or depart. They **sowed** magnetic mines in the channels and seas; they sent repeated waves of hostile aircraft, sometimes more than a hundred strong in one formation, to cast their bombs upon the single **pier** that remained, and upon the sand dunes upon which the troops had their eyes for shelter. Their U-boats, one of which was sunk, and their motor launches took their toll of the vast traffic which now began. For four or five days an intense struggle reigned. All their armored divisions—or what Was left of them—together with great masses of **infantry** and **artillery**, hurled themselves in vain upon the ever-narrowing, ever-contracting appendix within which the British and French Armies fought.

10 Meanwhile, the Royal Navy, with the willing help of countless merchant seamen, **strained every nerve** to embark the British and Allied troops; 220 light warships and 650 other vessels were engaged. They had to operate upon the difficult coast, often in adverse weather, under an almost ceaseless hail of bombs and an increasing concentration of artillery fire. Nor were the seas, as I have said, themselves free from mines and **torpedoes**. It was in conditions

such as these that our men carried on, with little or no rest, for days and nights on end, making trip after trip across the dangerous waters, bringing with them always men whom they had rescued. The numbers they have brought back are the measure of their devotion and their courage. The hospital ships, which brought off many thousands of British and French wounded, being so plainly marked were a special target for Nazi bombs; but the men and women on board them never **faltered** in their duty.

11   Meanwhile, the Royal Air Force, which had already been intervening in the battle, so far as its range would allow, from home bases, now used part of its main metropolitan fighter strength, and struck at the German bombers and at the fighters which in large numbers protected them. This struggle was **protracted** and fierce. Suddenly the scene has cleared, the crash and thunder has for the moment—but only for the moment—died away. A miracle of **deliverance**, achieved by **valor**, by perseverance, by perfect discipline, by faultless service, by resource, by skill, by unconquerable **fidelity**, is manifest to us all. The enemy was hurled back by the retreating British and French troops. He was so roughly handled that he did not hurry their departure seriously. The Royal Air Force engaged the main strength of the German Air Force, and **inflicted** upon them losses of at least four to one; and the Navy, using nearly 1,000 ships of all kinds, carried over 335,000 men, French and British, out of **the jaws of death** and shame, to their native land and to the tasks which lie immediately ahead. We must be very careful not to assign to this deliverance the attributes of a victory. Wars are not won by **evacuations**. But there was a victory inside this deliverance, which should be noted. It was gained by the Air Force. Many of our soldiers coming back have not seen the Air Force at work; they saw only the bombers which escaped its protective attack. They underrate its achievements. I have heard much talk of this; that is why **I go out of my way** to say this. I will tell you about it.

12   This was a great trial of strength between the British and German Air

Forces. Can you conceive a greater objective for the Germans in the air than to make evacuation from these beaches impossible, and to sink all these ships which were displayed, almost to the extent of thousands? Could there have been an objective of greater military importance and significance for the whole purpose of the war than this? They tried hard, and they were beaten back; they were frustrated in their task. We got the Army away; and they have paid fourfold for any losses which they have inflicted. Very large formations of German aeroplanes—and we know that they are a very brave race—have turned on several occasions from the attack of one-quarter of their number of the Royal Air Force, and have dispersed in different directions. Twelve aeroplanes have been hunted by two. One aeroplane was driven into the water and cast away by the mere charge of a British aeroplane, which had no more ammunition. All of our types—the Hurricane, the Spitfire and the new Defiant—and all our pilots have been **vindicated** as superior to what they have at present to face.

13 When we consider how much greater would be our advantage in defending the air above this Island against an overseas attack, I must say that I find in these facts a sure basis upon which practical and reassuring thoughts may rest. I will pay my tribute to these young airmen. The great French Army was very largely, for the time being, cast back and disturbed by the **onrush** of a few thousands of armored vehicles. May it not also be that the cause of civilization itself will be defended by the skill and devotion of a few thousand airmen? There never has been, I suppose, in all the world, in all the history of war, such an opportunity for youth. The Knights of the Round Table, the Crusaders, all fall back into the past—not only distant but **prosaic**; these young men, going forth every morn to guard their native land and all that we stand for, holding in their hands these instruments of **colossal** and shattering power, of whom it may be said that

Every morn brought forth a noble chance

And every chance brought forth a noble knight,

deserve our gratitude, as do all the brave men who, in so many ways and on so many occasions, are ready, and continue ready to give life and all for their native land.

14   I return to the Army. In the long series of very fierce battles, now on this front, now on that, fighting on three fronts at once, battles fought by two or three divisions against an equal or somewhat larger number of the enemy, and fought fiercely on some of the old grounds that so many of us knew so well—in these battles our losses in men have exceeded 30,000 killed, wounded and missing. I take occasion to express the sympathy of the House to all who have suffered **bereavement** or who are still anxious. The President of the Board of Trade [Sir Andrew Duncan] is not here today. His son has been killed, and many in the House have felt the **pangs** of affliction in the sharpest form. But I will say this about the missing: We have had a large number of wounded come home safely to this country, but I would say about the missing that there may be very many reported missing who will come back home, some day, in one way or another. In the confusion of this fight it is inevitable that many have been left in positions where honor required no further resistance from them.

15   Against this loss of over 30,000 men, we can set a far heavier loss certainly inflicted upon the enemy. But our losses in material are enormous. We have perhaps lost one-third of the men we lost in the opening days of the battle of 21st March, 1918, but we have lost nearly as many guns—nearly one thousand—and all our transport, all the armored vehicles that were with the Army in the north. This loss will impose a further delay on the expansion of our military strength. That expansion had not been proceeding as far as we had hoped. The best of all we had to give had gone to the British Expeditionary Force, and although they had not the numbers of tanks and some articles of equipment which were desirable, they were a very well and

finely equipped Army. They had the first-fruits of all that our industry had to give, and that is gone. And now here is this further delay. How long it will be, how long it will last, depends upon the exertions which we make in this Island. An effort the like of which has never been seen in our records is now being made. Work is proceeding everywhere, night and day, Sundays and week days. Capital and Labor have cast aside their interests, rights, and customs and put them into the common stock. Already the flow of munitions has leaped forward. There is no reason why we should not in a few months overtake the sudden and serious loss that has come upon us, without retarding the development of our general program.

16 Nevertheless, our thankfulness at the escape of our Army and so many men, whose loved ones have passed through an agonizing week, must not blind us to the fact that what has happened in France and Belgium is a colossal military disaster. The French Army has been weakened, the Belgian Army has been lost, a large part of those fortified lines upon which so much faith had been reposed is gone, many valuable mining districts and factories have passed into the enemy's possession, the whole of the Channel ports are in his hands, with all the tragic consequences that follow from that, and we must expect another blow to be struck almost immediately at us or at France. We are told that **Herr** Hitler has a plan for invading the British Isles. This has often been thought of before. When Napoleon lay at Boulogne for a year with his flat-bottomed boats and his Grand Army, he was told by someone, "There are bitter weeds in England." There are certainly a great many more of them since the British Expeditionary Force returned.

17 The whole question of home defense against invasion is, of course, powerfully affected by the fact that we have for the time being in this Island incomparably more powerful military forces than we have ever had at any moment in this war or the last. But this will not continue. We shall not be content with a defensive war. We have our duty to our Ally. We have to

reconstitute and build up the British Expeditionary Force once again, under its **gallant** Commander-in-Chief, Lord Gort. All this is in train; but in the interval we must put our defenses in this Island into such a high state of organization that the fewest possible numbers will be required to give effective security and that the largest possible potential of offensive effort may be realized. On this we are now engaged. It will be very convenient, if it be the desire of the House, to enter upon this subject in a secret Session. Not that the government would necessarily be able to reveal in very great detail military secrets, but we like to have our discussions free, without the restraint imposed by the fact that they will be read the next day by the enemy; and the Government would benefit by views freely expressed in all parts of the House by Members with their knowledge of so many different parts of the country. I understand that some request is to be made upon this subject, which will be readily **acceded** to by His Majesty's Government.

<u>18</u>   We have found it necessary to take measures of increasing **stringency**, not only against enemy aliens and suspicious characters of other nationalities, but also against British subjects who may become a danger or a nuisance should the war be transported to the United Kingdom. I know there are a great many people affected by the orders which we have made who are the passionate enemies of Nazi Germany. I am very sorry for them, but we cannot, at the present time and under the present stress, draw all the distinctions which we should like to do. If **parachute** landings were attempted and fierce fighting attendant upon them followed, these unfortunate people would be far better out of the way, for their own sakes as well as for ours. There is, however, another class, for which I feel not the slightest sympathy. Parliament has given us the powers to put down Fifth Column activities with a strong hand, and we shall use those powers subject to the supervision and correction of the House, without the slightest hesitation until we are satisfied, and more than satisfied, that this **malignancy** in our

midst has been effectively **stamped out.**

19 Turning once again, and this time more generally, to the question of invasion, I would observe that there has never been a period in all these long centuries of which we boast when an absolute guarantee against invasion, still less against serious raids, could have been given to our people. In the days of Napoleon the same wind which would have carried his transports across the Channel might have driven away the blockading fleet. There was always the chance, and it is that chance which has excited and befooled the imaginations of many Continental tyrants. Many are the tales that are told. We are assured that novel methods will be adopted, and when we see the originality of malice, the ingenuity of aggression, which our enemy displays, we may certainly prepare ourselves for every kind of novel **stratagem** and every kind of brutal and **treacherous maneuver.** I think that no idea is so **outlandish** that it should not be considered and viewed with a searching, but at the same time, I hope, with a steady eye. We must never forget the solid assurances of sea power and those which belong to air power if it can be locally exercised.

20 I have, myself, full confidence that if all do their duty, if nothing is neglected, and if the best arrangements are made, as they are being made, we shall prove ourselves once again able to defend our Island home, to **ride out** the storm of war, and to outlive the menace of tyranny, if necessary for years, if necessary alone. At any rate, that is what we are going to try to do. That is the resolve of His Majesty's Government—every man of them. That is the will of Parliament and the nation. The British Empire and the French Republic, linked together in their cause and in their need, will defend to the death their native soil, aiding each other like good comrades to the utmost of their strength. Even though large tracts of Europe and many old and famous States have fallen or may fall into the grip of the Gestapo and all the **odious apparatus** of Nazi rule, we shall not flag or fail. We shall go on to the end,

we shall fight in France, we shall fight on the seas and oceans, we shall fight with growing confidence and growing strength in the air, we shall defend our Island, whatever the cost may be, we shall fight on the beaches, we shall fight on the landing grounds, we shall fight in the fields and in the streets, we shall fight in the hills; we shall never surrender, and even if, which I do not for a moment believe, this Island or a large part of it were **subjugated** and starving, then our Empire beyond the seas, armed and guarded by the British Fleet, would carry on the struggle, until, in God's good time, the New World, with all its power and might, steps forth to the rescue and the liberation of the old.

Vocabulary

peril ['perəl] n.	a venture undertaken without regard to possible loss or injury 危险,冒险
Operation Dynamo	"发电机"作战计划
evacuation [i,vækju'eʃən] n.	the act of evacuating; leaving a place in an orderly fashion; especially for protection 撤退
malign [mə'lain] vt.	speak unfavorably about 诽谤,污蔑
vehemently ['viəməntli] ad.	in a vehement manner 竭尽全力地
euphoria [juː'fɔːriə] n.	a feeling of great (usually exaggerated) elation 兴高采烈
under orders	奉命
Generalissimo [,dʒenərə'lisiməu] n.	the officer who holds the supreme command 总司令,大元帅
scythe [saið] n.	an edge tool for cutting grass; has a long handle that must be held with both hands and a curved blade that moves parallel to the ground 长柄大镰刀
assort [ə'sɔːt] vt.	arrange or order by classes or categories 分级,归为一类
ammunition [,æmju'niʃ(ə)n] n.	projectiles to be fired from a gun 弹药,军火
shore up	支撑,加固
lorry ['lɔri] n.	a large truck designed to carry heavy loads; usually without sides 卡车,货车
battalion [bə'tæliən] n.	an army unit usually consisting of a headquarters and three or more companies 营,军营,军队,部队
Brigadier [,brigə'diə] n.	a general officer ranking below a major general 陆军准将

spurn [spə:n] vt.	reject with contempt 唾弃
forlorn [fə'lɔ:n] a.	marked by or showing hopelessness 被遗弃的
capitulate [kə'pitjuleit] vi.	surrender under agreed conditions 屈服，认输，有条件投降
ignominious [,ignə'miniəs] a.	(used of conduct or character) deserving or bringing disgrace or shame 可耻的
flank [flæŋk] n.	the side of military or naval formation 侧翼
plenipotentiary [,plenipə'tenʃəri] n.	a diplomat who is fully authorized to represent his or her government 全权代表
sow [səu] vt.	place (seeds) in or on the ground for future growth 散布，使密布
pier [piə] n.	a platform built out from the shore into the water and supported by piles; provides access to ships and boats 码头
infantry ['infəntri] n.	an army unit consisting of soldiers who fight on foot 步兵团
artillery [ɑ:'tiləri] n.	large but transportable armament 大炮
strain every nerve	竭力
torpedo [tɔ:'pi:dəu] n.	鱼雷
falter ['fɔ:ltə] v.	the act of pausing uncertainly 迟疑，退缩
protracted [prə'træktid] a.	relatively long in duration 拖延的
deliverance [di'livərəns] n.	recovery or preservation from loss or danger 释放，解救
valor ['vælə] n.	the qualities of a hero or heroine; exceptional or heroic courage when facing danger (especially in battle) 英勇
fidelity [fi'deliti] n.	the quality of being faithful 忠诚
inflict [in'flikt] vt.	impose something unpleasant 给予打击
the jaws of death	鬼门关
evacuation [i,vækju'eiʃən] n.	the act of removing the contents of something 疏散
go out of one's way	特地的，不怕麻烦的
vindicate ['vindikeit] vt.	show to be right by providing justification or proof 证明……正确，证明……无辜
onrush ['ɔnrʌʃ] n.	(military) an offensive against an enemy (using weapons) 突袭
prosaic [prə'zeik] a.	not fanciful or imaginative 平凡的
colossal [kə'lɔsl] a.	so great in size or force or extent as to elicit awe 巨大的
bereavement [bi'ri:vmənt] n.	state of sorrow over the death or departure of a loved one 丧失亲人

pang [pæŋ] n.   a sudden sharp feeling 剧痛；苦闷
Herr [hɛə] n.   〔德〕先生
gallant ['gælənt] a.   having or displaying great dignity or nobility 英勇的
accede [əkˈsiːd] vi.   take on duties or office 加入，同意
stringency ['strinʤənsi] n.   conscientious attention to rules and details 严格，说服力
parachute ['pærəˈʃut] n.   rescue equipment consisting of a device that fills with air and retards your fall 降落伞
malignancy [məˈlignənsi] n.   quality of being disposed to evil; intense ill will 恶意
stamp out   扑灭
stratagem ['strætəʤəm] n.   an elaborate or deceitful scheme contrived to deceive or evade 策略，计谋
treacherous ['tretʃərəs] a.   dangerously unstable and unpredictable 危险的
maneuver [məˈnuvə] n.   a military training exercise 演习，调遣
outlandish [ˌautˈlændiʃ] a.   conspicuously or grossly unconventional or unusual 古怪的
ride out   安全度过
odious ['əudiəs] a.   unequivocally detestable 可憎的
apparatus [ˌæpəˈreitəs] n.   equipment designed to serve a specific function 装置，设备
subjugated ['sʌbdʒugeitid] a.   reduced to submission 屈服的

Unit 8

Literature

Text A A Rose for Emily
Text B Solitude
Text C The Waste Land

Text A

A Rose for Emily[①]

William Faulkner

I

1 When Miss Emily Grierson died, our whole town went to her funeral: the men through a sort of respectful affection for a fallen monument, the women mostly out of curiosity to see the inside of her house, which no one save an old man-servant—a combined gardener and cook—had seen in at least ten years.

2 It was a big, squarish frame house that had once been white, decorated with **cupolas** and spires and **scrolled** balconies in the heavily lightsome style of the seventies, set on what had once been our most select street. But garages and cotton gins had **encroached** and **obliterated** even the **august** names of that

---

① Excerpted from William Faulkner's short story collection *These 13*.

neighborhood; only Miss Emily's house was left, lifting its stubborn and coquettish decay above the cotton wagons and the gasoline pumps—an eyesore among eyesores. And now Miss Emily had gone to join the representatives of those august names where they lay in the **cedar-bemused** cemetery among the ranked and anonymous graves of Union and Confederate soldiers who fell at the battle of Jefferson.

3   Alive, Miss Emily had been a tradition, a duty, and a care; a sort of hereditary obligation upon the town, dating from that day in 1894 when Colonel Sartoris, the mayor—he who fathered the edict that no Negro woman should appear on the streets without an apron—**remitted** her taxes, the **dispensation** dating from the death of her father on into perpetuity. Not that Miss Emily would have accepted charity. Colonel Sartoris invented an involved tale to the effect that Miss Emily's father had loaned money to the town, which the town, as a matter of business, preferred this way of repaying. Only a man of Colonel Sartoris' generation and thought could have invented it, and only a woman could have believed it.

4/5   When the next generation, with its more modern ideas, became mayors and **aldermen**, this arrangement created some little dissatisfaction. On the first of the year they mailed her a tax notice. February came, and there was no reply. They wrote her a formal letter, asking her to call at the sheriff's office at her convenience. A week later the mayor wrote her himself, offering to call or to send his car for her, and received in reply a note on paper of an **archaic** shape, in a thin, flowing calligraphy in faded ink, to the effect that she no longer went out at all. The tax notice was also enclosed, without comment.

5   They called a special meeting of the Board of Aldermen. A deputation waited upon her, knocked at the door through which no visitor had passed since she ceased giving china-painting lessons eight or ten years earlier. They were admitted by the old Negro into a dim hall from which a stairway mounted into still more shadow. It smelled of dust and disuse—a close, **dank** smell. The Negro led them into the **parlor**. It was furnished in heavy, leather-covered furniture. When the Negro opened the blinds of one window, they could see that the leather was cracked; and when they sat down, a faint dust rose **sluggishly** about their thighs, spinning with slow motes in the single sun-ray. On a **tarnished** gilt easel before the fireplace stood a crayon portrait of Miss Emily's father.

6   They rose when she entered—a small, fat woman in black, with a thin gold chain descending to her waist and vanishing into her belt, leaning on an **ebony** cane with a tarnished gold head. Her skeleton was small and spare; perhaps that was why what would have been merely **plumpness** in another was obesity in her. She looked bloated, like a body long submerged in motionless water, and of that **pallid** hue. Her eyes, lost in the fatty ridges of her face, looked like two small pieces of coal pressed into a lump of dough as they moved from one face to another while the visitors stated their errand.

7   She did not ask them to sit. She just stood in the door and listened quietly until the spokesman came to a stumbling halt. Then they could hear the invisible watch ticking at the end of the gold chain.

8   Her voice was dry and cold. "I have no taxes in Jefferson. Colonel Sartoris explained it to me. Perhaps one of you can gain access to the city records and satisfy yourselves."

9   "But we have. We are the city authorities, Miss Emily. Didn't you get a notice from the sheriff, signed by him?"

10   "I received a paper, yes," Miss Emily said. "Perhaps he considers himself the sheriff . . . I have no taxes in Jefferson."

11   "But there is nothing on the books to show that, you see We must go by the—"

12   "See Colonel Sartoris. I have no taxes in Jefferson."

13   "But, Miss Emily—"

14   "See Colonel Sartoris." (Colonel Sartoris had been dead almost ten years.) "I have no taxes in Jefferson. Tobe!" The Negro appeared. "Show these gentlemen out."

II

15   So she vanquished them, horse and foot, just as she had **vanquished** their fathers thirty years before about the smell.

16   That was two years after her father's death and a short time after her sweetheart—the one we believed would marry her—had deserted her. After her father's death she went out very little; after her sweetheart went away, people hardly saw her at all. A few of the ladies had the **temerity** to call, but were not received, and the only sign of life about the place was the Negro man—a young man then—going in and out with a market basket.

17   "Just as if a man—any man—could keep a kitchen properly," the ladies said; so they were not surprised when the smell developed. It was another link between the gross, **teeming** world and the high and mighty Griersons.

18   A neighbor, a woman, complained to the mayor, Judge Stevens, eighty years old.

19   "But what will you have me do about it, madam?" he said.

20   "Why, send her word to stop it," the woman said. "Isn't there a law?"

21   "I'm sure that won't be necessary," Judge Stevens said. "It's probably just a snake or a rat that nigger of hers killed in the yard. I'll speak to him about it."

22   The next day he received two more complaints, one from a man who came in **diffident deprecation**. "We really must do something about it, Judge. I'd be the last one in the world to bother Miss Emily, but we've got to do something." That night the Board of Aldermen met—three graybeards and one younger man, a member of the rising generation.

23   "It's simple enough," he said. "Send her word to have her place cleaned

up. Give her a certain time to do it in, and if she don't..."

24 "Dammit, sir," Judge Stevens said, "will you accuse a lady to her face of smelling bad?"

25 So the next night, after midnight, four men crossed Miss Emily's lawn and **slunk** about the house like burglars, sniffing along the base of the brickwork and at the cellar openings while one of them performed a regular sowing motion with his hand out of a sack slung from his shoulder. They broke open the cellar door and **sprinkled** lime there, and in all the outbuildings. As they recrossed the lawn, a window that had been dark was lighted and Miss Emily sat in it, the light behind her, and her upright torso motionless as that of an idol. They crept quietly across the lawn and into the shadow of the locusts that lined the street. After a week or two the smell went away.

26 That was when people had begun to feel really sorry for her. People in our town, remembering how old lady Wyatt, her great-aunt, had gone completely crazy at last, believed that the Griersons held themselves a little too high for what they really were. None of the young men were quite good enough for Miss Emily and such. We had long thought of them as a tableau, Miss Emily a slender figure in white in the background, her father a spraddled **silhouette** in the foreground, his back to her and clutching a horsewhip, the two of them framed by the back-**flung** front door. So when she got to be thirty and was still single, we were not pleased exactly, but **vindicated**; even with **insanity** in the family she wouldn't have turned down all of her chances if they had really materialized.

27 When her father died, it got about that the house was all that was left to her; and in a way, people were glad. At last they could pity Miss Emily. Being left alone, and a pauper, she had become humanized. Now she too would know the old thrill and the old despair of a penny more or less.

28 The day after his death all the ladies prepared to call at the house and

offer condolence and aid, as is our custom Miss Emily met them at the door, dressed as usual and with no trace of grief on her face. She told them that her father was not dead. She did that for three days, with the ministers calling on her, and the doctors, trying to persuade her to let them dispose of the body. Just as they were about to resort to law and force, she broke down, and they buried her father quickly.

29   We did not say she was crazy then. We believed she had to do that. We remembered all the young men her father had driven away, and we knew that with nothing left, she would have to cling to that which had robbed her, as people will.

III

30   She was sick for a long time. When we saw her again, her hair was cut short, making her look like a girl, with a vague resemblance to those angels in colored church windows—sort of tragic and **serene.**

31   The town had just let the contracts for paving the sidewalks, and in the summer after her father's death they began the work. The construction company came with riggers and mules and machinery, and a foreman named Homer Barron, a Yankee—a big, dark, ready man, with a big voice and eyes lighter than his face. The little boys would follow in groups to hear him cuss the riggers, and the riggers singing in time to the rise and fall of picks. Pretty soon he knew everybody in town. Whenever you heard a lot of laughing anywhere about the square, Homer Barron would be in the center of the group. Presently we began to see him and Miss Emily on Sunday afternoons driving in the yellow-wheeled buggy and the matched team of bays from the livery stable.

32   At first we were glad that Miss Emily would have an interest, because the ladies all said, "Of course a Grierson would not think seriously of a Northerner, a day laborer." But there were still others, older people, who

said that even grief could not cause a real lady to forget noblesse oblige—without calling it *noblesse oblige*. They just said, "Poor Emily. Her kinsfolk should come to her." She had some kin in Alabama; but years ago her father had fallen out with them over the estate of old lady Wyatt, the crazy woman, and there was no communication between the two families. They had not even been represented at the funeral.

33   And as soon as the old people said, "Poor Emily," the whispering began. "Do you suppose it's really so?" they said to one another. "Of course it is. What else could..." This behind their hands; rustling of craned silk and satin behind **jalousies** closed upon the sun of Sunday afternoon as the thin, swift clop-clop-clop of the matched team passed: "Poor Emily."

34   She carried her head high enough—even when we believed that she was fallen. It was as if she demanded more than ever the recognition of her dignity as the last Grierson; as if it had wanted that touch of earthiness to reaffirm her **imperviousness**. Like when she bought the rat poison, the **arsenic**. That was over a year after they had begun to say "Poor Emily," and while the two female cousins were visiting her.

35   "I want some poison," she said to the druggist. She was over thirty then, still a slight woman, though thinner than usual, with cold, haughty black eyes in a face the flesh of which was strained across the temples and about the eyesockets as you imagine a lighthouse-keeper's face ought to look. "I want some poison," she said.

36   "Yes, Miss Emily. What kind? For rats and such? I'd recom—"

37   "I want the best you have. I don't care what kind."

38   The druggist named several. "They'll kill anything up to an elephant. But what you want is—"

39   "Arsenic," Miss Emily said. "Is that a good one?"

40   "Is... arsenic? Yes, ma'am. But what you want—"

41   "I want arsenic."

42	The druggist looked down at her. She looked back at him, erect, her face like a strained flag. "Why, of course," the druggist said. "If that's what you want. But the law requires you to tell what you are going to use it for."

43	Miss Emily just stared at him, her head **tilted** back in order to look him eye for eye, until he looked away and went and got the arsenic and wrapped it up. The Negro delivery boy brought her the package; the druggist didn't come back. When she opened the package at home there was written on the box, under the skull and bones: "For rats."

IV

44	So the next day we all said, "She will kill herself"; and we said it would be the best thing. When she had first begun to be seen with Homer Barron, we had said, "She will marry him." Then we said, "She will persuade him yet," because Homer himself had remarked—he liked men, and it was known that he drank with the younger men in the Elks' Club—that he was not a marrying man. Later we said, "Poor Emily" behind the jalousies as they passed on Sunday afternoon in the glittering buggy, Miss Emily with her head high and Homer Barron with his hat cocked and a cigar in his teeth, reins and whip in a yellow glove.

45	Then some of the ladies began to say that it was a disgrace to the town and a bad example to the young people. The men did not want to interfere, but at last the ladies forced the Baptist minister—Miss Emily's people were Episcopal—to call upon her. He would never **divulge** what happened during that interview, but he refused to go back again. The next Sunday they again drove about the streets, and the following day the minister's wife wrote to Miss Emily's relations in Alabama.

46	So she had blood-kin under her roof again and we sat back to watch developments. At first nothing happened. Then we were sure that they were to be married. We learned that Miss Emily had been to the jeweler's and ordered a man's toilet set in silver, with the letters H. B. on each piece. Two days later we learned that she had bought a complete outfit of men's clothing, including a nightshirt, and we said, "They are married." We were really glad. We were glad because the two female cousins were even more Grierson than Miss Emily had ever been.

47   So we were not surprised when Homer Barron—the streets had been finished some time since—was gone. We were a little disappointed that there was not a public blowing-off, but we believed that he had gone on to prepare for Miss Emily's coming, or to give her a chance to get rid of the cousins. (By that time it was a cabal, and we were all Miss Emily's allies to help circumvent the cousins.) Sure enough, after another week they departed. And, as we had expected all along, within three days Homer Barron was back in town. A neighbor saw the Negro man admit him at the kitchen door at dusk one evening.

48   And that was the last we saw of Homer Barron. And of Miss Emily for some time. The Negro man went in and out with the market basket, but the front door remained closed. Now and then we would see her at a window for a moment, as the men did that night when they sprinkled the lime, but for almost six months she did not appear on the streets. Then we knew that this was to be expected too; as if that quality of her father which had **thwarted** her woman's life so many times had been too **virulent** and too **furious** to die.

49   When we next saw Miss Emily, she had grown fat and her hair was turning gray. During the next few years it grew grayer and grayer until it attained an even pepper-and-salt iron-gray, when it ceased turning. Up to the day of her death at seventy-four it was still that vigorous iron-gray, like the hair of an active man.

50   From that time on her front door remained closed, save for a period of six or seven years, when she was about forty, during which she gave lessons in china-painting. She fitted up a studio in one of the downstairs rooms,

where the daughters and granddaughters of Colonel Sartoris' contemporaries were sent to her with the same regularity and in the same spirit that they were sent to church on Sundays with a twenty-five-cent piece for the collection plate. Meanwhile her taxes had been remitted.

51   Then the newer generation became the backbone and the spirit of the town, and the painting pupils grew up and fell away and did not send their children to her with boxes of color and tedious brushes and pictures cut from the ladies' magazines. The front door closed upon the last one and remained closed for good. When the town got free postal delivery, Miss Emily alone refused to let them fasten the metal numbers above her door and attach a mailbox to it. She would not listen to them.

52   Daily, monthly, yearly we watched the Negro grow grayer and more **stooped**, going in and out with the market basket. Each December we sent her a tax notice, which would be returned by the post office a week later, unclaimed. Now and then we would see her in one of the downstairs windows—she had evidently shut up the top floor of the house—like the carven torso of an idol in a **niche**, looking or not looking at us, we could never tell which. Thus she passed from generation to generation—dear, inescapable, impervious, **tranquil**, and **perverse.**

53   And so she died. Fell ill in the house filled with dust and shadows, with only a **doddering** Negro man to wait on her. We did not even know she was sick; we had long since given up trying to get any information from the Negro.

54   He talked to no one, probably not even to her, for his voice had grown harsh and rusty, as if from disuse.

55   She died in one of the downstairs rooms, in a heavy walnut bed with a curtain, her gray head propped on a pillow yellow and moldy with age and lack of sunlight.

V

56   The Negro met the first of the ladies at the front door and let them in, with their hushed, **sibilant** voices and their quick, curious glances, and then he disappeared. He walked right through the house and out the back and was not seen again.

57   The two female cousins came at once. They held the funeral on the second day, with the town coming to look at Miss Emily beneath a mass of bought flowers, with the crayon face of her father musing profoundly above the bier and the ladies sibilant and **macabre**; and the very old men—some in their brushed Confederate uniforms—on the porch and the lawn, talking of Miss Emily as if she had been a contemporary of theirs, believing that they had danced with her and courted her perhaps, confusing time with its mathematical progression, as the old do, to whom all the past is not a diminishing road but, instead, a huge meadow which no winter ever quite touches, divided from them now by the narrow bottle-neck of the most recent decade of years.

58   Already we knew that there was one room in that region above stairs which no one had seen in forty years, and which would have to be forced. They waited until Miss Emily was decently in the ground before they opened it.

59   The violence of breaking down the door seemed to fill this room with **pervading** dust. A thin, **acrid pall** as of the tomb seemed to lie everywhere upon this room decked and furnished as for a bridal: upon the **valance** curtains of faded rose color, upon the rose-shaded lights, upon the dressing table, upon the delicate array of crystal and the man's toilet things backed with tarnished silver, silver so tarnished that the **monogram** was **obscured**. Among them lay a collar and tie, as if they had just been removed, which, lifted, left upon the surface a pale **crescent** in the dust. Upon a chair hung the

suit, carefully folded; beneath it the two mute shoes and the discarded socks.

60   The man himself lay in the bed.

61   For a long while we just stood there, looking down at the profound and fleshless grin. The body had apparently once lain in the attitude of an embrace, but now the long sleep that outlasts love, that conquers even the **grimace** of love, had cuckolded him. What was left of him, rotted beneath what was left of the nightshirt, had become **inextricable** from the bed in which he lay; and upon him and upon the pillow beside him lay that even coating of the patient and **biding** dust.

62   Then we noticed that in the second pillow was the **indentation** of a head. One of us lifted something from it, and leaning forward, that faint and invisible dust dry and acrid in the nostrils, we saw a long strand of iron-gray hair.

Vocabulary

cupola ['kju:pələz] n.   a roof or part of a roof that is shaped like a dome 穹顶

scroll [skrəul] v.   a round shape formed by a series of concentric circles 使……成卷形

encroach [in'krəutʃ] v.   impinge or infringe upon 侵蚀

obliterate [ə'blitəreit] v.   do away with completely, without leaving a trace 使消失

august [ɔ:'gʌst] a.   profoundly honored 令人敬畏的

cedar ['si:də(r)] n.   durable aromatic wood of any of numerous cedar trees 雪松

bemused [bi'mju:zd] a.   perplexed by many conflicting situations or statements; filled with bewilderment 茫然的, 不知所措的

remit ['ri:mit] v.   release from (claims, debts, or taxes) 赦免

dispensation [ˌdispen'seiʃn] n.   an exemption from some rule or obligation 特许

aldermen ['ɔ:ldəmən] n.   members of the governing body of a city 市议员

archaic [a:'keiik] a.   so extremely old as seeming to belong to an earlier period 古色古香的

dank [dæŋk] a.   unpleasantly cool and humid 阴湿的

parlor [ˈpɑːlə] n.		a room in a private house or establishment where people can sit and talk and relax 客厅
sluggishly [ˈslʌgiʃli] ad.		very slowly 缓慢地,迟钝地
tarnish [ˈtɑːniʃ] v.		make dirty or spotty, as by exposure to air; also used metaphorically (使)失去光泽
ebony [ˈebəni] n.		hard dark-colored heartwood of the ebony tree 黑檀
plumpness [ˈplʌmpnəs] n.		the bodily property of being well rounded 饱满度
pallid [ˈpælid] a.		abnormally deficient in color as suggesting physical or emotional distress 苍白的,病态的
vanquish [ˈvæŋkwiʃ] v.		come out better in a competition, race, or conflict 征服
temerity [təˈmerəti] n.		fearless daring 鲁莽,冒失
teeming [ˈtiːmiŋ] a.		abundantly filled with especially living things 丰富的
diffident [ˈdifidənt] a.		showing modest reserve 踌躇的
deprecation [depriˈkeiʃən] n.		the act of expressing disapproval 强烈不赞成
slunk [slʌŋk] v.		walk stealthily; slunk is the past tense and past participle of slink 偷偷溜走
sprinkle [ˈspriŋkl] v.		distribute loosely 洒,撒
silhouette [ˌsiluˈet] n.		an outline of a solid object (as cast by its shadow) 轮廓,剪影
flung [flʌŋ] v.		throw with force or recklessness; flung is the past tense and past participle of fling 猛扔
vindicate [ˈvindikeit] v.		show to be right by providing justification or proof 证明……正确
insanity [inˈsænəti] n.		relatively permanent disorder of the mind 疯狂
condolence [kənˈdəuləns] n.		an expression of sympathy with another in grief 同情
serene [səˈriːn] a.		characterized by absence of emotional agitation 沉静的
jalousies [ʒæˈluːziːz] n.		a blind with adjustable horizontal slats 百叶窗
imperviousness [imˈpəːviəsnis] a.		resistance to penetration 不通透性,不受外界干扰
arsenic [ˈɑːsnik] n.		a white powdered poison 砒霜
tilt [tilt] v.		to incline or bend from a vertical position 倾斜
divulge [daiˈvʌldʒ] v.		make known to the public information that was previously known only to a few people or that was meant to be kept a secret 暴露,揭发
thwart [θwɔːt] v.		hinder or prevent (the efforts, plans, or desires) of 挫败
virulent [ˈvirələnt] a.		extremely poisonous or injurious 剧毒的
furious [ˌfjuəriəs] a.		marked by extreme anger 狂怒的

stoop [stu:p] v.	carry oneself, often habitually, with head, shoulders, and upper back bent forward 驼背
niche [nitʃ] n.	a small concavity 壁龛
tranquil ['træŋkwil] a.	characterized by absence of emotional agitation 安静的
perverse [pə'və:s] a.	resistant to guidance or discipline 有悖常情的
doddering ['dɔdəriŋ] a.	mentally or physically infirm with age 蹒跚的
sibilant ['sibilənt] a.	of speech sounds produced by forcing air through a constricted passage 发咝咝声的
macabre [mə'ka:brə] a.	shockingly repellent; inspiring horror 令人毛骨悚然的
pervading [pə'veidiŋ] a.	spread throughout 弥漫的
acrid ['ækrid] a.	strong and sharp 辛辣的,刺鼻的
pall [pɔ:l] n.	burial garment in which a corpse is wrapped 棺罩
valance ['væləns] n.	a decorative framework to conceal curtain fixtures at the top of a window casing 短帷幔
monogram ['mɔnəgræm] n.	a graphic symbol consisting of two or more letters combined (usually your initials) 字母组合
obscure [əb'skjuə(r)] v.	make less visible or unclear 使……模糊不清
crescent ['kresnt] n.	any shape resembling the new moon in shape 月牙形
grimace [gri'meis] n.	a contorted facial expression 鬼脸
inextricable [ˌinik'strikəbl] a.	incapable of being disentangled or untied 无法摆脱的
bide [baid] v.	dwell 停留
indentation [ˌinden'teiʃn] n.	the formation of small pits in a surface 凹进

I. Vocabulary Building

uni-/mono-: one

e. g., monocycle, monotone, monarchy, monochrome, monochromic, Unitarianism, unique, unicode, unicorn, unicellular

bi-/di-: two

e. g., diatomic, dioxide, dilemma, dichotomize, dichromatic, bicycle, binocular, bilingual, biennial, biannual

tri-: three

e. g., tricycle, triangle, tripod, triple, triad, triplet, trishaw, tristate, tristimulus, trisyllable

II. Discussion

Discuss the following questions with your own words.

1. In the story of "A Rose for Emily", what are the dark and sinister themes that characterized the Old South?

2. In order to reflect the 1930's stagnant mindset and decaying of the South, what images have the author employed to convey this message?

3. As is depicted in the passage, what are the visible traces or evidences that betray Emily's innermost desperate need to cling to tradition and show her refusal for change?

4. In this story, William Faulkner examines the issue of progressive change in the face of old tradition. What is your attitude towards the new technologies such as new mail service, cotton gins, and garages which replace the archaic and luxuriant houses of the golden age for Emily?

5. As is portrayed in the story, "Miss Emily a slender figure in white in the background, her father a spraddled silhouette in the foreground, his back to her and clutching a horsewhip, the two of them framed by the back-flung front door."(Para. 26) What is your interpretation of the painting? Do you agree that control is a persistent theme throughout the story?

III. Translation A

Translate the following sentences selected from the text into Chinese.

1. When the next generation, with its more modern ideas, became mayors and aldermen, this arrangement created some little dissatisfaction. (Para. 4)

2. When the Negro opened the blinds of one window, they could see that the leather was cracked; and when they sat down, a faint dust rose sluggishly about their thighs, spinning with slow motes in the single sun-ray. On a tarnished gilt easel before the fireplace stood a crayon portrait of

Miss Emily's father. (Para. 5)

3. The next day he received two more complaints, one from a man who came in diffident deprecation. (Para. 22)

4. It was as if she demanded more than ever the recognition of her dignity as the last Grierson; as if it had wanted that touch of earthiness to reaffirm her imperviousness. (Para. 34)

5. Now and then we would see her in one of the downstairs windows—she had evidently shut up the top floor of the house—like the carven torso of an idol in a niche, looking or not looking at us, we could never tell which. (Para. 52)

IV. Translation B
Translate the following passage into Chinese.

I have a great deal of company in my house; especially in the morning, when nobody calls. Let me suggest a few comparisons, that some one may convey an idea of my situation. I am no more lonely than the loon in the pond that laughs so loud, or than Walden Pond itself. What company has that lonely lake, I pray? And yet it has not the blue devils, but the blue angels in it, in the azure tint of its waters. The sun is alone, except in thick weather, when there sometimes appear to be two, but one is a mock sun. God is alone—but the devil, he is far from being alone; he sees a great deal of company; he is legion. I am no more lonely than a single mullein or dandelion in a pasture, or a bean leaf, or sorrel, or a horse-fly, or a bumblebee. I am no more lonely than the Mill Brook, or a weathercock, or the north star, or the south wind, or an April shower, or a January thaw, or the first spider in a new house. (Excerpted from Text B)

V. Writing Exercise

Isolation and decay are the dark dominant themes that characterize the story "A Rose for Emily". Emily is desperately alone, yet always being watched and hence found herself like a castle virtually under siege by the townspeople. Moreover, her manipulative father contributes to her isolation while he was alive or even after he had passed. Please write an essay upon Miss Emily's fate as well as the root reason for her personal tragedy, which might explain away her failure in coping with the social transformation in her days.

Text B

Solitude①

Henry David Thoreau

1   With thinking we may be beside ourselves in a **sane** sense. By a conscious effort of the mind we can stand **aloof** from actions and their consequences; and all things, good and bad, go by us like a **torrent**. We are not wholly involved in Nature. I may be either the driftwood in the stream, or Indra in the sky looking down on it. I may be affected by a theatrical exhibition; on the other hand, I may not be affected by an actual event which appears to concern me much more. I only know myself as a human **entity**; the scene, so to speak, of thoughts and affections; and am sensible of a certain doubleness by which I can stand as remote from myself as from another. However intense my experience, I am conscious of the presence and criticism of a part of me, which, as it were, is not a part of me, but spectator, sharing no experience, but taking note of it, and that is no more I than it is you. When the play, it may be the tragedy, of life is over, the spectator goes his way. It was a kind of fiction, a work of the imagination only, so far as he

---

①   Excerpted from Henry David Thoreau's *Walden, or Life in the Woods*.

was concerned. This doubleness may easily make us poor neighbors and friends sometimes.

<u>2</u>   I find it wholesome to be alone the greater part of the time. To be in company, even with the best, is soon wearisome and **dissipating**. I love to be alone. I never found the companion that was so companionable as solitude. We are for the most part more lonely when we go abroad among men than when we stay in our **chambers**. A man thinking or working is always alone, let him be where he will. Solitude is not measured by the miles of space that intervene between a man and his fellows. The really diligent student in one of the crowded hives of Cambridge College is as solitary as a **dervish** in the desert. The farmer can work alone in the field or the woods all day, hoeing or chopping, and not feel lonesome, because he is employed; but when he comes home at night he cannot sit down in a room alone, at the mercy of his thoughts, but must be where he can "see the folks," and recreate, and as he thinks **remunerate** himself for his day's solitude; and hence he wonders how the student can sit alone in the house all night and most of the day without ennui and "the blues"; but he does not realize that the student, though in the house, is still at work in his field, and chopping in his woods, as the farmer in his, and in turn **seeks** the same recreation and society that the latter does, though it may be a more **condensed** form of it.

<u>3</u>   Society is commonly too cheap. We meet at very short intervals, not having had time to acquire any new value for each other. We meet at meals three times a day, and give each other a new taste of that old **musty** cheese that we are. We have had to agree on a certain set of rules, called **etiquette** and politeness, to make this frequent meeting tolerable and that we need not come to open war. We meet at the post-office, and at the sociable, and about the fireside every night; we live thick and are in each other's way, and **stumble** over one another, and I think that we thus lose some respect for one another. Certainly less frequency would suffice for all important and hearty

communications. Consider the girls in a factory—never alone, hardly in their dreams. It would be better if there were but one inhabitant to a square mile, as where I live. The value of a man is not in his skin, that we should touch him.

4   I have heard of a man lost in the woods and dying of **famine** and exhaustion at the foot of a tree, whose loneliness was relieved by the **grotesque** visions with which, owing to bodily weakness, his diseased imagination surrounded him, and which he believed to be real. So also, owing to bodily and mental health and strength, we may be continually cheered by a like but more normal and natural society, and come to know that we are never alone.

5   I have a great deal of company in my house; especially in the morning, when nobody calls. Let me suggest a few comparisons, that some one may convey an idea of my situation. I am no more lonely than the loon in the pond that laughs so loud, or than Walden Pond itself. What company has that lonely lake, I pray? And yet it has not the blue devils, but the blue angels in it, in the **azure tint** of its waters. The sun is alone, except in thick weather, when there sometimes appear to be two, but one is a mock sun. God is alone—but the devil, he is far from being alone; he sees a great deal of company; he is **legion**. I am no more lonely than a single **mullein** or **dandelion** in a **pasture**, or a bean leaf, or sorrel, or a horse-fly, or a bumblebee. I am no more lonely than the Mill Brook, or a weathercock, or the north star, or the south wind, or an April shower, or a January thaw, or the first spider in a new house.

6   I have occasional visits in the long winter evenings, when the snow falls fast and the wind howls in the wood, from an old settler and original **proprietor**, who is reported to have dug Walden Pond, and stoned it, and **fringed** it with pine woods; who tells me stories of old time and of new eternity; and between us we manage to pass a cheerful evening with social

mirth and pleasant views of things, even without apples or **cider**—a most wise and humorous friend, whom I love much, who keeps? himself more secret than ever did Goffe or Whalley; and though he is thought to be dead, none can show where he is buried. An elderly dame, too, dwells in my neighborhood, invisible to most persons, in whose **odorous** herb garden I love to stroll sometimes, gathering simples and listening to her fables; for she has a genius of unequalled **fertility**, and her memory runs back farther than mythology, and she can tell me the original of every fable, and on what fact every one is founded, for the incidents occurred when she was young. A **ruddy** and **lusty** old dame, who delights in all weathers and seasons, and is likely to outlive all her children yet.

7   The indescribable innocence and **beneficence** of Nature—of sun and wind and rain, of summer and winter—such health, such cheer, they afford forever! and such sympathy have they ever with our race, that all Nature would be affected, and the sun's brightness fade, and the winds would sigh **humanely**, and the clouds rain tears, and the woods shed their leaves and put on mourning in midsummer, if any man should ever for a just cause grieve. Shall I not have intelligence with the earth? Am I not partly leaves and vegetable mould myself?

8   What is the pill which will keep us well, **serene, contented**? Not my or thy great-grandfather's, but our great-grandmother Nature's universal, vegetable, **botanic** medicines, by which she has kept herself young always, outlived so many old Parr in her day, and fed her health with their decaying fatness. For my **panacea**, instead of one of those **quack vials** of a mixture dipped from Acheron and the Dead Sea, which come out of those long shallow black-schooner looking wagons which we sometimes see made to carry bottles, let me have a draught of **undiluted** morning air. Morning air! If men will not drink of this at the fountainhead of the day, why, then, we must even bottle up some and sell it in the shops, for the benefit of those

who have lost their **subscription** ticket to morning time in this world. But remember, it will not keep quite till noonday even in the coolest **cellar**, but drive out the stopples long ere that and follow westward the steps of Aurora. I am no worshipper of Hygeia, who was the daughter of that old herb-doctor æsculapius, and who is represented on monuments holding a serpent in one hand, and in the other a cup out of which the serpent sometimes drinks; but rather of Hebe, cup-bearer to Jupiter, who was the daughter of Juno and wild lettuce, and who had the power of restoring gods and men to the vigor of youth. She was probably the only thoroughly sound-conditioned, healthy, and **robust** young lady that ever walked the globe, and wherever she came it was spring.

Vocabulary

sane [sein] a.	mentally healthy; free from mental disorder 心智健全的
aloof [əˈluːf] ad.	remote in manner 疏离地
torrent [ˈtɔrənt] n.	a violently fast stream of water (or other liquid) 急流
entity [ˈentəti] n.	that which is perceived or known or inferred to have its own distinct existence (living or nonliving) 实体
dissipating [ˈdisipeitiŋ] a.	waste money, time, or effort in a foolish way 浪费（金钱、时间或精力）
chamber [ˈtʃeimbə(r)] n.	a natural or artificial enclosed space 室，卧室，会客室
dervish [ˈdəːviʃ] n.	an ascetic Muslim monk; a member of an order noted for devotional exercises 苦行僧
remunerate [riˈmjuːnəreit] v.	make payment to; compensate 酬劳
seek [siːk] v.	make an effort or attempt 追求
condense [kənˈdens] v.	become more compact or concentrated 浓缩
musty [ˈmʌsti] a.	stale and unclean smelling 发霉的，陈腐的
etiquette [ˈetiket] n.	rules governing socially acceptable behavior 礼节，规矩
stumble [ˈstʌmbl] v.	encounter by chance 偶然碰见
famine [ˈfæmin] n.	a severe shortage of food (as through crop failure) resulting in violent hunger and starvation and death 饥饿
grotesque [grəuˈtesk] a.	abnormal and hideous; ludicrously odd 怪诞的
azure [ˈæʒə(r)] n.	a light shade of blue 蔚蓝

tint [tɪnt] n.	a quality of a given color that differs slightly from a primary color 色彩,色泽	
legion ['liːdʒən] n.	a vast multitude 众多	
mullein ['mʌlɪn] n.	plants of the genus Verbascum having large usually woolly leaves and terminal spikes of yellow or white or purplish flowers 毛蕊花	
dandelion ['dændɪlaɪən] n.	herbs having long tap roots and deeply notched leaves and bright yellow flowers followed by fluffy seed balls 蒲公英	
pasture ['paːstʃə(r)] n.	a field covered with grass or herbage and suitable for grazing by livestock 牧场	
proprietor [prə'praɪətə(r)] n.	(law) someone who owns (is legal possessor of) a business 所有人,业主	
fringe [frɪndʒ] v.	adorn with a fringe 围绕	
mirth [məːθ] n.	great merriment 欢笑	
cider ['saɪdə(r)] n.	a beverage made from juice pressed from apples〔美〕苹果汁,〔英〕苹果酒	
odorous ['əudərəs] a.	having a natural fragrance 有气味的	
fertility [fə'tɪlətɪ] n.	the property of producing abundantly and sustaining growth 肥沃,〈生〉繁殖力	
ruddy ['rʌdɪ] a.	inclined to a healthy reddish color often associated with outdoor life 红润的	
lusty ['lʌstɪ] a.	vigorously passionate 健壮的	
beneficence [bɪ'nefɪsns] n.	the quality of being kind or helpful or generous 仁慈	
humanely [hjuː'meɪnlɪ] ad.	in a humane manner 富人情地	
serene [sə'riːn] a.	characterized by absence of emotional agitation 安详的	
contented [kən'tentɪd] a.	satisfied or showing satisfaction with things as they are 满意的,满足的	
botanic [bə'tænɪk] a.	relating to plants or botany 植物的	
panacea [ˌpænə'siːə] n.	hypothetical remedy for all ills or diseases; once sought by the alchemists 万灵药	
quack [kwæk] n.	an untrained person who pretends to be a physician and who dispenses medical advice 江湖郎中	
vial ['vaɪəl] n.	a small bottle that contains a drug 药水瓶	
undiluted [ˌʌndaɪ'luːtɪd] a.	not reduced in strength or concentration or quality or purity 未搀水,纯粹的	
subscription [səb'skrɪpʃn] n.	agreement expressed by (or as if expressed by) signing your name 订阅	

cellar ['selə(r)] n. an excavation where root vegetables are stored 地窖
robust [rəʊ'bʌst] a. physically strong 精力充沛的

Text C

The Waste Land①

T. S. Eliot

I. The Burial of the Dead

April is the cruellest month, breeding
Lilacs out of the dead land, mixing
Memory and desire, stirring
Dull roots with spring rain.
Winter kept us warm, covering
Earth in forgetful snow, feeding
A little life with dried **tubers.**
Summer surprised us, coming over the Starnbergersee②
With a shower of rain; we stopped in the colonnade,
And went on in sunlight, into the Hofgarten③,
And drank coffee, and talked for an hour.
Bin gar keine Russin, stamm' aus Litauen, echt deutsch④.
And when we were children, staying at the **archduke's**,

---

① Excerpted from T. S. Eliot's *The Waste Land*.
② 地名,施坦贝尔格湖。
③ 地名,霍夫加登。Hofgarten is German for "court garden" and refers to the gardens of a noble family, usually a reigning prince or sovereign.
④ 德语,意为:"我不是俄国人,我是立陶宛来的,是地道的德国人。"

My cousin's, he took me out on a sled,

And I was frightened. He said, Marie,

Marie, hold on tight. And down we went.

In the mountains, there you feel free.

I read, much of the night, and go south in the winter.

What are the roots that clutch, what branches grow

Out of this stony rubbish? Son of man①,

You cannot say, or guess, for you know only

A heap of broken images, where the sun beats,

And the dead tree gives no shelter, the cricket no relief,

And the dry stone no sound of water. Only

There is shadow under this red rock,

(Come in under the shadow of this red rock),

And I will show you something different from either

Your shadow at morning **striding** behind you

Or your shadow at evening rising to meet you;

I will show you fear in a handful of dust.

> *Frisch weht der Wind*
>
> *Der Heimat zu*
>
> *Mein Irisch Kind,*
>
> *Wo weilest du*②?

"You gave me **hyacinths** first a year ago;

"They called me the hyacinth girl."

—Yet when we came back, late, from the Hyacinth garden,

Your arms full, and your hair wet, I could not

---

① In his notes, Eliot cites Ezekiel 2:1. "Son of man, stand upon thy feet, and I will speak to thee."

② Eliot's Note 31. V. Tristan und Isolde, I, verses 5-8. 意为:"风吹得很轻快,吹送我回家去,爱尔兰的小孩,你在哪里逗留?"

Speak, and my eyes failed, I was neither

Living nor dead, and I knew nothing,

Looking into the heart of light, the silence.

Oed' und leer das Meer①.

Madame Sosostris, famous **clairvoyante**,

Had a bad cold, nevertheless

Is known to be the wisest woman in Europe,

With a wicked pack of cards. Here, said she,

Is your card, the drowned Phoenician Sailor,②

(Those are pearls that were his eyes. Look!)

Here is Belladonna③, the Lady of the Rocks,

The lady of situations.

Here is the man with three **staves**, and here the Wheel,④

And here is the one-eyed merchant, and this card,

Which is blank, is something he carries on his back,

Which I am forbidden to see. I do not find

The Hanged Man. Fear death by water.

I see crowds of people, walking round in a ring.

Thank you. If you see dear Mrs. Equitone,

Tell her I bring the horoscope myself:

One must be so careful these days.

Unreal City,

Under the brown fog of a winter dawn,

A crowd flowed over London Bridge, so many,

---

① 德语,意为:"荒凉而空虚是那大海。"
② 腓尼基水手。
③ The literal meaning of this word is "beautiful lady", who is frequently associated with Leonardo da Vinci's **Madonna of the Rocks**.
④ The man with the three staves and the wheel are authentic Tarot cards.

I had not thought death had undone so many.
Sighs, short and **infrequent**, were **exhaled**,
And each man fixed his eyes before his feet.
Flowed up the hill and down King William Street,
To where Saint Mary Woolnoth① kept the hours
With a dead sound on the final stroke of nine.
There I saw one I knew, and stopped him, crying "Stetson!
"You who were with me in the ships at Mylae②!
"That **corpse** you planted last year in your garden,
"Has it begun to sprout? Will it bloom this year?
"Or has the sudden frost disturbed its bed?
"Oh keep the Dog far hence, that's friend to men,
"Or with his nails he'll dig it up again!
"You! **hypocrite** lecteur! - mon semblable, - mon frere!"③

II. A Game of Chess

The Chair she sat in, like a **burnished** throne,
Glowed on the marble, where the glass
Held up by standards wrought with fruited vines
From which a golden Cupidon④ **peeped** out
(Another hid his eyes behind his wing)
Doubled the flames of seven branched **candelabra**⑤
Reflecting light upon the table as
The glitter of her jewels rose to meet it,
From satin cases poured in rich **profusion**;

---

① A church located in the city of London.
② 地名，梅拉河。
③ 法语，意为："虚伪的读者！——我的同类——我的兄弟！"
④ 小爱神。
⑤ 七枝光烛台。

In **vials** of ivory and coloured glass

Unstoppered, **lurked** her strange **synthetic perfumes**,

Unguent, **powdered**, or liquid - troubled, confused

And drowned the sense in odours; stirred by the air

That freshened from the window, these **ascended**

In fattening the prolonged candle-flames,

Flung their smoke into the laquearia①,

Stirring the pattern on the **coffered** ceiling.

Huge sea-wood fed with **copper**

Burned green and orange, framed by the coloured stone,

In which sad light a **carved** dolphin swam.

Above the **antique mantel** was displayed

As though a window gave upon the **sylvan** scene

The change of Philomel②, by the **barbarous** king

So rudely forced; yet there the nightingale

Filled all the desert with **inviolable** voice

And still she cried, and still the world pursues,

"Jug Jug" to dirty ears.

And other **withered** stumps of time

Were told upon the walls; staring forms

Leaned out, leaning, hushing the room enclosed.

Footsteps **shuffled** on the stair.

Under the firelight, under the brush, her hair

Spread out in **fiery** points

Glowed into words, then would be savagely still.

My nerves are bad to-night. Yes, bad. Stay with me.

---

① 屋顶的镶板。
② 人名,菲洛梅尔(赵萝蕤译本中译为"翡绿眉拉")。本义指"夜莺"。

"Speak to me. Why do you never speak. Speak.
"What are you thinking of? What thinking? What?
"I never know what you are thinking. Think."

I think we are in rats' **alley**

Where the dead men lost their bones.

"What is that noise?"

   The wind under the door.

"What is that noise now? What is the wind doing?"

   Nothing again nothing.

    "Do

"You know nothing? Do you see nothing? Do you remember

"Nothing?"

 I remember

Those are pearls that were his eyes.

"Are you alive, or not? Is there nothing in your head?"

    But

O O O that Shakespeherian Rag[①]—

It's so elegant

So intelligent

"What shall I do now? What shall I do?"

I shall rush out as I am, and walk the street

"With my hair down, so. What shall we do to-morrow?

"What shall we ever do?"

   The hot water at ten.

And if it rains, a closed car at four.

And we shall play a game of chess,

---

① Eliot's adapted version of a popular song, published in 1921.

Pressing lidless eyes and waiting for a knock upon the door.

When Lil's husband got **demobbed**, I said—
I didn't **mince** my words, I said to her myself,
HURRY UP PLEASE ITS TIME
Now Albert's coming back, make yourself a bit smart.
He'll want to know what you done with that money he gave you
To get yourself some teeth. He did, I was there.
You have them all out, Lil, and get a nice set,
He said, I swear, I can't bear to look at you.
And no more can't I, I said, and think of poor Albert,
He's been in the army four years, he wants a good time,
And if you don't give it him, there's others will, I said.
Oh is there, she said. Something o' that, I said.
Then I'll know who to thank, she said, and give me a straight look.
HURRY UP PLEASE ITS TIME①
If you don't like it you can get on with it, I said.
Others can pick and choose if you can't.
But if Albert makes off, it won't be for lack of telling.
You ought to be ashamed, I said, to look so antique.
(And her only thirty-one.)
I can't help it, she said, pulling a long face,
It's them pills I took, to bring it off, she said.
(She's had five already, and nearly died of young George.)
The chemist said it would be alright, but I've never been the same.
You are a proper fool, I said.
Well, if Albert won't leave you alone, there it is, I said,
What you get married for if you don't want children?

---

① Closing time, as announced at a pub.

HURRY UP PLEASE ITS TIME

Well, that Sunday Albert was home, they had a hot **gammon**,

And they asked me in to dinner, to get the beauty of it hot—

HURRY UP PLEASE ITS TIME

HRRY UP PLEASE ITS TIME

Goonight Bill. Goonight Lou. Goonight May. Goonight.

Ta ta. Goonight. Goonight.

Good night, ladies, good night, sweet ladies, good night, good night. ①

Vocabulary

lilac ['lailək] n.	any of various plants of the genus Syringa having large panicles of usually fragrant flowers 丁香花
tuber ['tjuːbə(r)] n.	various types of modified plant structures that are enlarged to store nutrients 块茎
archduke [ˌɑːtʃ'djuːk] n.	a sovereign prince of the former ruling house of Austria 大公
stride [straid] v.	walk with long steps 大踏步走
hyacinth ['haiəsinθ] n.	any of numerous bulbous perennial herbs 风信子
clairvoyante [kleəvɔ'iənt] n.	a clairvoyant is someone who claims to have power to perceive things that are not present to the senses 女占卜师
stave [steiv] n.	one of several thin slats of wood 狭板
infrequent [in'friːkwənt] a.	not occurring regularly 稀少的
exhale [eks'heil] v.	give out (breath or an odor) 呼出
corpse [kɔːps] n.	the dead body of a human being 尸体
hypocrite ['hipəkrit] n.	a person who professes beliefs and opinions that he does not hold 伪君子
burnish ['bəːniʃ] v.	polish and make shiny 擦亮
peep [piːp] v.	look furtively 窥视
profusion [prə'fjuːʒn] n.	the property of being extremely abundant 丰富
vial ['vaiəl] n.	a small bottle that contains a drug 小瓶

---

① In *Hamlet*: *Act IV*, the mad Ophelia's parting words to Queen and king, before her death.

unstoppered [ʌnsˈtɔpət] a.	(of a container) having the stopper removed 敞开口的
lurk [ləːk] v.	lie in wait, lie in ambush, behave in a sneaky and secretive manner 潜藏
synthetic [sinˈθetik] a.	prepared or made artificially 合成的
perfume [ˈpəːfjuːm] n.	a distinctive odor that is pleasant 香气
unguent [ˈʌŋgwənt] n.	semisolid preparation (usually containing a medicine) applied externally as a remedy or for soothing an irritation 油膏
powdered [ˈpaudəd] a.	consisting of fine particles 粉末状的
ascend [əˈsend] v.	travel up 上升
coffer [ˈkɔfə(r)] n.	an ornamental sunken panel in a ceiling or dome 镶板
copper [ˈkɔpə(r)] n.	a reddish-brown corrosion-resistant metallic element 铜
carve [kaːv] v.	engrave or cut by chipping away at a surface 雕刻
antique [ænˈtiːk] n.	belonging to or lasting from times long ago 古老的
mantel [ˈmæntl] n.	shelf that projects from wall above fireplace 壁炉架
sylvan [ˈsilvən] a.	characteristic of wooded regions 森林的,乡村的
barbarous [ˈbaːbərəs] a.	primitive in customs and culture 野蛮的
inviolable [inˈvaiələbl] a.	that cannot be transgressed or dishonored 不可侵犯的
withered [ˈwiðəd] a.	lean and wrinkled by shrinkage as from age or illness 枯萎的
shuffle [ˈʃʌfl] v.	walk by dragging one's feet 拖着脚走
fiery [ˈfaiəri] a.	like or suggestive of fire 火似的
alley [ˈæli] n.	a narrow street with walls on both side 胡同,小巷
demob [ˌdiːˈmɔb] v.	retire from military service 退伍
mince [mins] v.	make less severe or harsh 装腔作势地说
gammon [ˈgæmən] n.	ham 火腿